Broadsides & Bayonets

Broadsides & Bayonets

The Propaganda War of
the American Revolution

REVISED EDITION

by Carl Berger

PRESIDIO PRESS
SAN RAFAEL • CALIFORNIA

Library of Congress Catalogue Card Number 76-27182
ISBN 0-89141-006-6

Printed in the United States of America

to Rae Berger

Preface

In this book I have attempted to encompass the story of propaganda and subversion during the American Revolutionary War. The archives and literature of the Revolution contain many references to enemy "secret arts and machinations," some relating to incidents well known to historians, others touching on events long forgotten. This book for the first time brings them together in a single narrative and examines their role and importance.

During its eight-year progression the War for Independence gave birth to many divisive operations, well planned in some instances, and often involving minority groups on the scene as well as Englishmen and Americans. Drawn into the colonial struggle were French Canadians and German mercenaries, Indian tribes and Negro slaves, Irishmen, and other peoples. From the beginning it was a war of words as well as gunpowder, with each side seeking to subvert and weaken the enemy camp through carefully wrought arguments. It was a provocative war in which the atrocity story, kidnappings, false rumors, and bribery stirred the people. It was a conflict which inevitably spread to Europe and there engaged the talents of Benjamin Franklin and John Adams in America's first organized overseas propaganda campaign.

In reconstructing this story of wartime propaganda, I have been much less concerned with the important military operations that were conducted than with what was said and done in support of them, and also less concerned with the political disputes between Parliament and Congress than with the techniques of propaganda and subversion employed by each side. The reader will note that the word "propaganda" is used in this volume without evil connotations; that is, in accordance with the dictionary definition of: "any organized or concerted group effort or movement to spread particular doctrines, information, etc." The American Revolution was such a movement, which spread doctrines of liberty and independence throughout the world.

Broadsides and Bayonets was originally published in 1961. In preparing this revised edition, I have reorganized the text, expanded it, and incorporated additional contemporary illustrations obtained from the collections of the Library of Congress and the National Archives.

Carl Berger

Falls Church, Virginia
April 26, 1975

Acknowledgements

There are two general English-language studies dealing with what might be called the domestic side of the propaganda struggle, Arthur M. Schlesinger's *Prelude to Independence: The Newspaper War on Britain, 1764-1776* (1958) and Philip Davidson's *Propaganda and the American Revolution, 1763-1783* (1941). The emphasis in both is on the prewar pamphlet and newspaper competition between the Revolutionary leaders on one side, and the pro-English Tories and the British government on the other, for the hearts and minds of the American people. In the case of the present work, which concentrates on the war period, it follows a lead provided by Dr. Lyman H. Butterfield's article on "Psychological Warfare in 1776: The Jefferson-Franklin Plan to Cause Hessian Desertions." *Proceedings of the American Philosophical Society* (June 1950). Dr. Butterfield's article kindled the author's interest and subsequent research quickly uncovered evidence that the Hessians were not alone as targets for the subversive campaigns.

Contents

Illustrations

☆ 1 ☆

Propaganda
and Military Operations

AFTER YEARS OF growing American opposition to the arbitrary policies of the British government, the "Sons of Liberty" threw their famous tea party in Boston on December 16, 1773. When news of this latest act of opposition reached London in early 1774, the Parliament approved governmental measures to bring the rebellious colonists to heel. An American in London, William Lee, who followed the Parliamentary debates, wrote to his brother, Richard Henry Lee of Virginia, that the King "with his usual obstinacy and tyrannical disposition is determined, if it be possible, to enslave you all . . . ." Shortly afterwards, British naval vessels and troop reinforcements set sail for America. Their arrival was anticipated with anxiety. In Philadelphia, where the Continental Congress was meeting, John Adams wrote that: "The commencement of hostilities is exceedingly dreaded here."

During the winter of 1774-1775, before the war began, American loyalists and patriots found themselves arguing the question: Could the colonists ever hope to stand up against the trained regulars of Great Britain? The Tories, loyal to the King, warned the patriots against forcing a showdown. Americans, they said, would have no chance against the British troops and the contest would bring ruin to the colonies. The patriots were not convinced, especially such men as Charles Lee, a former British lieutenant colonel, who deprecated the loyalist claim of

1

English superiority in arms. Lee reminded the patriots of the beginnings of the French and Indian War with France a decade before. "Some of the most esteemed British regiments were sent over to this country," he wrote. "They were masters of their manual exercise, they fired together in platoons — but fatal experience taught us, that they knew not how to fight." Thus Lee recalled the shades of General Braddock!

Lee's views were published in February 1775 as an answer to some loyalist opinions disseminated by Dr. Myles Cooper, president of King's College, New York. Lee's arguments had great influence with the patriot side, especially his reminder of American expertness with firearms, "whereas the lower and middle people of England are, by the tyranny of certain laws, almost as ignorant in the use of a musket as they are of the ancient catapults."

Here was the beginning of the propaganda of the dreaded American marksmen, whose presence in parapets and battle lines was to cause British military commanders many anxious moments. In June 1775, following the clash at Lexington and Concord, one of the first acts of the Second Continental Congress was to issue a call to American riflemen to join the patriot army forming around Boston. On June 18 John Hancock informed Joseph Warren that ten companies of frontier riflemen from Pennsylvania, Maryland, and Virginia had been ordered to proceed immediately to Boston. "This is a good step," wrote Hancock, "and will be an excellent additional strength to our army. These are the finest marksmen in the world. They do execution with their rifle guns at an amazing distance."

Within a very short time more than 1,000 volunteer riflemen, dressed in the frontier hunting shirt and Indian-style breeches, were on their way to Boston. American newspapers went into excited panegyrics over them. For example, a writer in the *Pennsylvania Journal* told his readers on August 23:

These men have been bred in the woods to hardships and dangers from their infancy. They appear as if they were entirely unacquainted with, and had never felt the

2

passion of fear. With their rifles in their hands they assume a kind of omnipotence over their enemies. One cannot much wonder at this when we mention a fact which can be fully attested by several of the reputable persons who were eyewitnesses to it. Two brothers in the company [of riflemen] took a piece of board five inches broad and seven inches long, with a bit of white paper about the size of a dollar nailed in the center, and while one of them supported this board perpendicularly between his knees, the other, at a distance of upwards of sixty yards, and without any kind of rest, shot eight bullets through it successively, and spared a brother's thigh!

The riflemen began arriving in large numbers at the American camp at Cambridge in August 1775. Surgeon John Thacher noted in his journal: "They are now stationed on our lines, and their shots have frequently proved fatal to British officers and soldiers who expose themselves to view, even at more than double the distance of common musket-shot." During the Battle of Bunker Hill, of 2,300 officers and men who launched the British attack, more than 1,000 fell, 226 of them killed. Of that number, 19 officers were killed, 70 were wounded, and 8 of these died. Among them were Captains Percival and Sabine of the Marines, Captain Johnson of the Royal Irish Regiment, a Captain LeMoine, and Captain Chetwyn, son of Lord Chetwyn. On the American side, of 3,500 men, 38 were killed, 276 wounded, and 36 were missing. To reduce their losses, the British threw up a breastwork across the neck at the foot of Bunker Hill to secure their sentries and advanced guards. According to one account, the riflemen had "grown so terrible" to the British "that nothing is to be seen from their breast works but a hat . . . ."[1]

George Washington, the newly named Commander in Chief of the Continental Army, soon found that these executioners were unruly and undisciplined like most frontiersmen. They jumped in and out of the American lines on Prospect Hill at will, fired without orders, and often at such great distances as to waste scarce powder. In September, in an effort to establish his authority and some kind of discipline over these strong-willed men, Washington court-martialed an entire platoon of thirty-three riflemen, who were fined twenty shillings each for "disobedient and mutinous behavior."[2] The reputation of the riflemen declined further when some of the men deserted to the British.

Nevertheless, their recognized ability with the rifle was a military and propaganda asset which the Americans continued to invoke. In Virginia, for example, patriot forces met royal troops under Governor John Murray, Lord Dunmore, and defeated them in a skirmish at Hampton. The *Virginia Gazette* boasted that in this engagement "a rifle-man killed a man at a distance of 400 yards." The paper added ominously: "Take care, ministerial troops."

The claim of 400 yards may have been exaggerated. Charles Lee, appointed a major general, after traveling southward at the behest of Congress in 1776 to help the patriot defenders of Charleston, urged the local commander there to insist the riflemen stop firing at such great distances. "It is a certain truth," said Lee, "that the enemy entertain a most fortunate apprehension of American riflemen. It is equally certain that nothing can diminish this apprehension so infallibly as a frequent, ineffectual fire." Lee recommended that no man should fire at a distance greater than 150 yards. "In short," he advised the southerners, "they must never fire without almost a moral certainty of hitting their object."

In July 1776 Washington also sought to take advantage of British fears of the riflemen. When the problem arose of clothing his troops, Washington recommended that they all adopt the rifleman's hunting shirt with the long breeches. Not only was that costume cheap and utilitarian, he said, but it also constituted a dress "justly supposed to carry no small terror to the enemy, who thinks every such person a complete marksman."

The British, before they discovered they also had an important and effective weapon of terror in the bayonet, sought to match the American riflemen with German *jaegers*. About 1,000 of these mercenaries, trained to use rifle-barrel guns in boar hunting in the German forests, were among the nearly 30,000 German troops hired by Britain.

4

It was not until after the first battle of Long Island on August 27, 1776, that the Achilles heel of the riflemen was discovered. During the fight the British and German generals noted the basic weaknesses of the rifle — it took too long to reload and had no bayonet. American riflemen could scarcely get off several shots before the advancing columns of British and German infantry were upon them with the bayonet.

The disadvantages of the rifle versus the musket-with-bayonet also have been described as follows:

> The musket and bayonet were the weapons for the line of battle, where the target was not an individual, but another line, and when the lines closed the bayonet was ready for use. Firearms were very sensitive to the weather; after long-continued or heavy rain they were useless, and lack of a bayonet was then fatal. To take advantage of the rifle, fire must be opened at a longer range, and its accuracy utilized in aiming at individuals. It could not be used with the musket in the line of battle, for the smoke then prevented the rifleman from seeing his target, thus nullifying the principal advantage of the weapon.[3]

When these faults had been revealed, the rifle suddenly became a handicap. General William Howe, in preparing his British troops for the next battle, reminded them "of their evident superiority" with their bayonets and he recommended that they place "an entire dependence" on that weapon. As the campaign progressed, British leaders became so confident in their superiority that they ordered many an attack *with muskets unloaded*, leaving the troops no alternative but to use their bayonets against the terror-stricken American militia.

Now it was the British who boasted of a superior weapon which, in battle after battle, struck fear in the hearts of the amateur soldiers in the Continental army and sent them flying. The growing inhibitions of patriot forces elicited by the bayonet became an important psychological factor which Washington and his officers worked hard to overcome. However, it was not until 1778 — when bayonet practice was introduced into the Continental army by the German volunteer, Baron von Steuben — that progress was made in this direction.

5

A most revealing statement made in connection with this problem came from Major General Anthony Wayne, who exclaimed in a letter dated February 1778 to Richard Peters, former secretary of Congress' Board of War:

> I don't like rifles. I would almost as face an enemy with a good musket and bayonet without ammunition, as with ammunition without a bayonet. For although there are not many instances of bloody bayonets, yet I am confident that one bayonet keeps off another — and for the want of which the chief of the defeats we have met with ought in a great measure to be attributed. The enemy knowing the defenceless state of our riflemen rush on: They fly, mix with or pass through the other troops and communicate fears that is ever incident to a retiring corps. But it would be still better if good muskets and bayonets were put into the hands of good marksmen and rifles entirely laid aside. For my part I never wish to see one, at least without a bayonet. I don't give this as mere matter of opinion or speculation, but as matter of fact to the truth of which I have more than once been an unhappy witness.

Washington was of a like mind, and in July 1779 he assigned General Wayne the mission of seizing the British post at Stony Point, New York, using troops who were to advance with fixed bayonets and unloaded muskets. The operation was completely successful and the victory on July 16 a sure sign the Americans were slowly mastering their fears.

Although the musket with bayonet remained the primary infantry weapon throughout the Revolution, the rifle still retained its usefulness. This was well demonstrated in January 1781, when Brigadier General Daniel Morgan of the Long Rifles managed to utilize both rifles and muskets in a successful engagement. In the important battle of Cowpens, Morgan deployed his militia riflemen in the front line with orders to fire two volleys at "the men with the epaulets," and then to retire to the second line of militia. The latter troops were told of this plan to prevent panic at the sight of the retreating riflemen. The second line also was ordered to fire "low and deliberately" and then to retire when hard pressed to the rear of the main American formation, where they would re-form as a reserve.

Morgan's battle plan worked with devastating effect. The successive American withdrawals drew in the British troops under Lieutenant Colonel Banastre Tarleton, while the riflemen's fire took a deadly toll. At the critical moment, the main American formation was ready with its muskets and bayonets. The patriots at last seemed to have solved the problem of effectively utilizing both weapons in a single engagement.

Eight months later, in September 1781, while the American and French armies were on their march to the historic denouement of British forces under Major General Charles Cornwallis at Yorktown, the Commander in Chief used the occasion to encourage his troops "to place their principal reliance on the bayonet, that they may prove the vanity of the boast which the British make of their particular prowess in deciding battles with that weapon."

Although the rifle had declined in importance as a weapon of the line until Morgan's demonstration, it still was greatly feared in the hands of American partisans. "Their riflemen are terrible," complained a German officer. Indeed, Thomas Jefferson also expanded on that idea in a letter to a friend in Europe in 1778. He ascribed higher British casualties (more than double American losses, he said) as due to "our superiority in taking aim when we fire, every soldier in our Army having been intimate with his gun from his infancy."

So went the propaganda of the rifle and the bayonet.

+

This "weapons propaganda" was but one aspect of a general war of broadsides and bayonets waged during the years 1775-1783. The British government's last resort to armed force was, of course, their final argument in the dispute, the King and his advisors believing it would persuade the rebels to lay down their arms and submit. However, during the first year of the war, the British forces were under the severe handicap of being almost entirely on the military defensive. It was the patriots who pro-

7

duced what might be called the first propaganda broadside of the Revolution aimed at the enemy's troops.

Their target was the Royal Irish Regiment stationed in New York in the spring of 1775. Within days after news reached New York of the fighting at Lexington and Concord, an "English American" published a broadside addressed "To the Regular Soldiery of Great-Britain now on Service in the British American Colonies." It was a lengthy political exposition of the patriot viewpoint, dated May 1, 1775, which ended with an open invitation to the soldiers to desert:

> As the service on which you were sent here is dishonorable and injurious to your country, we have reason to think it is highly disagreeable to you. Therefore, in the name of the British colonies in general, I am authorized to assure you and all the British soldiery at present in America, that if you will quit the service and join your American brethren in opposing the wicked designs of the Ministry (or if you please, you shall not be required to draw your swords or take any active part in the contest). You shall be kindly received as brothers and friends and provided with a comfortable subsistence among us. You shall be sent with a proper escort to any part of the continent where you choose to retire — together with your wives, children and effects — or these shall be sent after you. You shall be protected against the Army and the military laws of Great Britain, which have no legal force in America.[4]

When reports of this and other American subversive efforts reached Boston, Lieutenant General Thomas Gage, the British Commander in Chief in North America, ordered the regiment withdrawn from New York. Early in June 1775, the unit prepared to leave but its departure was not without incident. According to Lieutenant Governor Cadwallader Colden, writing to Lord Dartmouth, Secretary of State for the American colonies, on June 7: "As soon as the troops marched from the barracks, several people began to harangue them, exhorting them to desert, and assuring them of sufficient protection. Two or three of these fellows had the hardiness to turn off with the arms from the ranks, and were immediately carried away by the people." They were probably the first soldiers to desert from either side during the Revolution.

The Royal Irish Regiment joined Gage's besieged forces in Boston, where during the summer of 1775 at least two other American propaganda sheets were distributed among the British troops. One was entitled, "An address to the Soldiers," and was a reprint of a document produced in London by a Whiggish "Old Soldier," who had addressed the troops as follows: "You are about to embark for America to compel your fellow-subjects there to submit to Popery and Slavery . . . ."[5] The other was a leaflet disseminated from rebel-controlled Prospect Hill, which made the following points:

PROSPECT HILL	BUNKER HILL
I. Seven Dollars a Month	I. Three Pence a Day
II. Fresh Provisions, and in Plenty	II. Rotten Salt Pork
III. Health	III. The Scurvy
IV. Freedom, Ease, Affluence and a good Farm	IV. Slavery, Beggary and Want

This leaflet was disseminated to the British troops by American patrols operating at night to avoid enemy detection and to get the leaflets into the hands of the rank and file before the officers could destroy them. The leaflets, wrapped around bullets "to make them fly well," were heaved into the British entrenchments on Bunker Hill.[6]

In Boston, General Gage struggled to counter patriot propaganda through various means, including a broadside he published on June 12, 1775, which denounced the whole rebel movement. In this tract, issued a few days before the Battle of Bunker Hill, Gage attacked the leaders of the rebellion as men with no interest in truth who had disseminated "the grossest forgeries, calumnies, and absurdities that ever insulted human understanding."

The American press, the General complained, "has been invariably prostituted to the most contrary purposes." And not only those "flagitious prints" but also "the popular harangues of the times" had taught men "to depend upon activity in treason for the security of their persons and properties; till, to complete the horrid profanation of terms and ideas, the name of God has been introduced in the pulpits to excite and justify devastation and massacre." So were the minds of men prepared for treason, Gage charged, especially by such persons as Samuel Adams and John Hancock, whom he now excluded from a general pardon offered "to all persons who shall forthwith lay down their arms, and return to the duties of peaceful subjects."

Publication of such a proclamation had been approved in London, but in view of the fact that British forces were isolated and on the defensive in Boston, it had little effect. Indeed, it became the subject of ridicule in the patriot press. Even in the House of Commons a member of the opposition party managed to get in a dig at "Gage's foolish and contemptible proclamation."[7]

A somewhat similar mishap occurred in May 1776 when Sir Henry Clinton appeared off the coast of North Carolina with a British fleet and body of troops and made an attempt to invade that state to restore the King's government. From his flagship, General Clinton dispatched a proclamation to the Americans in which he denounced "a most unprovoked and wicked rebellion" which, he said, had usurped the powers of government and had erected "a tyranny in the hands of Congresses and Committees of various denominations." Clinton allowed that he had authority to march against all such men as enemies of Britain. However, "from the principle of humanity," he offered free pardons to all who would lay down their arms and submit to British rule.

But having taken such an uncompromising stand, Clinton found he was unable to impose his will by force. He had expected to be reinforced by thousands of loyalist backcountry Scotch Highlanders in North Carolina. Instead, he learned that the Highlanders had risen prematurely and had been destroyed in a battle with the patriots at Moore's Bridge. Clinton also had been waiting for the arrival of British reinforcements sailing directly from England but they did not reach American waters until May 1776. His plan to pacify North Carolina aborted,

Clinton sailed southward where he attempted an unsuccessful assault on Charleston, South Carolina, in June. His calls to the people there to return to their duty also were ignored.

The first fully coordinated British effort to talk or force the Americans into laying down their arms did not begin until the arrival of the Howe brothers off the coast of America in the summer of 1776. Lord Howe, Vice Admiral of the British fleet, and Lieutenant General William Howe, successor to Gage, had been designated commissioners "for restoring peace to his majesty's colonies and plantations." Their campaign was initiated by Lord Howe as soon as his flagship, the *Eagle*, arrived off Massachusetts Bay on June 20. The Admiral promptly dispatched three sets of documents to the mainland: (1) letters to four royal governors who had fled for their safety to the refuge of British ships for fear of being seized by the patriots;[8] (2) a "Declaration" announcing the appointment of his brother and himself as commissioners, authorized to grant pardons to all who would speedily "return to their duty"; and (3) personal letters from Englishmen to their American friends, "placing the character of the Howes in the most amiable point of view, and recommending reconciliation with G. Britain."

These last-mentioned papers were sent to the rebel camp under a flag of truce, and Washington promptly forwarded them to Congress. Among them were several letters addressed to members of Congress, including one to Benjamin Franklin which he presented to that body. On August 20 Franklin wrote to Lord Howe that the proposal that the colonies submit to the crown of Great Britain was fruitless. "The time is past," he said. "One might as well propose it to France . . . ." Reacting to these various papers, the Continental Congress ordered the British "Declaration" published in order to "let the people see upon what terms reconciliation is proposed to them." The truth of the matter was, William Ellery of Rhode Island wrote, "the door is shut . . . . The sword must determine our quarrel."

On this occasion the British were quite prepared to wield the sword. Thus, between June and late August 1776, an armada of several hundred English transports arrived in lower New York

11

Bay, disembarking a grand army of 32,000 soldiers (including German mercenaries) — "the greatest expeditionary force Great Britain had ever sent out from its shores."[9] To oppose these trained professional troops the Americans had managed to muster about 19,000 colonists, most of them untrained militiamen.

The British Commander in Chief, General Howe, resorted to the printing press before launching military operations on Long Island. On August 23 he issued an appeal to the "loyal inhabitants of this island" who had been "compelled by the leaders in rebellion to take up arms against his Majesty's government." To any such person who would desert the American side and present himself at British army headquarters, Howe promised his protection. And, if the Americans chose to join the King's standard under arms, they would be given every encouragement.

Soon after this broadside was put into circulation, the first battle took place, sustaining the loyalist argument of the winter of 1774-1775. Washington's army all but collapsed and was sent reeling into a headlong retreat. General Howe had demonstrated British military superiority with ease, his army killing and capturing 1,000 rebels. Since the occasion seemed opportune to talk to the Americans again, the Howes sent one of their newly acquired prisoners, Major General John Sullivan, of New Hampshire, to Congress with a request for a parley. They suggested a meeting between the Admiral and a "private" group of Americans.

At first Congress balked at such unofficial talks, fearful of what John Adams called British "Machiavellian maneuvres." However, it was clear that if Congress refused even to confer, the loyalists and moderate Americans might criticize that body as "obstinate and so desirous of war and bloodshed" that it had refused even to listen to Lord Howe's peace proposals.[10] To prevent such a possible British appeal directly to the American people, Congress finally agreed to send a three-man delegation to meet with the Admiral. It selected John Adams, Benjamin Franklin, and Edward Rutledge.

This interview took place on September 11, 1776, on Staten Island. As it began, the delegation's fears that Lord Howe might somehow talk the Americans out of their revolution quickly evaporated. Howe was firm in his approach, but mild and quite

12

un-Machaivellian. The principal stumbling block to reconciliation with Britain, he said, was the two-month-old Declaration of
Independence, which had made it "absolutely impossible for me
to treat, or even confer upon that ground, or to admit the idea
in the smallest degree." But the Americans would not, could
not, retreat from independence. The conference predictably
ended in failure.

Diplomacy having failed, the Howe brothers unsheathed the
sword once again and, during the next several days, British regulars drove the Americans before them in clashes on Manhattan
at Kips' Bay and Harlem Heights. During the first skirmish
Washington's militiamen fled in panic: in the second, although
they did somewhat better, they were again forced from the field.

On September 19, while the British and German forces re-
grouped and fortified their newly won positions, the Howes
issued another appeal to "his Majesty's well-affected subjects"
and "the inhabitants at large." This propaganda broadside
declared (excerpts):

> Although Congress, whom the misguided *Americans*
> suffer to direct their opposition to a re-establishment of
> the constitutional government of these provinces, have dis-
> avowed every purpose of reconciliation not consonant with
> their *extravagant and inadmissable claim of Independence,*
> the King's Commissioners think fit to declare that they
> are equally desirous to confer with his Majesty's well-
> affected subjects upon the means of restoring the public
> tranquillity, and establishing a permanent union with every
> colony as a part of the British empire .... It is recom-
> mended to the inhabitants at large to reflect seriously
> upon their present condition and expectations, and judge
> for themselves whether it would be more inconsistent with
> their honor and happiness to offer up their lives as a sacri-
> fice to the unjust and precarious cause in which they are
> engaged, or return to their allegiance, accept the blessings
> of peace, and to be secured in a free enjoyment of their
> liberties and properties.

In this appeal to the colonists the British leaders seemed to
have hoped they could ignore Congress. As for the King's "well-

affected" subjects, these loyalists had already flocked in large numbers to British-controlled New York City where they conferred with the Howes on ways and means of crushing the rebellion.

The patriot side did not let the Howes' appeal of September 19 go unchallenged. A counterproclamation — almost a word-for-word parody of the British broadside — soon made an appearance. It insisted that the King's commissioners really wished "to confer with his Majesty's subjects (if any so weak and abandoned are to be found) upon the means of establishing a permanent tyranny over every colony, and fix them the ever-lasting slaves of the British empire." [11]

The political situation thus unchanged, General Howe set his army into motion again on October 12, 1776. Again Washington's forces were unable to meet the challenge. As they retreated to the north, Fort Washington and Fort Lee (named in honor of the Commander in Chief and his second in command) were besieged and fell into British hands. The loss of Fort Washington was a hard blow to the American cause. Captured with it were 230 officers and 2,600 soldiers, as well as a large number of guns, cannon, shells, and other equipment. By mid-November, with the American militia enlistments fast expiring and his army weakened by desertions, Washington fled into the Jerseys, carrying with him "the remains of a broken army." The enemy followed closely at his heels.

If ever the moment was ripe for a British propaganda offensive, the last days of November and early December 1776 was the time. As the rebel cause began to lose adherents, General Howe issued a new appeal to all Americans to come in and renew their allegiance to the King. In a tract published on November 30, he ordered those rebels in arms to disband and return to their homes. Other rebels, "assembled together under the name of General or Provincial Congresses, Committees, conventions, or other associations by whatever name or names known," were directed to cease all such "treasonable actings and doings." Further, Howe established a deadline — sixty days from the date of this proclamation — for the people to come in and obtain their "full and free pardon of all treason." Those who failed to do so by that date, it was clear, would face the traitor's gibbet.

Now, indeed, British propaganda took effect. As one English historian has put it: "New Jersey rose to this bait almost en masse."[12] A contemporary observer wrote: "A great many came to headquarters in Trenton, were accepted, and dismissed with a [paper] protection."[13]

The early weeks of December 1776 saw the rebel cause at its lowest ebb. In their extremity the Americans turned to an ancient propaganda technique in an effort to rally the people to greater defensive efforts. This was the atrocity story, which painted British and German troops in brutish colors. During their march through the countryside, the British and German contingents had been involved in a certain amount of looting, pillaging, and desecration. By the time American propagandists finished with these incidents, they had been somewhat expanded, especially as to sexual assaults. "The enemy," wrote a friend to Jefferson, "like locusts sweep the Jerseys . . . . They to the disgrace of a civilized nation ravish the fair sex, from the age of ten to seventy."[14]

A more detailed description of some of these incidents, published in December by orders of the Pennsylvania Council of Safety, was reported in an anonymous letter from an "officer of distinction in the American army" to a friend:

> Since I last wrote you this morning I have had an opportunity of hearing a number of the particulars of the horrid depredations . . . of the British army . . . . Besides the sixteen young women who had fled to the woods to avoid their brutality, and were seized and carried off, one man had the cruel mortification to have his wife and only daughter (a child of ten years of age) ravished; this he himself, almost choked with grief, uttered in lamentations to his friend, who told me of it, and also informed me that another girl of thirteen years of age was taken from her father's house, carried to a barn about a mile, there ravished and afterwards made use of by five or more of these brutes.

15

On April 18, 1777, a Congressional committee, which had been appointed to inquire into the conduct of British troops during their march through New York and New Jersey, brought in a four-point indictment of wanton devastation and destruction of property, inhuman treatment of prisoners, the "savage butchery of those who had submitted," and finally the "lust and brutality of the soldiers in abusing women." Concerning this last indictment, the committee reported it had received authentic information of "many instances of the most indecent treatment and actual ravishment of married and single women . . . ."

The theme of British-German sexual depravity was to be repeated by the Americans on numerous occasions, leading finally to an outraged cry of indignation in the Tory press: "The charge of 'deflowering defenceless women' is one of those deliberate, malicious falsehoods which are circulated by the rebels, purely to incense the inhabitants against the British troops."[15]

In late December 1776 a more positive note was injected into American propaganda by one of the most famous writers of the period. A few days before the battle of Trenton, *The American Crisis* by Thomas Paine came into Washington's hands. Paine, who was then serving as a volunteer in the American army, had earlier written the influential pamphlet, *Common Sense*. The opening words of his new appeal still reverberate in American ears:

> These are the times that try men's souls. The summer soldier and the sunshine patriot will, in this cruel crisis, shrink from the service of his country; but he that stands it now, deserves the love and thanks of man and woman. Tyranny, like hell, is not easily conquered; yet we have this consolation with us, that the harder the conflict, the more glorious the triumph.

Washington quickly perceived the effect Paine's words would have on his discouraged soldiers. He ordered the drums sounded and the troops assembled to hear their officers read from the pamphlet. "It was," comments one writer, "as wine to the weary patriots, giving them strength to endure the bitter winter winds that swept the Delaware and whipped them as they stumbled through the snow and sleet . . . to Trenton."[16]

The success of Washington's attack that followed at Trenton was a turning point in the war. Although General Howe at first dismissed it as of limited military significance, as it was, he soon became unhappily aware of Trenton's real meaning — in the area of patriot morale and confidence. In January 1777 he wrote to Lord George Germain, Secretary of State for the American colonies:

It is with much concern that I am to inform your Lordship, the unfortunate and untimely defeat at Trenton has thrown us further back than was at first apprehended, from the great encouragement given to the rebels. I do not now see a prospect of terminating the war, but by a general action.

This revealing statement is the key to Howe's early military strategy. He had not been thinking in terms of a general action; rather, he simply had been applying military pressure to give sustenance to earlier British arguments, hoping the combination would persuade the Americans to cease their resistance. But, with Trenton, the "bubble of British invincibility" was punctured. The effects of all the British military successes between August and December 1776 had been practically swept away. They were indeed not even back where they started, since the rebels had tasted an important victory and knew they could win, if conditions were right. Now it would take a great many more bayonets and a great many broadsides to prove to the rebels that Trenton was an accident of war. It would take "a general action," something the British government and General Howe had hoped to avoid.

+

A new phase of the propaganda war began in January 1777. Washington had been given unprecedented powers by Congress to deal with the crisis, and he proceeded to issue his own counterproclamation to the people. This broadside was aimed at Americans who, he said, had been influenced "by inimical motives, intimidated by the threats of the enemy, or deluded by a proclamation issued the 30th of November last, by Lord and

17

General Howe," who had taken oaths of allegiance to the throne. Washington ordered all such persons — in order to enable the patriots to distinguish "between the friends of America and those of Great Britain" — to travel immediately to his headquarters or any other general officer of the army, and surrender such British certificates and take the oath of allegiance to the United States. Those who refused to do so within thirty days were "to withdraw themselves and their families within the enemy's lines."

This proclamation, which had the effect of clearing American-controlled territory of Tories, brought Washington unexpected criticism from delegates in Congress. The New Jersey members in particular expressed alarm that the Commander in Chief was setting a dangerous precedent by assuming "the legislative and executive powers of government in all the states." Abraham Clark, one of the New Jersey delegates, argued: "We set out to oppose tyranny in all its strides, and I hope we shall persevere." In February a Congressional committee was appointed to examine this complaint. It found that Washington's proclamation had not interfered "with the laws or civil government of any state, but considering the situation of the army was prudent and necessary," and the matter was dropped.

Although military operations had come to a halt for the winter, in both camps propaganda planning went on. In March and April 1777, Howe's staff produced several new desertion appeals which were effective. The first appeal was dated March 17. It promised rebel soldiers who surrendered to the British army before May 1, that they would receive not only full pardons but that every man who brought in his weapons would be paid their full value. Further, any deserter who wished would be allowed to join a provincial corps being formed in the British army. The second appeal, dated April 21, promised 200 acres of land to every private who enlisted in the provincial corps and served for two years or for the duration of the war in North America.[17]

Early in May, in a letter to Congress, Washington reported that these British propaganda appeals had had "an unhappy influence on too many of the soldiers; in a particular manner on those who are not natives . . . . I could wish some means could be devised to cause more frequent desertions of their troops. Congress may think of some expedients. A larger bounty might have some effect."

To counter British efforts and prepare the American people for the impending "general action," Congress published a lengthy address on May 29, 1777, "To the Inhabitants of the United States." In this paper Congress reviewed the background of the struggle which, it said, began "because you would not be slaves." Said the Congress (excerpts):

Commissioners, at the head of *fleets* and *armies* were sent to restore *peace* to America. After their arrival they issued a proclamation containing a promise of pardon. A pardon implies a precedent crime. What crime was it which the pardon so graciously proferred was meant to extinguish? That of refusing to surrender your birthright and to be bound, in all cases, by the acts of the British parliament. To receive a pardon was to acknowledge that asserting essential rights of freemen was criminal; and to promise never to assert them any more . . . .

No middle line can now be drawn. Absolute and unconditonal submission to their power is the end, long intended . . . . Absolute and unconditional submission! These are terms to which your ears have been unaccustomed. It behooves you fully to understand their meaning . . . . The horrors of Asiatic slavery rush into your views . . . . You would be numbered among slaves . . . .

Congress warned further that the people should remain on guard against "the secret arts and machinations of emissaries" sent among them. Such persons, said Congress, "gain and transmit intelligence; they invent and propagate false and injurious reports; they create and foment jealousies between states and individuals; they magnify the power, numbers, and resources of the enemy; they undervalue yours. By these means, the timid are dismayed; and the honest but unsuspicious are misinformed and misled."

This address, a timely and effective reminder of the nature of the contest, was published just before two British armies began to move. In the north, Lieutenant General John Burgoyne began an invasion of the northern colonies from Canada in June, while the British army under Howe sailed from New York for an unknown destination, finally reappearing at the Head of Elk, Maryland, where the troops disembarked for a march against Philadelphia.

The day he landed in Maryland, August 27, 1777, Howe published another propaganda sheet whose purpose (as he later described in a letter to Lord George Germain, the colonial secretary) was: "To quiet the minds of the people at large in Pennsylvania and the countries to which it has relations . . . as well as . . . to disunite their army." In this broadside, Howe renewed his offer of pardon "to all such officers and private men" in the rebel army who surrendered "to any detachment of his Majesty's forces."

Washington immediately denounced the appeal as another attempt "to seduce the people to give up their rights and to encourage our soldiery to desert." At this time, however, the thought uppermost in Washington's mind was to force march his army so as to block the British advance on Philadelphia. On September 11 the maneuverings of the two forces led to the Battle of Brandywine, where Washington's army was once again thrashed and forced to retreat. Shortly thereafter, the British marched unmolested into undefended Philadelphia.

Howe had hoped the capture of Philadelphia would be a turning point in the struggle. Unfortunately for the English cause, the acquisition of Philadelphia was counterbalanced by military disaster in the north. In August 1777, Congress received word that a force of New England militiamen under John Stark had defeated part of Burgoyne's invading army at Bennington, Vermont. This news was immediately published by Congress in leaflet form and sent to Washington for distribution to his troops. Thanking Congress for the papers, Washington responded: "I doubt not but they will answer the good end which is intended by them. Every piece of good news circulated in this manner through the camp, will certainly inspirit the troops."

Several weeks later, he reported additional good news from the north to encourage his soldiers for an impending battle. In general orders read to the troops, Washington cited Major General Horatio Gates' victory over General Burgoyne at Saratoga and the surrender of the entire British force. Challenging his soldiers to do as well, he exhorted them: "The army, the main American army, will certainly not suffer itself to be outdone by their northern brethren . . . . Let it never be said that in a day of action you turned your backs on the foe. Let the enemy no longer triumph."

The next day, October 4, the main American army marched out to do battle with the British-German forces. For a time, in the ensuing battle of Germantown, it looked as if it would win. But the British rallied and Washington's army again was forced to retreat, losing about 1,000 men – killed, wounded, or made prisoner. The Americans had done so well in this battle, however, that morale was not seriously undone.

After Germantown, and before Washington brought his battered army to the bleak ground at Valley Forge, only the victory over Burgoyne brought comfort to the patriots. While Howe's army went into winter quarters in Philadelphia, where a round of dancing and parties began, Washington and his troops settled in at Valley Forge to wait out the harsh winter of 1777-1778.

+

The festive atmosphere in British-occupied Philadelphia seemed almost to have been deliberately invoked by Howe to demonstrate the rewards of loyalty and rebellion. Several times during the winter the British renewed their offers of pardon and other benefits to the rebel soldiers at Valley Forge if they would give up their struggle. These had great effect. By March 25, 1778, according to figures compiled by Joseph Galloway, Howe's Superintendent-General of Police, 1,134 soldiers and 354 sailors deserted the American armed forces and fled to Philadelphia, where they took the oath of allegiance to Great Britain. The bulk of these men, however, were foreign-born, consisting mostly of natives of Ireland, England, or Scotland.[18]

At Washington's suggestion an effort was made to counter the British appeal to deserters. On April 23, 1778, Congress issued

21

its own proclamation offering pardons to American loyalist soldiers serving with the British forces, if they returned to the state where they lived before June 10. Congress recommended that the citizens of the states receive "such returning penitents with compassion and mercy . . . ." It ordered 500 copies printed in English and 200 in German, and asked Washington to "take such measures as he shall deem most effectual for circulating the foregoing . . . amongst the American levies in the enemy's army."

There was apparently little reaction to the American offer of pardon. Meanwhile, British and loyalist planners, buoyed by the success of their appeal, launched another subversive effort against the American army. It involved the publication in the loyalist *Evening Post* in Philadelphia of a document purporting to be an official resolution of Congress, which declared that American militiamen who had enlisted or were drafted to serve for limited periods, nevertheless would be detailed beyond the stipulated times.

When this report reached Valley Forge, Washington acted immediately to counter it. In his general orders of April 23, 1778, which were read to the troops, Washington declared that the report "is as false as it is wicked and is intended to induce those who have already inlisted or have been drafted to desert and to intimidate others from engaging into the service of their country." He further declared:

Our enemies, finding themselves unable to reduce us by force of their arms, are now practicing every insidious art to gain time and disunite us, but the General hopes that men who have struggled with every difficulty and encountered every danger are not to be conquered by artifices which are so easily exposed. It is necessary to give warning to such weak men as might otherwise be deluded by the traitorous promises of the enemy that, under pretence of sending deserters from this army passage free to Great Britain or Ireland, there to be set at large, they confine them on board ship with a view either to force them into their service as seamen or transport them as recruits to some garrison.

Within a few days these propaganda incidents were forgotten in the patriot excitement over the important and stirring news received from Europe. France had recognized the independence of the United States! On May 2 a great celebration broke out in the American camp. In British-occupied Philadelphia the same news threw a dark shadow over all English prospects in America.

Prior to the arrival of the news of France's decision to recognize the United States, Washington had received from the British governor of New York City, William Tryon, a draft of Prime Minister Frederick North's "conciliatory bills." They constituted a belated attempt by the British government to prevent the signing of the French-American alliance. North offered important concessions to the Americans to restore old ties — everything, in fact, but complete independence. To sell these proposals, Lord North appointed peace commissioners who were ordered to sail to America to negotiate with the rebels "to reunite the British empire."

After studying the papers sent him by Tryon, Washington dispatched them to Congress with the comment that they were obviously "meant to poison the minds of the people and detach the wavering, at least, from our cause." But unsure of their significance, he urged Congress to investigate and expose the new British move.

Washington's negative reaction was reflected in the actions of Congress. On April 22 that body adopted a resolution which declared that if the papers were authentic, they indicated a loss of British confidence in their ability to conquer America. In any event the concessions (which included doing away with all taxation) were no longer important. The Continental Congress decided that it would not hold any conference or meet with any commissioners "unless they shall, as preliminary thereto, either withdraw their fleets and armies, or else, in positive and express terms, acknowledge the independence of the said states." To demonstrate its confidence, Congress ordered the British proposals printed "for the public information," despite the fact they seemed to have been "industriously circulated by the emissaries of the enemy in a partial and secret manner."

The same day Congress acted, Washington received "an extra-ordinary and impertinent request" from Governor Tryon, who asked that copies of the bills be disseminated among the officers and men of the American army. On the twenty-sixth Washington replied to Tryon that he would indeed circulate the bills among his soldiers, "in whose fidelity to the United States I have the most perfect confidence." He enclosed a copy of a newspaper showing Congress' resolve to publish the bills in any event, and also sent Tryon several American propaganda papers, requesting they be disseminated among the soldiers of the British army. That was a game two could play.

The new British effort at conciliation had gotten off to a bad start. When the new peace commissioners — the Earl of Carlisle, William Eden, and George Johnstone — arrived in occupied Philadelphia in early June 1778, they learned to their dismay that the British force was preparing to evacuate the city and that Congress had firmly rejected the new proposals. The unhappy commissioners were forced to join the retreat to New York. Subsequently, they sent various secret agents, such as one John Berkenhout, to Philadelphia to sound out influential Americans on the British proposals. These efforts proved unsuccessful and some of the agents were jailed. Other subversive operations also failed. The rebel leaders remained impervious to British arguments.

In a final desperate effort to succeed in their mission, the commissioners decided to take their case directly to the American people in the fall of 1778. Beginning on October 3, they launched a large-scale propaganda campaign (called by one commissioner "a last dying speech"). By land and sea they sent great numbers of a "Manifesto and Proclamation" to all members of Congress, to members of state assemblies and conventions, to ministers of the gospel, to governors of various states, to officers of the Continental army, to chief justices and judges of the American courts and to the people in general.

In this "Manifesto" the commissioners reminded the Americans that Congress had, in the beginning, asked only for redress of grievances and had denied any desire to become independent. But having been granted all it had asked, it had enlarged its

24

demands and was insisting on independence. Congress, declared the commissioners, had no authority "either to reject our offers without the previous consideration and consent of the several assemblies and conventions of their constituents, or to refer us to pretended sovereign treaties, which have never yet been ratified by the people of this continent."

The commissioners then proceeded to appeal over the head of Congress to the local assemblies suggesting direct negotiations; to the "free inhabitants" under arms suggesting they join the British army; to ministers of the gospel, commending Britain to them as their best guarantee of religious liberty and Protestantism. Having thus flung their net widely, the commissioners' tone, at the end of their "dying speech," grew threatening. They warned:

> The policy, as well as the benevolence of Great Britain, have thus far checked the extremes of war, when they tended to distress people still considered as our fellow-subjects, and to desolate a country shortly to become again a source of mutual advantage: but when that country professes the unnatural design not only of estranging herself from us, but of mortgaging herself and her resources to our enemies, the whole contest is changed . . . .
>
> Under such circumstances, the laws of self-preservation must direct the conduct of Great Britain: and if the British Colonies are to become an accessory to France, will direct her to render that accession of as little avail as possible to her enemy.

The final decision in the dispute, said the commissioners, was up to the American people. They concluded by again offering full pardons to any colonist who applied under the terms of the "Manifesto" for forty days from the date of the document, or until November 11, 1778.

The initial reaction of Congress to this lengthy propaganda appeal was to forbid its dissemination, which was a reversal of its previous confident attitude towards the conciliatory bills. On October 16 it ordered all authorities to seize and suppress the "seditious" papers whenever and wherever they were found. Washington had misgivings about Congress' reaction. In a letter he suggested that "the avenues and channels in which [the papers] may be conveyed are so various and numerous that no exertions will be found sufficient entirely to prevent the evil." The Commander in Chief also felt that the attempt to suppress the British offer might, in the end, have more bad effects than a free circulation of them, made "with proper strictures."[19]

Washington had also quickly noted the "implied threat" in the "Manifesto" of a change of military operations "to one of a more predatory and destructive kind." The British may have done this, he suggested, "only in terrorem; but it is possible that it may be intended as a serious principle of practice." Reacting to this threat, Congress warned the people on October 10 that "there is every reason to expect" that Britain would "as the last effort, ravage, burn and destroy every city and town on this continent they can come at." Congress recommended Americans living in exposed areas which might be attacked to immediately build huts thirty miles from their homes, where they could take refuge in an emergency. It further suggested that if such enemy operations did take place, the patriots should retaliate by setting fire and destroying the properties of refugee loyalists.

Several weeks later, on October 30, Congress issued its own threatening "manifesto." Taking note of the British intimidations that devastation would follow rejection of the latest offer, it announced its firm resolve "that if our enemies presume to execute their threats, or persist in their present career of barbarity, we will take such exemplary vengeance as shall deter others from a like conduct." Printed copies of this resolution were sent to Washington and, after setting his secret agents in motion, he informed Congress on November 6 that the British authorities in New York City would soon "be possessed of some of the copies and of the newspapers that contain them."

In November, despite American warnings, a British vessel sailing with a cargo of manifestoes "under a flag of truce" was shipwrecked on the coast of New Jersey. The Americans seized its commander, Lieutenant Christopher Hele, and his entire crew and imprisoned them. Their incarceration triggered written protests from Admiral James Gambier of the British navy. On

November 28 Congress informed the admiral that "as the manifestoes on board that vessel were of a seditious nature, and intended to open an unwarrantable correspondence, their being covered by a flag of truce is by no means an extenuation of the offence." Congress further argued that rights under a flag of truce were "forfeited" when employed in "illicit practices." In denouncing the Congress on this issue a Hessian officer wrote: "Everyone trembles at the thought of such despotic power . . . ."[20]

By the end of 1778 it had become clear to the British commissioners that their "Manifesto" and all their efforts had failed. Their propaganda answered by counterpropaganda, their emissaries arrested, and their peace offerings rejected, the commissioners finally gave up the struggle and returned to England in December.

+

Having been unsuccessful in their campaigns in the north and failing equally in the middle colonies despite Howe's early military successes, British commanders turned their attention hopefully to the "weak" end of the American chain, the southern colonies, where a new phase of the war now began. The idea in the minds of both civilian and military authorities in New York was that if just one province could be subdued, and a royal government restored, "then everyone believes all provinces would prefer peace to war."[21]

This phase of the conflict began with the capture of Savannah, Georgia, on December 29, 1778, by Lieutenant Colonel Archibald Campbell and a combined British-German-loyalist force of 3,500 men. The seizure of Savannah and the routing of the patriot militia seemed to have brought about a complete submission of Georgia. Finally, Great Britain had a pacified province.

In consolidating their newly won position, the British army turned its attention once again to the printing press. One broadside, dated January 4, 1779, formally announced "to all his Majesty's faithful subjects of the southern provinces, that a fleet and army . . . are actually arrived in Georgia for their protection, to which they are desired to repair without loss of time, and by uniting their force under the royal standard, rescue their friends from oppression, themselves from slavery." On January 11 a second paper offered a reward for the capture of the "ring-leaders of sedition, and some skulking parties from the rebels of Carolina." A third document also was issued, a combination of an oath of allegiance and "safe conduct pass," to be signed by Americans who submitted.

These papers, backed by British military superiority, were highly effective and Colonel Campbell reported with satisfaction to Lord Germain that "the inhabitants from all parts of the province flock with their arms to the standard, and cordially embrace the terms which have been offered." On March 4 the British reestablished a royal government and on March 24 further announced that Georgia was formally "at the peace of his Majesty."

While the British army consolidated its hold on Georgia, in July 1779 several important military and propaganda operations were taking place in the north. The first involved a punitive raid into Connecticut on the third anniversary of the adoption of the Declaration of Independence by a British force of 2,600 men. The raiders, who plundered and burned as they marched, simultaneously disseminated a propaganda paper titled, "Address to the Inhabitants of Connecticut." The document warned the people that they lay entirely at the mercy of British forces, whose control of the seas allowed them to land at will, and it then posed the question: "Why then will you persist in a ruinous and ill-judged resistance?"

These broadsides were distributed by Admiral Sir George Collier and former New York governor Major General Tryon, at the suggestion of General Clinton. Tryon later reported to Clinton that the effects of the propaganda sheets could not be determined "till there are some further operations and descents upon their coasts. Many copies... were left behind at Newhaven and at Fairchild."

But if the reaction of at least one delegate to the Congress was any indication, the raid had an effect "directly contrary" to what was intended. Americans, wrote James Duane, could never "be worked to submission by cruelty and devastation. Their aversion to their destroyers will become deeper rivetted; and their efforts to defend themselves more strenuous and decisive."

Congress was so angered by the raid that a committee of retaliation was created "to take the most effectual means to carry into execution the manifesto of October 30, 1778, by burning and destroying the towns belonging to the enemy in Great Britain and the West Indies." A directive to Benjamin Franklin in Paris was drafted, instructing him to hire incendiaries "to set fire in the capital of the British Dominions, particularly the royal palace, and to such other towns in Great Britain as may be most expedient, and that as soon as some great object of this sort can be accomplished you do in a proper manifesto avow the same as having been done by the order of Congress."

It is not certain this directive was ever sent to Franklin, but similar instructions on retaliatory measures did reach him, and certain invasion plans and others were coordinated with the French.

Several weeks after the Connecticut raid, General Wayne restored American spirits with his capture of the British fort at Stony Point, New York. What particularly encouraged the patriots was the cold efficiency with which Wayne's troops attacked with unloaded muskets, using only the bayonet. They killed 63 enemy troops and captured 543, while losing 15 killed and 83 wounded, including General Wayne, whose skull was grazed by a musket ball. Exulting over this victory, the *New Hampshire Gazette* wrote on July 27:

> Nothing can exceed the spirit and intrepidity of our brave countrymen in storming and carrying . . . Stony Point. It demonstrates that the Americans have soldiers equal to any in the world; and that they can attack and vanquish the Britons in their strongest works. No action during the war, performed by the British military, has equalled this coup de main.

Sir Henry Clinton confessed that the success of the American operation was "a very great affront to us, the more mortifying since it was unexpected and possibly avoidable." In Philadelphia the French minister to the United States, Conrad Alexandre

Gerard, was greatly impressed. He suggested that telling the story of Stony Point overseas would "much elevate the ideas of Europe about the military qualities of the Americans."

Distressed "by the aggravating circumstances of the loss of the whole garrison" (General Clinton's words), the British tried to put the best face on it, and at least one loyalist writer tried to counter American propaganda on the event by noting in the *New York Gazette:*

> Can any one be so stupid as to imagine that such a trifling affair could be in any way decisive at present, or influence the conduct of Britain? Or are incidents of this kind unusual in the course of war? I could mention several instances where outposts belonging to the greatest generals that ever led armies into the field, have been attacked and carried; and in wars, too, where those generals have been most successful. People who are so easily elevated, betray their own weakness.

Nevertheless, this first American clear-cut victory in a long time sweetened the patriots' labors for several months to come.

+

Still the year 1779 ended on a dismal note for the Americans. In October a combined French-American force tried but failed to oust the British forces from Savannah; and in December General Clinton sailed south from New York with an army of 8,500 men, with Lord Cornwallis second in command. In February the troops landed thirty miles south of Charleston, South Carolina, and shortly thereafter placed that port town under siege. On May 12, 1780, this siege ended with the surrender of Charleston in "one of the greatest disasters suffered by the Americans during the whole war."[22] The British captured more than 5,400 prisoners and huge amounts of materials and weapons. Among the prize prisoners were three signers of the Declaration of Independence: Arthur Middleton, Edward Rutledge, and Thomas Heyward, Jr., all South Carolinians. All three were imprisoned at St. Augustine, Florida, until July 1781.

30

British broadsides detailing the event were promptly disseminated into the interior, which propaganda, General Clinton
later wrote, "soon had the happy effects, as numbers with their
arms came in every day to headquarters from the remotest parts
of the province, many of them bringing in their former oppressors." Now South Carolina as well as Georgia seemed to have
submitted.

Meanwhile, in the north — where operations appeared at a
standstill — the British renewed their desertion appeals to the
soldiers of Washington's army at Morristown. Thus, one leaflet
addressed "To the Soldiers in the Continental Army, 1780"
declared that:

> The time is at length arrived when all the artifices and
> falsehoods of the Congress and of your commanders can
> no longer conceal from you the misery of your situation;
> you are neither Clothed, Fed, nor Paid; your numbers are
> wasting away by Sickness, Famine, Nakedness, and rapidly
> so by the period of your stipulated Services . . . . this is
> then the moment to fly away from slavery and fraud.

Continuing in this vein the leaflet announced that the troubles
between Ireland and Great Britain had been settled (a statement
aimed at Washington's Irish-born soldiers) and urged both
American and foreign-born rebels to "join your real friends."
The leaflet concluded: "you are told that you are surrounded
by a numerous militia, this is also false — associate then together, make use of your firelocks and join the British army, where
you will be permitted to dispose of yourselves as you please."

A copy of this leaflet — the only one found in the Morristown
camp, although Washington was certain many copies had been
dispersed by British agents and picked up by the troops — was
sent to Congress. Washington offered the opinion that this
propaganda had had "a considerable effect" on the soldiers.

The morale of the main American army, at a low ebb in the
spring of 1780, was further depressed by the news of the fall of
Charleston. It became apparent, after the news of the seemingly
complete submission of the southerners reached the north, that
only the dispatch of new American forces could prevent the loss

31

of the entire south. Prior to Charleston's fall, Washington had sent a small force of 1,400 men under Baron de Kalb to give aid to the southerners. The crisis in South Carolina moved Congress to inject itself into the military picture; it ordered the hero of Saratoga, Horatio Gates, to take immediate command of all American operations in the southern department.

Late in July 1780 Gates arrived in North Carolina where he assumed command from de Kalb. On August 4, in one of his first moves to bolster morale and encourage the southerners, Gates issued a broadside announcing his approach with "a numerous, well appointed and formidable army" to deal with the "insulting" British. One hundred copies were printed for distribution by his advancing columns.[23] Unfortunately for General Gates, on August 16 his mixed force of regulars and militiamen (about 4,100 men) was defeated in the Battle of Camden and swept from the field by Cornwallis' regiments. Early in the melee Gates fled precipitously, leaving de Kalb to fight on until he was mortally wounded.

This defeat, which greatly tarnished General Gates' reputation, was somewhat offset in October by the important patriot victory at King's Mountain over a loyalist force, the American Volunteers, led by Major Patrick Ferguson of the British army. Ferguson had become infamous for his plundering raids in the Carolinas as well as his threats to the frontier settlers if they did not stop opposing the King's rule. The frontiersmen decided not to wait for Ferguson to come to them but to fight him in his own territory. More than 1,400 of them turned out to pursue Ferguson's troops to King's Mountain, South Carolina, where they destroyed the American loyalist troops in a remarkable battle in which Ferguson was slain. Of the enemy force of about 1,000 men, 157 were killed, a similar number were badly wounded, and nearly 700 taken prisoner. The patriots lost 90 men killed or wounded.

The battle of King's Mountain had the effect of slowing Cornwallis' invasion of North Carolina. Congress, in the meantime, disappointed by Gates' performance, turned over to Washington the problem of choosing his successor. The Commander in Chief named Major General Nathanael Greene, a happy choice. Greene immediately rode south to take over the southern "army" — 2,300 infantrymen on paper, of whom only 1,480 were present and fit for duty.

+

While these military events unfolded in the Carolinas, in the north there occurred the defection to the British side of one of the best fighting generals on the American side, Benedict Arnold. The fiery Arnold's treason was discovered accidently on September 25, 1780, while he was engaged in a plot with British officials to deliver West Point to the enemy. Before the plot was fully exposed, he fled to the British camp, leaving behind his unfortunate contact, British adjutant general, John André, who was seized as a spy by Washington and hanged.

The Arnold defection gave birth to two propaganda appeals to his former associates, addresses which showed the hand of loyalist ghost-writers. The first, addressed to "the inhabitants of America," was a general statement by Arnold in which he attempted to explain the motives which had led him "to join the King's arms." It contained no word of his negotiations with General Clinton for monies and emoluments for his treason. Instead, he lamented that Britain's offers of reconciliation and peace had been ignored by Congress, which had joined with France, "the enemy of the Protestant faith."

These unconvincing arguments were followed several weeks later by Arnold's second address "To the Officers and Soldiers of the Continental Army who have the real Interest of their Country at Heart, and who are determined to be no longer the Tools and Dupes of Congress, or of France." Dated October 20, this subversive document invited the Americans to desert and join the British army. It stated that:

> His Excellency, Sir Henry Clinton has authorized me to raise a corps of cavalry and infantry, who are to be clothed, subsisted and paid as the other corps are in the British service, and those who bring in horses, arms, or accoutrements are to be paid their value, or have liberty to sell them. To every non-commissioned officer and private

a bounty of three guineas will be given, and as the Commander-in-Chief is pleased to allow me to nominate the officers, I shall with infinite satisfaction embrace this opportunity of advancing men whose valor I have witnessed, and whose principles are favorable to a union with Britain and true American liberty.

After making this offer, Arnold's tone changed as he continued:

Friends, fellow soldiers, and citizens, arouse and judge for yourselves — reflect on what you have lost — consider to what you are reduced, and by your courage repel the ruin that still threatens you .... What is America but a land of widows, beggars, and orphans? — and should the parent nation cease her exertions to deliver you, what security remains to you for the enjoyment of the consolations of that religion for which your fathers braved the ocean, the heathen, and the wilderness? ...

But what need of arguments to such as feel infinitely more misery than language can express? I therefore only add my promise of the most affectionate welcome and attention to all who are disposed to join me.

When the first Arnold address appeared, Washington sent a copy to Congress and commented mildly: "I am at a loss which to admire most, the confidence of Arnold in publishing, or the folly of the enemy in supposing that a production signed by so infamous a character will have any weight with the people of these states, or any influence upon our affairs abroad." But when the second appeal addressed to his soldiers arrived, Washington was far more annoyed at what he termed "this unparalleled piece of assurance." It would, he said sharply, only "add to the detestation" the soldiers felt for Arnold.

The British attempt to use Arnold to subvert the rebel army continued unabated for many weeks. On October 25 the New York *Royal Gazette* reprinted Arnold's address to the American army and continued to reprint it in every issue, twice a week, through December.[24] The patriot press countered with a flow of words which placed Arnold beyond redemption in American eyes. Burned in effigy and reviled as the personification of evil, he was soon held in "utmost abhorrence and detestation."[25] Many of his former colleagues longed to lay hands upon him and a plan to that effect was shortly set in motion by Washington, who hoped to see him hanged.

Copies of Arnold's address in one form or another also made their way into the encampment of the Pennsylvania line near Morristown, New Jersey, commanded by Wayne. On December 16, 1780, Wayne wrote to the President of Pennsylvania, Joseph Reed, to advise that his "poorly clothed, badly fed, and worse paid" troops were being "worked upon" by enemy proclamations. Two weeks later, in the evening of January 1, 1781, the troops mutinied over their poor living conditions, their lengthy service, and no pay. They fired muskets, killing one officer, wounding two, and seized control of the cannon.

General Wayne and two of his aides tried to reason with them. But the mutineers replied they had been wronged and "were determined to see themselves righted . . . ." Wayne asked them what they intended to do and pleaded with them not to "attempt to go to the enemy." They replied that was not their intent, that they would hang any man who would attempt it and, "for that, if the enemy should come out in consequence of this revolt, they would turn back and fight them." Thus assured, Wayne told the men he would accompany them, whereupon they marched off to present their grievances to Congress.[26]

It did not take long for news of the mutiny to reach General Clinton in New York. He immediately ordered the British grenadiers and light infantry, and three battalions of Hessian troops to march toward the mutineers "to favor the revolt." He also sent two undercover agents to Princeton, where the mutineers had halted on January 3, to assure them "that in this struggle for their just rights and liberties," they would be helped by a body of British troops. Further, Clinton suggested that if they laid down their arms they would be pardoned for all past offenses, be paid all their back pay due them by Congress, and "not be required to serve unless they chuse it."

But the British had misread their sentiments. The Pennsylvania troops had not changed their attitude toward Great Britain. As proof of this, they seized the two British spies who brought them "a written invitation promising them great rewards if they would march" towards the British forces which would provide them cover. A board of sergeants declared that they despised "a treachery and meanness like that of Benedict Arnold, that their views were honorable, and their loyalty to the cause of their country unalterable." When President Reed came to Princeton, he was received with respect and brought with him the response from Congress dealing with their complaints, which they accepted. They also delivered to authorities the two spies sent from Clinton, who were tried by a board of officers, condemned, and executed on January 11. In late January 1781 a similar rising of Jersey troops also occurred. Washington immediately sent a force to subdue them, executing a few of the ringleaders on the spot.

+

The excitement in the north had temporarily diverted American attention from the critical military situation in the Carolinas, where Cornwallis' force appeared to be invincible, despite Daniel Morgan's victory at Cowpens on January 17. With the very existence of the southern American army constantly threatened by Cornwallis, General Greene sought security in Virginia. His movement to all intents left the entire area from the Virginia border to Florida ostensibly in British hands. Whereupon, Cornwallis retired to Greensboro where he issued a new broadside inviting all "faithful and loyal subjects to repair, without loss of time, with their arms and ten days' provisions, to the royal standard . . . ." When Greene slipped back into North Carolina to do battle and was defeated at Guilford Courthouse, the British general issued a second broadside announcing his "complete victory" over the rebels and calling upon the people to surrender and receive British protection.[27]

Despite these victories, however, the Americans did not return to their former allegiance. Cornwallis wrote to Clinton: "Many of the inhabitants rode into camp, shook me by the hand, said they were glad to see us and to hear that we had beat Greene,

36

and then rode home again. I could not get 100 men . . . to stay with us even as militia." There was good reason for this. Although Cornwallis had won every battle he had fought, his army had paid too high a price. His tents were full of wounded and the entire army looked much bedraggled. To the hardheaded North Carolinians, it did not look much like a victorious army. And it was not. Cornwallis had already lost the campaign. He was deep in hostile country, through which his march seemed to have had no perceptible effect. The stage was set for his fateful retreat to Yorktown.

Greene, on the other hand, who had not yet won a battle, turned southward to liberate the Carolinas. He quickly demonstrated that the British conquests had been a mirage. One British strongpoint fell after another, until by May 1781, Lieutenant Colonel Lord Francis Rawdon, the commander at Charleston, found himself trying to explain why the King's troops had relinquished "for the present" parts of South Carolina. In a paper disseminated in the backcountry, Lord Rawdon said: "We trust it is unnecessary for us to exhort the loyal inhabitants of those districts to stand firm in their duty and principles; or to caution them against the insidious artifices of an enemy who must shortly abandon to their fate those unfortunate people whom they have deluded into revolt."

But these words could not conceal the fact that the game was ending for Britain. Four months later, at Yorktown, Cornwallis and his army found themselves cornered and besieged by a combined French-American army of 16,000 men under the rebel commander, George Washington; their escape by sea blocked by the French fleet. On October 18, 1781, Cornwallis surrendered.

During the two remaining war years after the denouement at Yorktown, while the peace negotiations went on, only minor military actions took place. During this period the British were almost entirely on the military and propaganda defensive. Now it was their army that became the target for American offers of "pardon and protection" to any Americans "who may have been seduced from their allegiance to Congress."[28] Washington easily entered into the subversive game and, in an attempt to break up a British corps of American deserters, issued a pardon "to all our deserters in the service of the enemy, who will return to their colors."

At besieged Savannah the Americans also invoked an ancient propaganda technique, prevailing upon an English deserter, one Henry Pumphrey, to write a "seductive" letter to his former comrades. In this letter Pumphrey advised them "to escape from bondage and tyranny to liberty and happiness." He referred them to an offer of the governor of Georgia, who promised free lands and other rewards to any British soldier who defected.

These little operations, of course, were only the backwash of the prolonged struggle, whose outcome had already been settled at Yorktown.

☆ 2 ☆

American Propaganda
and the Struggle
for Canada

E IGHT MONTHS BEFORE the war began on the plains of
Boston, fifty-six predominantly middle-aged Americans gathered
together in Philadelphia in the First Continental Congress to
consult "on the present state of the Colonies." For seven weeks,
beginning on September 5, 1774, the delegates argued and
debated "the unwise, unjust, and ruinous policy" of Great
Britain. In late October, after adopting various anti-Parliamentary
resolves and issuing several important papers, they adjourned
peaceably. One of those state papers was an appeal to the King
for redress of grievances; another was a lengthy and indignant
Address to the People of Great Britain; and a third was an
Address to the Inhabitants of the Province of Quebec.

The last document is of particular interest because it marked
the beginning of an American propaganda campaign to bring
Canada over to the side of the colonies. This campaign was
highly successful in subverting the new and tenuous allegiance
of the French Canadians to the British government, especially
after the entry of France into the war in 1788. The combined
French-American verbal assault on the Canadian mind was so
effective that the British authorities in Canada were placed
almost entirely on the defensive. Indeed, the British government
was so worried over the impact of the ideas emanating from
the south that it attempted to seal off the province from the

colonies. With English bayonets the British made a futile attempt to create an eighteenth-century "Iron Curtain" to halt the movement of American agitators and propaganda into that uneasy territory.

+

To understand why American propaganda to the north was so successful, we must review briefly Canada's population complexion. Most of the white inhabitants of Canada at the time of the Revolution were of French descent, adherents of the Roman Catholic faith and tenant farmers by occupation. They had come under British rule as a result of England's victory over France in the French and Indian War (Seven Years' War). By 1763 the prolific French-Canadian population had reached an estimated 70,000 persons, while the English residents totalled scarcely 400 people, these being mostly traders from the southern colonies or discharged British soldiers.[1]

During the decade after 1763, the British military government — overseeing a large and formerly hostile Canadian population with but a small force of regular troops — was troubled by fears of a popular uprising. Rumors of Canadian plots were reported periodically to London by members of the British minority. In 1768 the military governor, Sir Guy Carleton, although unable to discover any of the supposed subversive plots, wrote to the London government that "there was no doubt of their secret and natural affection for France," an affection which he said would continue so long as they were excluded from all appointments in the British service. Carleton was referring specifically to the French-Canadian seigneurs and clergy, the privileged minority which had dominated the peasant class under French rule but which had lost much of its power under Britain.

It was clear London would have to "conciliate the affections of the conquered" in order to insure its rule. There was subsequently initiated a governmental study which led, in 1774, to the passage by Parliament of the famed Quebec Act. This act, which had become known as "the Magna Carta of the French

40

Canadians," guaranteed to the inhabitants the free exercise of their religion and French judicial procedure. It also provided for an advisory council to the British governor, to be composed of seventeen to twenty-six members, chosen from among the French-Canadian nobility and clergy. In addition, the act extended the boundaries of Quebec south to the Ohio, and west to the Mississippi.

The Quebec Act was not well received by Americans, especially its boundary provisions which would have had the effect of blocking American expansion into the western territories. This was the situation when the colonists learned with surprise that many of the Canadian peasants also were not pleased with the act. On the contrary, wrote a "Gentleman in Montreal" to a New York friend: "The Canadians, in general, are greatly alarmed at being put under their former laws, of which they had long severely felt the bad effects; though the French noblesse and gentry, indeed, are very well pleased with the new act, which restores the old, as they expect to lord it over the industrious farmer and trader, and live upon their spoils, as they did before the conquest."[2]

It was under these circumstances that the first propaganda address of the Continental Congress was promulgated. In what was to be its procedure in producing propaganda documents throughout the war, Congress appointed a committee composed of Thomas Cushing of Massachusetts, Richard Henry Lee of Virginia, and John Dickinson of Pennsylvania to write the first appeal to the people of Quebec for support against Parliament. It was Dickinson's famous pen which produced the address dated October 26, 1774, in which Congress suggested to the Canadians "whether it may not be expedient for you to meet together, in your several towns and districts, and select deputies who, after meeting in a Provincial Congress, may choose delegates to represent your province in the Continental Congress."

As to their differences in religion, Congress argued smoothly:

> We are too well acquainted with the liberality of sentiment distinguishing your nation, to imagine the difference in religion will prejudice you against a hearty amity with us. You know that the transcendent nature of freedom

elevates those who unite in her cause, above all such low-minded infirmities. The Swiss Cantons furnish a memorable proof of this truth. Their union is composed of Roman Catholic and Protestant states, living in the utmost concord and peace with one another.

Responsibility for translating this American address into French was given to the delegates from Pennsylvania, who were also directed to have it printed and disseminated in Canada with the help of agents of New Hampshire, New York, and Massachusetts.

There were, however, a number of flaws in this initial propaganda to Canada. One of these was the undeveloped political consciousness of the Canadians, resulting largely from their feudal background and the fact that many of the peasants could not read. A pro-American writer in Montreal, after receiving English-language copies of Congress' address, predicted the Canadians would "avoid taking any part in the matter" because "they have been so little accustomed to speak or think on subjects of that kind," and were also afraid "of giving the smallest offence to government."[3]

There was still another important flaw in this address, connected with Congress' simultaneous appeal to the people of Great Britain. In this latter appeal, which was written largely by John Jay, Congress had attacked the Quebec Act on religious grounds, professing astonishment "that a British Parliament should ever consent to establish in that country a *Religion* that had deluged your island in blood, and dispersed impiety, bigotry, persecution, murder, and rebellion, through every part of the world."

Congress' faux pas soon came home to roost. A letter from Montreal described what happened:

> The Address from the Continental Congress attracted the notice of some of the principal Canadians; it was soon translated into very tolerable French. The decent manner in which the religious matters were touched; the encomiums on the French nation, flattered a people fond of compliments. They begged the translator, as he had succeeded so well, to try his hand on that Address to the

People of Great Britain. He had equal success in this, and read his performance to a numerous audience. But when he came to that part which treats of the new modelling of the province; draws a picture of the Catholic religion . . . they could not contain their resentment, nor express it but in broken curses. "Oh! the perfidious, double-faced Congress . . . ."4

Because they had failed to coordinate their propaganda, the Americans created ill-feeling instead of goodwill for their cause. However, they continued to address the Canadians. Prior to Congress' adjournment on October 26, 1774, the task of corresponding with the northern province was turned over to that important agency of American propaganda, the Boston Committee of Correspondence. Several months later, in February 1775, this committee received and accepted a proposal from one John Brown that he and other agents be sent to Canada to obtain intelligence and to spread American viewpoints.

To help him on his mission, the Boston Committee supplied him with a stock of American patriotic propaganda pamphlets, as well as a number of letters to English friends in Montreal, including a letter to the Canadians from that master agitator, Samuel Adams. Adams' letter, dated February 21, 1775, was a lengthy review of colonial grievances which contained the hopeful sentence: "The enemies of American liberty will surely be chagrined when they find that the people of Quebec have in common with other Americans the true sentiments of liberty."

Brown headed north accompanied by several frontiersmen and they distributed American literature in the hamlets on the way. In feeling out the sentiments of the Canadians, Brown found that while they were not unfriendly to the colonies, they preferred "to stand neuter." Reaching Montreal in March 1775, Brown immediately contacted the pro-American faction in the town. He also had the brashness to apply to Governor Carleton for a public printing of the address of Congress — which was refused. On March 29 Brown sat down to write a report to Sam Adams on the political conditions he had found in Canada. In his letter, he revealed "a profound secret." Wrote Brown: "The fort at Ticonderoga must be seized as soon as possible should hostilities be committed by the King's Troops." He confided that some New Hampshire patriots had made plans "to do" the business.

The business was done indeed. On May 10, 1775 — three weeks after the opening clash of the war at Lexington and Concord — a loose band of New Hampshire colonials led by Ethan Allen and Benedict Arnold, then a thirty-four-year-old militia captain, attacked and seized Ticonderoga. Two days later Crown Point, a few miles to the north, also fell into American hands. The headlong rush carried the colonials into Canadian territory in the vicinity of St. Johns.

The day Ticonderoga was seized, the Second Continental Congress was reconvening in Philadelphia, and some days later that body was startled to learn of this first American offensive action of the war. However, in a resolution adopted May 18 Congress quickly justified the seizures by claiming knowledge of "indubitable evidence that a design is formed by the British ministry of making a cruel invasion from the province of Quebec upon these colonies." However, having no military plans at this point, Congress ordered that all captured stores taken at Ticonderoga and Crown Point be removed further south for their security.

Reviewing the event a few days later, Congress felt it might be wise to address the Canadians again, not only to justify the seizure of the two forts but to calm any fears they might have concerning American intentions. On May 29, 1775, Congress published another propaganda broadside, addressed this time *To the Oppressed Inhabitants of Canada*, in which it declared that the fate of the Protestant and Catholic colonies were strongly linked together, and it once more invited the Canadians to "join with us in resolving to be free." Argued Congress (excerpts):

By . . . your present form of government, or rather present form of tyranny, you and your wives and your children are made slaves. You have nothing that you can call your own, and all the fruits of your labor and industry may be taken from you whenever an avaricious governor and a rapacious council may incline to demand them. You are liable by the edicts to be transported into foreign countries to fight battles in which you have no interest, and to spill your blood in conflicts from which neither honor nor emolument can be derived . . . .

We are informed you have already been called upon to · waste your lives in a contest with us. Should you, by complying in this instance, assent to your new establishment, and a war break out with France, your wealth and your sons may be sent to perish in expeditions against their Islands in the West Indies.

It cannot be presumed that these considerations will have no weight with you, or that you are so lost to all sense of honor. We can never believe that the present race of Canadians are so degenerate as to possess neither the spirit, the gallantry, nor the courage of their ancestors . . . .

Permit us again to repeat that we are your friends, not your enemies, and be not imposed upon those who may endeavor to create animosities. The taking of the fort and military stores at Ticonderoga and Crown Point . . . was dictated by the great law of self-preservation.

One thousand copies of this address, translated into French, were sent into Canada via agents.

At this initial stage of the war — with the siege of British troops in Boston not yet underway — Congress was defense-minded and had no Canadian invasion plans. This attitude was particularly frustrating to at least one New Englander, firebrand Ethan Allen, who in his eagerness to march north, sought the support of the New York Provincial Congress. In a letter to that body on June 2, he declared: "I will lay my life on it, that with fifteen hundred men and a proper train of artillery, I will take Montreal." Allen argued there was an "unspeakable advantage in directing the war into Canada, that instead of turning the Canadians and Indians against us (as is wrongly suggested by many), it would unavoidably attach and connect them to our interest. Our friends in Canada can never help us till we first help them, except in a passive or inactive manner."

The northern colonials kept agitating for a Canadian expedition, but the Continental Congress was slow in making up its mind. In the meantime, several additional propaganda papers were being sent into Canada. One was a formal address from the

New York Provincial Congress, dated June 2, 1775, which told the Canadian people that the key issue between Britain and her colonies "is whether they are subjects, or whether they are slaves" and beseeched the inhabitants "not to be imposed on" by British wiles.

Another message on June 4 was sent by Ethan Allen to "Our worthy and respectable Countrymen and Friends, the French People of Canada." In this appeal Allen sought to reassure the Canadians that the Americans had entered their country with not the least desire to injure or molest them or their property. American soldiers, he said, were under orders not to harm any Canadians "on pain of death." He declared that there was no real conflict between Americans and Canadians.

> You are sensible that war has already commenced between England and the Colonies . . . . But pray, is it necessary that the Canadians and the inhabitants of the English Colonies should butcher one another?
>
> God forbid. There is no controversy subsisting between you and them. Pray let old England and the Colonies fight it out; and you, Canadians, stand by and see what an arm of flesh can do.

The effect of this American propaganda, which aimed at alienating the French Canadians from the British government, was great and the British commander, General Carleton, soon found his position seriously undermined. Writing on June 7 to Lord Dartmouth (Britain's Secretary of State for the colonies), Carleton complained that throughout Canada insubordination was growing, "the minds of the people [being] poisoned by the same hypocrisy and lies practiced with so much success in the other provinces, and which their emissaries and friends here have spread abroad with great art and diligence." In his letter to Dartmouth, Carleton enclosed samples of recent American propaganda, including the address of the New York Provincial Congress of June 2, and a copy of a scrap of paper reportedly placed under the doors of French-Canadian homes throughout the country, which warned: "Honi soit qui mal y pense, A lui qui ne suivra le bon chemin. Baston."[5] (Evil to him who evil thinks, who does not follow the right way. Boston.)

On June 9 — with British control over the province rapidly slipping away — Carleton issued a proclamation establishing martial law. In his proclamation Carleton attacked the "traitorous invasion" of Canada, and denounced the Americans for "falsely and maliciously giving out" that they had come only to prevent the Canadians "from being taxed and oppressed," and for spreading "false and seditious reports, tending to inflame the minds of the people, and alienate them from his Majesty."

+

In Philadelphia the American Congress slowly came around to establishing a policy towards Canada. The opinion of the New England colonials carried the day; that is, the view that the American cause would be enhanced by an invasion of Canada.[6] The "great question," John Adams had said, was whether to push north with an army "sufficient to break the power of Governor Carleton, to overawe the Indians, and to protect the French .... It seems to be the general conclusion that it is best to go, if we can be assured that the Canadians will be pleased with it and join."

On June 27, 1775 — only a few days after Congress learned of the bloody Battle of Bunker Hill — it reached a decision. Instructions were issued to the newly appointed northern commander, Major General Philip Schuyler, to "immediately take possession of St. Johns, Montreal and any other parts" of Canada that he could. The attitude of the Canadians, however, remained of crucial importance. A previous condition, "a *sine qua non* of marching into Canada," wrote Samuel Chase to Schuyler, "is the friendship of the Canadians. Without their consent and approbation, it is not [to] be undertaken."

In the months that followed — while Schuyler and his second in command, Irish-born Brigadier General Richard Montgomery, struggled to collect supplies and an army of 1,200 men — the British fought to counteract the impact of American propaganda. But it was already very late. "There is no persuading the country people here of their danger," wrote a British loyalist from Canada. "Emissaries of the rebels have made them believe

47

that they are only come into the country to protect them from heavy taxes, which the Parliament designs to lay upon them. This, and the remembrance of what they suffered last war, makes them very desirous of observing a strict neutrality."[7]

Under the circumstances a strict neutrality was pro-American in effect, since it prevented General Carleton from calling out the Canadian militia to reinforce his meager forces (which totalled only 550 British regulars, scattered throughout five posts). Of this situation a British officer wrote from Quebec: "General Carleton is, I believe, afraid to order out the militia, lest they should refuse to obey," which would further undermine his authority. Added the officer: "In short, the Quebec bill is of no use; on the contrary, the Canadians talk of that damned absurd word liberty."[8]

In the last days of August 1775, General Montgomery began to move the hastily recruited American expedition slowly northward. As part of this invasion planning, on September 5 the ailing General Schuyler affixed his signature to a new propaganda message in French *To the Inhabitants of Canada.*

Addressing himself to his northern "friends and countrymen," Schuyler expressed his confidence that the Canadians would be pleased "that the Grand Congress have ordered an army into Canada, to expel from thence if possible, those British troops which, now acting under the orders of a despotic ministry, would wish to enslave their countrymen." The general assured the Canadians Congress would never have adopted such a severe measure if it had not been convinced "that it would be perfectly agreeable with you." Congress had judged Canadian feelings by their own: "They could not conceive that anything but the force of necessity could induce you tamely to bear the insult and ignominy that is daily imposed on you, or that you could calmly sit by, and see those chains forging which are intended to bind you, your posterity, and ours, in one common and eternal slavery." To secure both Americans and Canadians from such a dreadful bondage, declared Schuyler, was the only goal of Congress.

Copies of Schuyler's address travelled forward with the army; and as the Americans pushed on, they were delighted to find the Canadians both friendly and helpful. Ethan Allen, who had gone ahead to Chambly, wrote from there: "The news of my being in this place excited many captains of the militia and respectable gentlemen of the Canadians to visit and converse with me, as I gave out I was sent by General Schuyler to manifest his friendly intentions towards them, and delivered the General's written manifesto to them to the same purpose."

By mid-September, after several setbacks, Montgomery managed to put St. Johns under siege. It turned into a very lengthy affair. As the days dragged on into weeks, Allen and John Brown were sent ahead to gather together several bodies of Canadians who were beginning to volunteer for American service in substantial numbers.

In October, Allen reached Longueuil across the St. Lawrence river from Montreal. Gazing at the peaceful town, his old dream of a great exploit seized him. Coming together with Brown's party Allen concocted a plan to cross the river and make an immediate assault. On the night of October 24, 1775, the Montreal attack was set in motion, but somehow it miscarried. General Carleton, then in Montreal checking defenses, rallied some English and Canadian citizens and, together with 150 soldiers, he managed to surround Allen and forty of his men. Outnumbered, and with retreat cut off, Allen surrendered and was taken prisoner.

The capture of Ethan Allen, "the Notorious New Hampshire Incendiary," was less a military defeat than a great propaganda blow against the Americans. It immediately affected the attitude of the Canadians; they began to have second thoughts about committing themselves to the American side. "The Canadians seemed to grow cool and fearful and some went off," reported one American, while another writer, a Montreal loyalist, exulted: "This little action had changed the face of things. The Canadians before were nine-tenths for the Bostonians. They are now returned to their duty; many [are now] in arms for the King and the parishes, who had been otherwise."[9]

Fortunately for the Americans, the Allen incident was soon overtaken by more favorable events. On November 2, 1775 — after a fifty-five day siege — the British commander at St. Johns surrendered the post to General Montgomery, and this important event soon began to have an opposite effect. As the news spread through the many parishes south of the St. Lawrence, the Canadians once more began to rally to the Americans.

Montgomery pushed on towards Montreal as soon as he was able to reorganize his force. On November 11 he crossed the St. Lawrence, landing above the town, where his column was greeted by four nervous citizens who came to inquire as to his intentions. Montgomery took a firm stand. In a written reply, he expressed anxiety for the fate of Montreal, should it become necessary for him to open his batteries on the town. "When I consider the dreadful consequences of a bombardment," he said, "the distress that must attend a fire (at this season especially) when it is too late to repair the damage which must ensue, how many innocent people must suffer . . . ." After continuing in this threatening vein, Montgomery urged the citizens "to soften the heart of the Governor" and surrender the town and thus avoid disaster.

But there was little need for this psychological ploy. General Carleton, having estimated that his small force would be unable to defend Montreal, had already fled the town. The following day Montreal peacefully surrendered and was swiftly occupied by the Americans.

+

During the period Montgomery was busy at St. Johns and Montreal, further east the Americans had unleashed a second invasion of Canada aimed at capturing Quebec, the first town of the province. The plan for this second invasion evolved in General Washington's headquarters at Cambridge, where the Commander in Chief was just beginning the long task of forming an army from the mixed provincial volunteers around Boston. By August 20 the Cambridge invasion plan was so far advanced that Washington was able to communicate it to Schuyler. The idea, wrote Washington, was "to penetrate into Canada by way of the Kennebeck River, and so to Quebec by a route ninety miles [actually 150] below Montreal."

The Boston Massacre, March 5, 1770

Paul Revere's engraving showing British troops firing on the helpless populace.

Patrick Henry

Thomas Paine

George III

King of England and target of many American broadsides.

Admiral Lord Richard Howe

General Sir William Howe

BLOODY BUTCHERY BY THE BRITISH TROOPS:

OR, THE

RUNAWAY FIGHT OF THE REGULARS.

The Battle of Concord, April 19, 1775

Newspaper account of British butchery.

Thomas Jefferson

A clever propagandist.

Major General John Sullivan

Major General Charles Lee

Joseph Brant

Mohawk chief allied with the British.

Washington's plan was to detach a small volunteer force of 1,000 men from the army at Boston. To lead the expedition Washington personally chose Benedict Arnold, who had first come to public attention at Ticonderoga and Crown Point.

Arnold was given the rank of colonel and immediately threw himself into the job of preparing for the northern trek. Notice of the expedition appeared in Washington's general orders of September 5, 1775. The Commander in Chief, in preparing his formal instructions to Arnold, showed concern over the attitude of the Canadians. He cautioned Arnold to consider himself as marching, "not through an enemy's country but that of our friends and brethren." Severe disciplinary action was recommended against any soldier "so base and infamous as to injure any Canadian or Indian." The troops were to be warned likewise to "avoid all disrespect" to the Catholic faith of the Canadians.

Washington also decided to address the Canadians directly to reassure them as to American intentions. His staff quickly drew up a new appeal *To the Inhabitants of Canada.* In this address Washington explained that the army under Schuyler had been sent to Canada "not to plunder but to protect you; to animate and bring forth those sentiments of freedom you have disclosed."

> To cooperate with this design and to frustrate those cruel and perfidious schemes which would deluge our frontier with the blood of women and children, I have detached Colonel Arnold into your country, with a part of the army under my command. I have enjoined upon him, and I am certain that he will consider himself, and act as in the country of his patrons and best friends. Necessaries and accommodations of every kind which you may furnish, he will thankfully receive and render full value. I invite you therefore as friends and brethren to provide him with such supplies as your country affords; and I pledge myself not only for your safety and security, but for ample compensation. Let no man desert his habitation. Let no man flee as before an enemy.

Arnold left Cambridge before the French translations of Washington's address were printed. These were forwarded to him on his march north, and he began distributing the broad-side upon reaching the first Canadian settlements. Arnold's experience with the Canadians was similar to that of the Americans in the west. On October 27 Arnold wrote to Washington from Chaudiere Pond that the Canadian attitude was friendly and that they "will very gladly receive us."

Early in November, while anxiously awaiting word from Arnold, Washington learned that some of the provincial troops at Cambridge were planning to divert themselves with what he termed "the ridiculous and childish custom of burning the effigy of the pope." In his general orders dated November 5, Washington expressed amazement "that there should be officers and soldiers in this army so void of common sense as not to see the impropriety of such a step at this juncture, at a time when we are soliciting . . . the friendship and alliance of the people of Canada . . . . At such a juncture and in such circumstances, to be insulting their religion is so monstrous as not to be suffered or excused."

On November 9 Arnold and his reduced column of 600 men, after a tortuous forty-five-day march, straggled out of the wilderness at Point Levi, across the river from Quebec. On the thirteenth, after locating some boats, they crossed the river and bivouaced on the Plains of Abraham, a mile and a half from the town. The next day Arnold called upon the British lieutenant governor, Hector T. Cramahe, to surrender. An emissary carrying a flag of truce approached the walls with Arnold's demand for "the immediate surrender of the town, fortifications, &c., of Quebec to the forces of the United Colonies under my command; forbidding you to injure any of the inhabitants of the town in their persons or property, as you will answer the same at your peril."[10]

The British, however, had adopted a policy of nonrecognition of the American rebels, and gunfire from the walls sent Arnold's men into a fast retreat. The next day, thinking a mistake might have been made, Arnold sent another flag of truce but it also was fired upon. In a subsequent small diversion, he marched his troops "bravado-like" to within a short distance of the walls, where they "gave 3 huzzas" which was answered by some cheering from within the town, and then they retired. Obviously too weak to take Quebec by force, Arnold retired twenty miles up the river to await Montgomery and the American troops from Montreal.

Within Quebec there was a great deal of anxiety among the British, caused not only by the appearance of Arnold's troops outside the walls but also by the pro-American "fifth column" inside. Of this situation, a British officer of the Quebec garrison noted:

> The success of the rebels under Mr. Montgomery induced many people in Quebec to show their sentiments, and, indeed, to act as if no opposition might be made against the rebel forces. A thousand different intimidating reports were industriously spread abroad concerning their numbers. Our enemies within the walls catched every favorable opportunity to work on the minds of such English and Frenchmen as were not confirmed in their principles. They spoke of their fears. Our force, said they, is nothing, theirs is great and grows daily. Be wise and remain neuter, that you may secure good treatment from those who will undoubtedly take the town sooner or later.[11]

These subversive activities put the British on the defensive, although they made efforts to counteract this American propaganda. The Americans, the British countered, were simply highwaymen, "rebel banditti" who had come into Canada looking only for loot and plunder. These arguments, however, were not very convincing; the Canadians were unmoved and continued to stand aside to watch the outcome of the struggle.

On November 19 an important event boosted British morale out of its depressed state. On that day General Carleton, who had "escaped from Montreal by paddling with his hands," slipped into Quebec to the "unspeakable joy of the garrison," which saw safety in his presence.[12] Carleton quickly took charge and one of his first moves was to try to purge Quebec of its pro-American elements. On November 22 he issued a proclamation ordering all those who would not serve actively in arms to defend the town, to evacuate in four days "under pain of being treated as rebels and spies." This order proved effective; a number of the disaffected and their families filed from town in the next few days, and the British garrison was indirectly strengthened.

It was not until December 2 that Montgomery arrived at Arnold's camp and took charge of operations. The combined American force stood at about 800 men, while the British defenders were able to call on more than twice that number (that is, including civilians). Montgomery was faced with a crucial decision, whether to "siege, invest or storm." The first two choices seemed impractical because the town had provisions to last eight months and the harsh Canadian winter had already begun. Montgomery's thoughts thus turned to the problem of storming the walls.

First, however, he was willing to try a propaganda assault. Aware that flags of truce would not be honored, Montgomery prepared letters to General Carleton and to the principal merchants of the town, calling for the surrender of the garrison. He used an old woman, who begged admission to the town, to deliver the letters. But the British governor refused to receive them: he had the papers burned and sent the woman back with the word that he would receive no communication from a rebel.

Several days later Montgomery pursued his psychological warfare campaign by means of an ancient instrument. On the evening of December 12, he had copies of his letter fired into the town tied to Indian arrows. One letter to the inhabitants informed them of American surrender terms and painted the dreadful consequences of a refusal ("a city in flames, carnage, confusion, plunder"). The other letter was addressed to Carleton and threatened him with immediate death unless he gave up the city. To back up his threats, Montgomery mounted several batteries on a height within 700 yards of the city walls.

There was no response to these tactics, however, and on December 16 Montgomery issued a final, fierce surrender demand, dispatched again by messenger. In this document he pointed out to Carleton the weakness of the garrison, while

54

noting that the American soldiers were "accustomed to success, confident of the righteousness of the cause they are engaged in, inured to danger and fatigue, and so highly incensed at your inhumanity . . . and the ungenerous means employed to prejudice them in the minds of the Canadians, that it is with difficulty that I restrain them . . . . Should you persist in an unwarrantable defence, the consequences be upon your own head. Beware of destroying stores of any sort . . . . If you do, by Heavens, there will be no mercy shown."

Montgomery's latest messenger was promptly jailed. The letter was poor psychology to use on Carleton, a competent officer who was well aware of the importance of retaining Quebec. As long as Britain held Quebec, Canada would remain unconquered.

Propaganda and threats having failed, the sword alone could resolve the issue. During the early morning hours of December 31 − in a blinding snowstorm − the people of Quebec were roused to meet the American assault. At first there was much confusion, until it became clear the two real American attacks were centered on the lower town. The British rallied; a number of Americans were caught in a trap and surrendered, others were slaughtered. In the fighting Arnold suffered a leg wound and General Montgomery fell mortally wounded. The Americans were beaten off.

When news of the failure at Quebec, and especially of the death of Montgomery, spread through the parishes of Canada, the American cause began to lose adherents. This was a quite natural thing; it was a matter of self-preservation for the Canadians to choose, if they could, the winning side. Congress immediately recognized the impact the event must have on the Canadians. On January 24, 1776, after the unexpected news had reached Philadelphia, Congress drew up another address to the Canadians in an effort to counter the effects of the Quebec failure.

The best of causes are subject to vicissitudes; and disappointments have ever been inevitable. Such is the lot of

55

human nature. But generous souls, enlightened and warmed with the sacred fire of liberty, become more resolute as difficulties increase; and surmount, with irresistible ardor, every obstacle that stands between them and the favourite object of their wishes.

We will never abandon you to the unrelenting fury of your and our enemies. Two battalions have already received orders to march to Canada, a part of which are now on their route. Six additional battalions are raising in the United Colonies, for the same service . . . . The whole of these troops will probably arrive in Canada before the Ministerial army under General Carleton can receive any succours.

Congress further urged Arnold to maintain the siege, and this was done. But the situation was somewhat ridiculous in that an American force of not more than 500 worn-out soldiers were besieging a garrison of about 1,600 men. Yet despite British military superiority, Carleton made no move to drive the Americans away. The British General's inactivity was partly the result of his complete disillusionment with the Canadians. Their "neutrality" coupled with American propaganda had had an impact on the British leader. He was content to sit safe within the walls of Quebec until reinforcements arrived from Britain.

The situation continued to deteriorate for the Americans. They had lost the aura of successful conquerors, and soon the presence and demands of the American troops in the country began to irritate the Canadians. In March 1776 a thoroughly alarmed Congress decided to dispatch a three-man commission to Montreal to obtain firsthand information on conditions. Named to the commission were Benjamin Franklin, Samuel Chase, and Charles Carroll. The commissioners were directed to reassure the Canadians that Congress would persist in the struggle against Britain, and that it was to Canada's interest "to cultivate a friendly intercourse with these colonies."[13]

The commission was also directed to set up "a free press" in Canada to publish "such pieces as may be of service to the cause of the United Colonies." To this end Congress agreed to pay the expenses of Fleury Mesplet, a French printer in Philadelphia, to remove himself, his family, and his printing press to Canada. (It was on Mesplet's press that Congress' three French-language propaganda broadsides of October 1774, May 1775, and January 1776 were printed).[14] In still another move aimed at winning the allegiance of the Canadians, Congress persuaded the Reverend John Carroll, a Roman Catholic priest and a cousin of Charles Carroll, to accompany the commission to Canada. He was to try to influence the clergy to change over to the American side. The inclusion of Reverend Carroll was considered by the American patriots to be "a master-stroke of policy."[15]

Not until late April 1776 did the commissioners and their party reach Montreal, then under the military command of Arnold. They found the situation greatly deteriorated: the army had become extremely unpopular with the Canadians, having no hard cash to pay for supplies. Some of the Canadians had been forced to accept paper certificates in lieu of cash, and had been cheated and abused. On May 8, 1776, the commission wrote to Congress: "If money cannot be had to support your army here with honor, so as to be respected instead of being hated by the people, we report it as our firm and unanimous opinion that it is better immediately to withdraw it."

Congress, however, could not easily give up its dream of uniting Canada to the colonies: it immediately ordered $300,000 be sent northward and it requested the commission to publish another address to the Canadians, assuring them that Congress would give ample redress for any misconduct by any of the American soldiers.

Meanwhile, in Montreal Reverend Carroll met a wall of resistance in attempting to win over the French-Canadian clergy. The clerics said they were quite satisfied with British rule, and argued that the Quebec Act favored their national traditions. Further, they said, they had not forgotten the address of Congress to the people of Britain which had denounced the Roman Catholic faith. Carroll was also unable to counter their statement that there was not a single colony in which the Roman Catholic church and clergy had such privileges as in Canada.[16]

The situation facing the Americans was well summed up by Moses Hazen, a former resident of Canada who had joined the patriot side. In a letter to General Schuyler from Montreal on April 1, Hazen wrote:

You are not unacquainted with the friendly disposition of the Canadians when General Montgomery first penetrated into the country; the ready assistance which they gave on all occasions, by men, carriages, or provisions, was most remarkable. Even when he was before Quebec many parishes offered their services in the reduction of the fortress, which were at that time thought unnecessary. But his most unfortunate fate, added to other incidents, had caused such a change in their disposition, that we no longer look upon them as friends but on the contrary waiting an opportunity to join our enemies. That no observations of my own may remain obscure, I beg leave to observe that I think the clergy, or guardians of the souls and conductors of the bodies of these enthusiasts, have been neglected, perhaps in some instances ill used. Be that as it will, they are unanimous, though privately, against our cause, and I have too much reason to fear many of them, with other people of consequence, have carried on a correspondence the whole winter with General Carleton in Quebec, and are now plotting our destruction. The peasantry in general have been ill used. They have in some instances been dragooned with the point of the bayonet to supply wood for the garrison at a lower rate than the current price . . . . And in a more material point, they have not seen sufficient force in the country to protect them. These matters furnish very strong arguments to be made use of by our enemies. With respect to the better sort of people, both French and English, seven-eighths are Tories, who would wish to see our throats cut, and perhaps would readily assist in doing it.

So drastically had American fortunes declined that the next important decision on Canada's future was made by the British. On May 6 five ships arrived at Quebec carrying troop reinforcements from England and, thus bolstered, Carleton ordered out

58

the greatest part of his garrison "to see what those mighty boasters were about." He found the Americans making a headlong retreat, and the five months' siege of Quebec was brought to an abrupt end.

In the next few weeks, following an unsuccessful American effort to seize the strongpoint at Three Rivers, it became clear the whole American position in Canada was threatened. On June 13 Arnold wrote: "The junction of the Canadas with the colonies is at an end. Let us quit them and secure our own country before it is too late." Montreal was abandoned and the slow retreat began, first to Ile aux Nois and finally, in the early days of July 1776, to Crown Point, from whence the invasion of Canada had begun ten months before.

+

Following the American retreat, Carleton's major task was to consolidate his position with the French Canadians. He wisely adopted a policy of leniency towards them, as well as towards "his Majesty's deluded subjects of the neighboring provinces," and he offered medical aid to any who needed help plus the promise of "free liberty to return to their respective provinces" when their health was restored. To the citizens of liberated Montreal, however, he hammered home the theme that "the people's greatest enemies" were the American colonists whose "flattering and perverted use of words" had undermined the governmental structure.[17] American propaganda had left its scars.

Carleton also thought to use Americans captured in recent battles to spread British propaganda in the south. Early in August 1776 he paroled 147 American prisoners and sent them to New York in the hopes, he wrote, "that the confinement they have undergone may have brought them to a sense of their past crimes and that this proof given to the rebels still in arms that the way to mercy is not shut to them, the contrary being inculcated by their chiefs, and those who have an interest in fomenting the disorders of the country, may tend to work a favorable change in their minds."

Carleton's show of clemency — his demonstration that the British did not kill their prisoners — had the desired effect. A few months later, as the British and American armies maneuvered at New York and in New Jersey, an American chaplain with the patriot forces tried to counter the influence of the prisoner release by warning the American troops that: "General Carleton's late conduct was only designed to deceive; his clemency is to be dreaded."[18] There was nothing ahead, he said, but victory or death. So must all soldiers be convinced.

But if the British in Canada thought they were now free from American propaganda, they were rudely awakened early in August 1776 when the Americans dispatched an officer northward carrying some new resolutions of Congress dealing with treatment of prisoners. Carleton was stirred to great anger by those papers, and his anger spilled over into his general orders of August 7, a copy of which was handed to the American emissary.

In this order Carleton directed his subordinate officers to inform all British personnel "that letters or messages from rebels, traitors in arms against their King, rioters, disturbers of the peace, plunderers, robbers, assassins or murderers, are on no occasion to be admitted. That should emissaries of such lawless men again presume to approach the army, whether under the name of flag-of-truce men or ambassadors, except when they come to implore the King's mercy, their persons shall be immediately seized and committed to close confinement, in order to be proceeded against as the law directs; their papers and letters for whomsoever, even for the Commander-in-Chief, are to be delivered to the Provost Marshall, that, unread and unopened, they may be burned by the hands of the common hangman."

Carleton plainly had had enough of American revolutionaries. "Let their crimes," he said, "pursue these faithless, bloody-minded men, who assert that black is white and white is black."[19]

Carleton had good reason to cry out against American propaganda, whose lingering effects were seen in the difficulty which his new subordinate, Major General John Burgoyne, had in trying to recruit Canadians for his regiment. Burgoyne, who had arrived with the British reinforcements, wrote to Lord George Germain (the new colonial secretary) and attributed his recruiting troubles partly "to the poison which the emissaries of the rebels have thrown into their mind." As a result, only a handful of Canadians accompanied the British forces when they went on the offensive against the Americans on Lake Champlain in the fall of 1776.

In October, in an important naval battle near Valcour Island, Carleton's gunboats defeated an improvised American navy under Benedict Arnold. British control of the lake forced the patriots to abandon Crown Point. However, Arnold's resistance had so delayed the British that Carleton was forced to call a halt to operations for the winter. Thus the Americans retained Ticonderoga through the winter of 1776-1777.

+

It was during this long Canadian winter that the restless General Burgoyne returned to England, where he found his opinions and views about the American war in great demand. Burgoyne had ideas in abundance, and a natural ambition which led him to submit to the King a paper entitled "Thoughts for Conducting the War from the Side of Canada." In this plan he proposed an attack against Ticonderoga with a British force which he envisioned would include 2,000 Canadians and 1,000 Indian auxiliaries. After seizing Ticonderoga, the army would continue south by way of Lake George and the Hudson River Valley to Albany, New York. The main invasion would be supported by an auxiliary expedition marching on Albany by a western route.

The King and the ministry approved Burgoyne's plan, and when he returned to Quebec in May 1777, it was as commander of a combined British-German expeditionary force. He superseded Carleton, who was ordered to remain behind as governor of Canada. Almost at once, however, Burgoyne's neat little plan began to go awry. He discovered the Canadians were still determined on neutrality; he was able to obtain only 150 of his hoped-for 2,000 men. Still it was an impressive army of 7,123 rank and file which, in June 1777, began the historic march that was to end ingloriously at Saratoga.

The great political and propaganda value which accrued to the American cause by Burgoyne's surrender contributed mightily to Washington's ultimate victory. Saratoga not only brought French recognition of American independence and subsequent participation in the war, but gave a tremendous lift to American morale and revitalized American propaganda in Canada.

On the other hand, when the news reached England there was shock and disbelief. According to a London correspondent, writing on December 9, 1777: "The account of General Burgoyne's treaty with Mr. Gates, arriving when the two Houses of Parliament were sitting, and in the warmth of high debate, the friends of government were much confounded and staggered by such a shock; but you cannot imagine how furiously, illiberally, and indecently opposition triumphed on the occasion, opening and roaring like so many bull dogs against administration. The King was greatly affected; but . . . soon declared that such a cause could never be given up, that this loss must be retrieved by greater and more vigorous exertions, and that he would sell all his private estates before he would desert his loyal American subjects."[20] But this was wishful thinking, particularly with regards to the situation in Canada. From the time of Burgoyne's surrender to the end of war, the British remained on the defensive in the north.

Subsequently, when the Second Continental Congress adopted the Articles of Confederation in November 1777, the delegates inserted a paragraph which would allow Canada to join the new union by simply acceding to the new arrangement. On November 29 Congress appointed a committee to translate the Articles into the French language. The committee also was directed to prepare another address to the Canadians and to develop a plan for disseminating these new propaganda papers, in hopes they would "conciliate the affections of the Canadians toward these United States."

In December the committee brought in a partial report, but the following month, January 1778, Congress decided to do more than propagandize; it seized on a hastily conceived plan to undertake a new military "irruption" into Canada. The plan called for a contingent of French officers to join the northward march in the hope they would be able to persuade the Canadians to come over en masse to the American side.

Within a few months, however, reality reasserted itself when it became evident that neither supplies nor men were available and that it was too late in the season to organize an expedition. On March 13, having been informed of these problems, Congress ordered the plan set aside.

One of the French officers who had been involved in this wild scheme was the youthful Marquis de Lafayette, who had gone to New York to undertake preparations for what he hoped would be a campaign of glory. After surveying the situation in Albany, and noting the lack of all necessities, Lafayette reluctantly concluded that the expedition was impractical. However, news of his presence near the Canadian border added a further dimension to British fears.

In the months that followed, the entrance of France into the war naturally contributed to the apprehensions in British quarters over the security of Canada. Parliament acted to prohibit all intercourse between it and the southern colonies, and Carleton was given strict instructions to watch out for American emissaries and to seize any papers they might carry. Carleton needed no such directive. What he and his successors tried to do, according to one historian, was to build "a voice-proof wall on the frontier, with gates of bronze and no latchstring," in an effort to keep out the subversive Americans and their "unnatural" allies, the French.

But this feeble eighteenth-century attempt at an "Iron Curtain" had too many gaps in it to be effective. Indeed, in the fall of 1778 one of the most subversive propaganda appeals of the entire war was filtered into the Canadian countryside. The writer of this appeal was a Frenchman, Charles Henri Theodat, Comte d'Estaing, Admiral of the French fleet sent to aid the Americans, who had dropped anchor in Boston in October.

During his stay in Boston d'Estaing was visited by some Canadian Indian chiefs of the Penobscot and Nova Scotia tribes. They had come, they explained, "to see with their own eyes" whether it was true that France had joined the American cause.[21] To the Admiral it seemed that a golden opportunity had presented itself to use the Indians to carry back into Canada an appeal to the French Canadians. He thereupon drew up a declaration "in the name of the King of France," dated October 28, 1778, which was printed on his ship's press. Addressing the Canadians, d'Estaing declared (excerpts):

> You were born French, you never could cease to be French. The late war . . . has wrested from you that which is most dear to all men, even the name of your country. To compel you to bear arms of parricides against it, must be the completion of misfortunes . . . .

> As a French gentleman, I need not mention to those among you who were born such as well as myself, that there is but one august House in the universe under which the French can be happy and serve with pleasure . . . I shall not excite your regrets for those qualifications, those marks of distinction, those decorations, which, in our manner of thinking, are precious treasures, but which by our common misfortune the American French . . . are now precluded. These, I am bold to hope, and to promise, their zeal will very soon procure to be diffused among them. They will merit them, when they *dare to become the friends of our allies.*

> I shall not ask the military companions of the Marquis de Levi, those who shared his glory, who admired his talents and genius for war, who loved his cordiality and frankness, the principal characteristics of our nobility, whether there be other names in other nations among which they would be better pleased to take their own.

> Can the Canadians who saw the brave Montcalm fall in their defence, can they become the enemies of his nephews? Can they fight against their former leaders, and arm themselves against their kinsmen? At the bare mention of their names, the weapons would fall from their hands.

I shall not observe to the Ministers of the altars, that their evangelic efforts will require the special protection of Providence to prevent faith being diminished by example, by worldly interest, and by sovereigns whom force has imposed upon them, and whose political indulgence will be lessened proportionably as those sovereigns shall have less to fear. I shall not observe that it is necessary for religion that those who preach it should form a body in the State; and that in Canada no other body would be more considered, or have more power to do good than that of the priests . . . .

I shall not urge a whole people, that to *join* with the United States is to secure their own happiness; since a whole people, when they acquire the right of thinking and acting for themselves, must know their own interest; but I will declare, and I now formally declare in the name of his Majesty, who has authorized and commanded me to do it, that all his former subjects in North America who shall no more acknowledge the supremacy of Great Britain, may depend upon his protection and support.

Admiral d'Estaing's subtle propaganda appeal — aimed at the clergy and nobility, as well as the peasants — was followed in December 1778 by a letter from Lafayette to the Indian tribes of Canada, announcing France's adherence to America and urging them to also desert the British cause.

News of these French appeals spread quickly. The British Commander in Chief, Sir Henry Clinton, when he heard of them, was certain that d'Estaing's broadside had "debauched" the Canadians. So was Carleton's successor as governor of Canada, General Frederick Haldimand, who was convinced the appeals would be very seductive to Canadian hearts. Especially worrisome was the effect of the propaganda on the two elements of the population Britain had previously relied upon, the nobility and clergy. Reporting his apprehensions to London, Haldimand·said that since it was learned France had entered the war and in particular "since the address of Count d'Estaing and a letter of M. de la Fayette to the Canadians and Indians have been circulated in the province, many of the priests have changed their opinions, and in case of another invasion I fear would adopt another system of conduct."

Both d'Estaing's address and Lafayette's letter were disseminated at a time when Congress was showing renewed interest in a northern expedition. This interest was stimulated by Lafayette, who conceived a new scheme for a combined French-American attack on Canada. To implement the plan, Congress agreed that Lafayette should return to France to seek the support of the French King. On October 22, 1778, Congress also sent instructions to Benjamin Franklin in Paris on the "Plan of an Attack Upon Quebec." The scheme called for cooperation of 4,000 or 5,000 French troops to sail in an invasion fleet up the St. Lawrence to seize Quebec, while at the same time, an American force would move northward in two columns to capture Montreal and the British post at Detroit.

On this occasion, Washington, who had been bypassed by Congress in all the planning for the abortive "irruption" (January-March 1778), was consulted, and promptly threw cold water on the whole idea. Not only did he express doubts about the ability of America to support an invasion of Canada, but he also privately expressed concern over future political complications that might arise should France again obtain a strong foothold in Canada.

Washington's arguments against the expedition, presented both in private and public letters, carried the day in Congress. On December 5, 1778, the same day d'Estaing's Canadian address was read to the Congress at the request of the French minister, a Congressional committee reported "the reasons assigned by the General against an expedition to Canada appear to the committee to be well founded, and to merit the approbation of Congress."

Congress accepted the recommendation. Several weeks later a letter was addressed to Lafayette to inform him of the decision. Congress felt, the letter stated, "that the arms of America should be employed in expelling the enemy from her own shores before the liberation of a neighbouring province is undertaken." Before this letter reached Lafayette, however, his ship had sailed for France. Not until five months later did he learn of the

American decision, but by that time other stimulating projects (the prospect of an invasion of England) were on his mind.

+

For the remainder of the war, the plan to win Canada was never far from the American consciousness and each renewal of discussion — whether real or for deceptive purposes — gave sustenance to British apprehensions in the north. To General Haldimand it was particularly galling when Canadians and Indians slipped out of the country to see the French fleet and return to spread tales of French victories and French superiority. "On many an occasion," Haldimand once wrote to Lord Germain, he had seen the "secret pleasure" on the faces of the Canadians, even as they made their bows to him. Meanwhile, American agents hovered on the frontier, agitating the people and disseminating additional copies of d'Estaing's address throughout the country.[22]

In May 1780, when Lafayette returned to America with the good news that a French army and fleet would shortly arrive, Washington undertook to utilize propaganda for strategic deception. In a conference with Lafayette, the General suggested the French nobleman issue several proclamations to the Canadians. One, Washington said, should indicate that a French fleet and army would soon arrive in the St. Lawrence River to cooperate with the Americans in a northern campaign, and urge them to join the allied arms and assist in making Canada a part of the American confederation. The other proclamation "should be drawn on the supposition of the fleet and army being already arrived, and should contain an animating invitation to arrange themselves under the allied banners."

To further confuse the British, Washington thought it would be useful to slip into the American press some items to the effect that the impending French naval and land forces would join with the American army in "a combined operation against New York."[23] This latter operation was the plan Washington actually hoped to implement.

Lafayette quickly complied with Washington's request and at least one proclamation is known to have been written, which Washington sent in great secrecy to Major General Benedict Arnold, the commander in Philadelphia, with the request that 500 copies be struck off. "The importance of this business," Washington wrote to Arnold, "will sufficiently impress you with the necessity of transacting it with every possible degree of caution. The printer is to be particularly charged not on any account to reserve a copy himself or to suffer one to get abroad."

Unfortunately, Washington had placed his secret document into the hands of a man already playing the role of traitor. Arnold sent a message to the British informing them of Lafayette's proclamation and of the impending French-American attack against Canada. In a sense this did not hurt Washington's plan and, in fact, seems to have furthered it. For example, as late as December 1780 (after Arnold's defection), General Clinton warned Haldimand:

> By intelligence late received an attempt against Canada is so far set as to render naval transactions on this coast improbable. As the French . . . will compose the principal part of the armament I am inclined to credit the accounts I heard of a combination being formed in Canada by the inhabitants to join them. As [the invaders] . . . will probably be obliged to trust to the country for supplies of flour and other provisions, I submit to Your Excellency whether it would not be of moment to take from the inhabitants every article of that sort except what may be absolutely requisite for the support of their families.[24]

Haldimand did not need Clinton's warning to stay alert as the news in Canada was equally alarming; disaffection was running rampant and the Canadians, he said, were persuaded "that a French fleet will soon show themselves" in the St. Lawrence.

There were, of course, no aggressive moves against Canada in 1780. However, the following spring a member of Congress, John Sullivan of New Hampshire, proposed to Congress that the army make a diversion in Canada which, if circumstances were favorable, might be turned into "a real attack." Sullivan asked Washington for an opinion. The General's letter of reply, which argued that the plan was impracticable, was intercepted by the British and published in the *London Gazette* on July 14, 1781. However, having received so many contradictory reports, it is not certain the British government was put entirely at ease.

By this late date the peace negotiations were underway and Congress, in planning for them, instructed Franklin to try to obtain Canada and Nova Scotia in any settlement, if he could. Pursuing these instructions in May 1782, Franklin suggested to the British representative that if Britain "should voluntarily offer to give up this province," it would undoubtedly have "an excellent effect" on the American people. Further, argued Franklin, Britain would otherwise be forced to spend a great deal of money to govern and maintain its forces in Canada, which expense would be eliminated by giving it up to the United States.[25] The British were unmoved by such arguments. What they had managed to hold by force for seven years, they would keep.

The lesson of the struggle for Canada, if the Americans thought at all about it, was a simple one. It was that propaganda and diplomatic maneuvers were no substitute for "an arm of flesh." When General Montgomery fell mortally wounded in the snows of Quebec, so did the American cause in Canada.

☆ **3** ☆

The Campaign to Win
the Indians' Allegiance

Besides the French Canadians, there was another people in North America who became a target for belligerent propaganda – the Indian inhabitants. Long before the outbreak of fighting at Lexington and Concord in April 1775, the Americans realized that their Indian neighbors on the frontiers might play a crucial role in any armed conflict with Great Britain. Early in the propaganda war between the patriots and loyalists, the latter invoked the threat of unnumbered tribes of savages fighting under the banner of the King. The colonists, with a long history of bloody frontier warfare with the Indians, recognized the need to gain the allegiance of the red men, or at least their neutrality.

Beginning in 1775, both sides were drawn into a complex propaganda struggle for the Indian mind. In this struggle, which involved economic and military as well as verbal propaganda, the British possessed certain advantages and the best arguments. The result was tragic for both the American frontier and the Indian nations.

When the Revolution began, the important Indian tribes were located in three general areas: (1) in northwestern New York, hunting grounds of the Iroquois confederation – the Six Nations of Mohawks, Oneidas, Tuscaroras, Onondagas, Cayugas, and Senecas; (2) in the Kentucky-Ohio territory, lands of a loose western confederation which included Shawnee, Miami, Potowatami, Delaware, and other tribes; and (3) in the Virginia-

71

Carolina-Georgia backcountry, home of the southern Indians, the Cherokees, Creeks, Chickasaws, and Choctaws.

Living among these Indians when the war began were British agents and Indian superintendents, serving as official representatives of the British government. In the Iroquois country the ruling family was the Johnsons. Before his death in 1774, Sir William Johnson, the Superintendent for Indian Affairs, was a man of great influence with the Six Nations. His power was passed on to his son, Sir John, and to his son-in-law, Colonel Guy Johnson, the latter succeeding as Superintendent. Elsewhere, at Detroit and in the southern territory, British officials such as John Stuart were able to bring personal influence to bear on the Indians in an effort to insure loyalty to the British crown.

+

The campaign to gain the Indians' support is connected to a long-forgotten issue of American history: the question of who first employed the savages in military operations. For this the American patriots bear the onus. The Indians were first brought into action by the patriots on a limited scale at Boston. These were the semicivilized warriors of the Stockbridge tribe, a remnant of a once powerful people living in the Berkshire hills of Massachusetts.

In the tense days and weeks before fighting broke out on the plains of Boston, the Massachusetts Provincial Congress sought the support of the Stockbridge Indians. A chief gave the tribe's reply on April 11, 1775.

> Brothers, [he told the patriots], whenever I see your blood running, you will soon find me about you to revenge my brothers' blood. Although I am low and very small, I will grip hold of your enemy's heel, that he cannot run so fast and so light, as if he had nothing at his heels. So then, if you please, I will take a run to the westward and feel the minds of the Six Nations, who have always looked this way for advice concerning all important news that comes from the rising sun . . . . If I find they are against you, I will try to turn their minds.

72

But before the Stockbridge could act as propaganda agents for the Americans, and "feel the minds" of the Iroquois, the war had begun. True to their promise, a number of warriors signed up at once as minutemen. By April 30 these Indians were spotted by the British at the ferry near Boston. This was all the British Commander in Chief, Thomas Gage, needed to spur him to seek full-fledged support of the savages on the frontiers. As early as the fall of 1774, Gage had alerted the various British agents in Indian country to prepare for trouble. Now, in the spring of 1775, with the siege of Boston underway, he reported to London: "We need not be tender of calling upon the savages, as the rebels have shown us the example by bringing as many Indians down against us here as they could collect." The British government quickly gave its official blessing to use of the Indians.

In Philadelphia it was clear to Congress that the colonists were at a serious disadvantage in any competition to win support of the frontier tribes. Not only were the Indians attached to the persons of the British superintendents, who could remind them of their grievances against American encroachments on their hunting grounds, but Britain also controlled the supplies of goods and necessities with which to buy continued Indian loyalty. In view of these handicaps, the best the Americans could hope for was a pledge of Indian neutrality.

On July 12, 1775, Congress adopted a plan to keep the Indians neutral. After expressing fears England "will spare no pains to excite the several nations of Indians to take up arms against these Colonies," Congress approved the creation of three departments for Indian affairs, northern, southern and middle. Five commissioners were named to the southern department, and three commissioners each for the other two. They were directed "to treat with the Indians . . . on behalf of the United colonies, in order to preserve the peace and friendship with the said Indians, and to prevent their taking part in the present commotions."

The northern commissioners laid immediate plans to convene a council fire with the Iroquois confederation at Albany. To help them in their discussions, Congress approved a long American policy statement, studded with patriot themes, to be presented to the Indians. On August 26 and 28, 1775, in sessions attended by General Schuyler and the northern commissioners, Oliver Wolcott, Colonel Turbutt Francis, and Volkert P. Douw, the address of Congress was read and translated for the Indians.

In outlining the history of the dispute between America and the King's "wicked counsellors," Congress made the following key statements: "Brothers and friends! We desire you will hear and receive what we have told you, and that you will open a good ear and listen to what we are going to say. This is a family quarrel between us and Old England. You Indians are not concerned in it. We don't wish you to take up the hatchet against the king's troops. We desire you to remain at home, and not join either side, but keep the hatchet buried deep." The patriots concluded with an attempt to anticipate and counter British propaganda. "This island," said Congress, "now trembles, the wind whistles from almost every quarter. Let us fortify our minds and shut our ears against false rumors. Let us be cautious what we receive for truth, unless spoken by wise and good men."

On August 31 a Mohawk chief arose to give the Iroquois reply. Standing before the council fire, he declared that the British had also desired them to "sit still." Therefore, he said, the following was the decision of the Six Nations: "Not to take any part, but, as it is a family affair, to sit still and see you fight it out; we beg you will receive this as infallible, it being our full resolution."

So it was the Iroquois pledged neutrality and Congress' Indian policy seemed to have borne fruit.

+

Although Congress had fixed its policy by August 1775, exceptions were made on an individual basis which made it seem the Americans were practicing deception. For example, Benedict Arnold during his march to Quebec in November 1775 persuaded some Canadian Indians to join his forces. In a meeting with these red men Arnold explained the American dispute with the King "and his wicked great men," and told them his

74

forces had entered Canada "to drive out the king's soldiers." He invited them to join, promising "one Portuguese per month, two dollars bounty and . . . provision, and the liberty to choose their own officers." Whereupon fifty Indians signed up to march with the Americans.

In general, however, the Americans sought to influence the northern Indians to remain on the sidelines. A useful agent in these attempts was the Reverend Samuel Kirkland, a Protestant missionary who had lived among the Oneidas and Tuscaroras. In the fall of 1775, Kirkland persuaded an important Oneida chief to visit Washington's camp at Cambridge. Washington, who clearly understood the importance of making a good impression on the Indian leader, did all he could to make the visit agreeable. But the best American propaganda in this instance was the sight of the British army shut up in Boston, surrounded by thousands of colonial militiamen.

Other Indians came to Washington's camp during this period, including leaders of the St. Francis and Caghnawagas of Canada. Washington found himself "a little embarrassed," as he put it in January 1776, when the visiting Caghnawagas offered to take up arms on America's behalf. In a letter to Schuyler, Washington commented that his embarrassment stemmed not so much "from the impropriety of encouraging these people to depart from their neutrality (accepting their own voluntary offer rather)," but because of the expense of supporting them. He added: "I am sensible that if they do not desire to be idle, that they will be for or against us. I am sensible also that no artifices will be left unessayed to engage them against us."

In his reply Schuyler suggested Washington try "to get decently rid of their offer" in some way without offending them. He verified Washington's view on supplies: "The expense we are at in the (northern) Indian department is now amazing; it will be more so when they consider themselves in our service." Washington finally resolved the problem by sending the Indians back to Canada with the promise he would call on them when help was needed.

By April 1776 Washington came to realize that as the American position deteriorated in Canada, it would be impossible to keep the Indians in a state of neutrality. In a letter to Congress, Washington asked whether it might not "be best immediately to engage them on our side, and to use our utmost endeavours to prevent their minds being poisoned by ministerial emissaries, which will ever be the case while a king's garrison is suffered to remain in their country."

Washington's fears were justified, since the British were beginning an active campaign to secure the assistance of their "old friends and allies, the Indians of the Six Nations."[1] In May 1776, Colonel John Butler and other British agents collected some chiefs of the Iroquois at Niagara in an effort to persuade them to break their vows of neutrality and join the British standard. Initially, the Indians resisted, answering that they were determined "to maintain peace with both the King and the Bostonians, and receive no axe from either." One important influence working on their minds apparently was the news of the British evacuation of Boston several months earlier. In an effort to counteract the significance of that withdrawal, the British told the Iroquois leaders:

> The King of England is very great and wise; he was never yet conquered. He has subdued both France and Spain. Pray, what can this handful in America do with such a King? The King is very subtle, he has deceived the Bostonians . . . . He ordered his forces continued at Boston till the Bostonians had collected all the cannon that could be found, from Philadelphia, New York, and even from Virginia, and brought them to that place. The Bostonians, having all their force and cannon collected, were about to destroy the town; but the King's officer commanding there forbade them, telling them he would leave it in a peaceful manner, as the purpose of his coming there was now answered. And now, brothers, you will soon hear that the King's ships have laid waste all their seaports, as they can make no resistance, having sent all their cannon and stores to Boston.[2]

Although the Indians may not have been impressed by these laborious arguments, Butler prevailed on them to send a delegation to talk with Colonel Guy Johnson, who had just returned from England with specific instructions to fully engage the Indians of the Iroquois confederation.

Meanwhile, Congress had not been idle. In April 1776 it turned its attention to a visiting delegation of Delawares of the middle department, headed by "Captain White Eyes." Hoping the Delawares could be used, Congress ordered a present of $300 plus two horses and saddles for Captain White Eyes. The Delaware chief was then urged to go among all the Indian nations to the westward, and to tell them "that we are determined to cultivate peace and friendship with them, and that we will endeavour, by making the best regulation in our power, to prevent any of our people wronging them in any manner, or taking their lands; and we will strive to put the trade between us on such a footing, as will secure the peace and promote the interest of all parties; and we expect that all the wise men of every Indian nation will use their influence for the same purpose."

By June 1776, however, Congress' hopes of peace and friendship with the Indians began to dim. With the bad news from Canada came word that the British were actively trying to recruit the savages of the Six Nations. On June 3, Congress decided to break away from its year-old policy of seeking Indian neutrality. On that day it authorized Washington to employ 2,000 Indians as auxiliaries to reinforce the northern army.[3]

+

In the now open competition between Americans and English for Indian support, both sides were aware that the greatest arguments that could be brought to bear on the tribesmen were economic ones. From London Germain wrote to General Carleton and announced that a considerable supply of goods suitable for presents was on its way to America "the better to enable you to prevail" on the Iroquois "to a general declaration in our favour."[4] The Americans, in desperate need of the same blankets, muskets, and knives which would buy Indian support, could only threaten dire revenge if the tribes took up the hatchet on the British side.

For example, when word reached the Americans that the

77

blood-thirsty Senecas were urging the Shawnees to attack the Virginia frontier, the Americans threatened their complete destruction. As Jefferson reported in August 1776: "We directed a declaration to be made to the six nations in general that if they did not take the most decisive measures for the preservation of neutrality we would never cease waging war with them while one was to be found on the face of the earth."

This threat may have temporarily deterred the Indians. In the late summer of 1776, however, an incident took place at British Detroit which bode no good for the patriots. It involved Captain White Eyes of the Delawares, and an American trader named William Wilson, who had gone into territory of the Wiandot tribe to spread the doctrines and messages of Congress. Wilson carried with him a written message to the Wiandots from Congress' agent in the middle department, George Morgan.

The Wiandots, who were under British influence, apparently notified the British lieutenant governor at Detroit, Henry Hamilton, who invited the two men to visit him for a friendly parley. Wilson and Captain White Eyes accepted. Once in Detroit, however, they found themselves the victims of an anti-American demonstration staged by Hamilton before a mixed gathering of savages. It began at the council meeting they were invited to, when Hamilton asked Wilson if he could see Morgan's message to the Wiandots. Wilson handed it over to the British leader, who read it slowly and then turned to the assembled savages to denounce the Americans as "enemies and traitors to my king." While the Indians watched, Hamilton dramatically tore up the American address and the gift belt that had accompanied it, and threw the pieces about the council house. Turning to Captain White Eyes, he ordered him to leave Detroit at once if he valued his life. It was a much-chagrined Delaware chief and American agent who speedily packed up and left the fort, their propaganda mission a failure.

The western Indians who had keenly observed Hamilton's little drama, vowed to him that they were ready to act immediately against the Americans. Hamilton, however, held them back, having received instructions that the savages should be held in readiness to cooperate with British forces the following spring. He told the assembled Indians "to content themselves with watchfully observing the enemy's motions."[5]

Although in the north and central territories British policy in 1776 was to hold off the Indians until the campaigns of 1777, a different policy was pursued in the south. There John Stuart, the Indian superintendent, stirred up the Cherokees, Creeks, and Chickasaws to attack the frontier settlements in the summer of 1776. Stuart did not need to be very persuasive to win over these Indians, many of whom had long-standing grievances against the land-grabbing colonists.

The British plan in the south in 1776 called for synchronization of naval operations along the Carolina-Georgia coast with Indian outbreaks on the frontier. The sole propaganda operation undertaken in this connection involved an attempt to subvert the frontiersmen. In May 1776, the British disseminated a propaganda letter along the Carolina frontier which held out safety and salvation to any Americans who would rally to the government. The letter stated it was not the King's intention "to set his friends and allies, the Indians, on his liege subjects. Therefore, whoever of you are willing to join his Majesty's forces as soon as they arrive at the Cherokee nation, by repairing to the King's standard, shall find protection, and their families and estates be secured from all danger whatever."

. This letter also revealed British military plans, as follows: "Should any of the inhabitants be desirous of knowing how they are to be kept free of every kind of insult or danger, inform them that his Majesty will immediately land an army in West Florida, and march them through the Creek nation to the Chickasaws, where five hundred warriors from each nation are to join them, then come by the Cherokees, (who have also promised their assistance), and then take possession of the frontiers of North Carolina and Virginia." This intelligence was interesting enough to cause excited preparations by the Americans to meet the impending attacks.

In July 1776 the first blow fell on settlers along the Holston River, when 700 Indians advanced against Watauga Fort and Eaton's Station. Both attacks, however, were beated off. This initiation of frontier warfare by the British and their tawny allies in a sense enhanced the patriot cause since, by striking the first blow, it turned southern opinion further against Britain and "the detestable villain, Stuart." Many Americans who had been lukewarm Tories turned Whig, according to one report from Charleston on July 21: "A number of the heads of the Tories in this province, when they heard of the breaking out of the Indians, wrote to our governor and told him they never dreamt the King would descend to such lawless and diabolical designs; that they were now willing to do everything in their power to assist their brethren in America. These are men of influence on the frontiers, and will be very useful against the Indians."

The British meanwhile were rebuffed by the patriots in their attempt to seize Charleston in late June 1775. The result on the frontier was that after the Indians retreated, the injured Americans determined to retaliate. In the fall of 1776, several hastily organized columns of Carolina militia, plus a force of Virginians, marched into Cherokee country, put villages and fields to the torch, and scattered the Indians.

In the north, when Washington received word of the successful American raid into Indian country, the Commander in Chief sought to press home its lessons to a tribe of Canadian Indians. In a message to the chiefs of the Passamaquoddy tribe, Washington wrote in December 1776:

> Brothers: I have a piece of news to tell you which I hope you will attend to. Our enemy, the King of Great Britain, endeavoured to stir up all the Indians from Canada to South Carolina against us. But our brethren of the Six Nations and their allies the Shawanese and Delawares, would not harken to the advice of the messengers sent among them, but kept fast hold of our ancient covenant chain. The Cherokees and Southern tribes were foolish enough to listen to them, and to take up the hatchet against us; upon which our warriors went into their country, burnt their houses, destroyed their corn, and obliged them to sue for peace and give hostages for their future good behavior.
>
> Now, brothers, never let the King's wicked counsellors turn your hearts against me and your brethren of this country. . . .

Washington was not alone in taking advantage of favorable events to spread friendly propaganda. On the British side, John Stuart, in an effort to recoup his fortunes among the defeated Cherokees, announced the defeat of Washington's army in late 1776 at New York and in New Jersey. Writing to the Indians early in 1777, Stuart said: "The King's army is victorious everywhere, and the rebels who bragged so much of their valor, fly before him like the deer before wolves and tigers. Their great army is dispersed and not finding protection in their strong forts and walls, have sought [safety] in inglorious flight. This we may reasonably expect will soon bring about a peace." But the news could not change the fact that the Cherokees had been thoroughly cowed by the Americans. In July, at the Treaty of "Long Island," they made peace with the Virginians and North Carolinians.

Two months later, James Robertson, an agent of North Carolina, visited the Cherokees and learned that Alexander Cameron, a British agent, had sent his deputy to Chicamauga with orders to inform the Indians "that Philadelphia was taken, and fourteen thousands of the Provincials killed, and that America in six weeks time would be in ye hands of the English." Whereupon, Robertson set about contradicting everything the British had told the Cherokees.[6]

+

Although the new year 1777 dawned on frontiers which were relatively quiet, British agents were able to persuade many tribes, particularly the Iroquois, to take up the hatchet against the Americans. The British plan called for using the Indians as auxiliaries with Burgoyne's army on the march from Canada, or to excite diversions on the frontiers. In the case of Burgoyne's army, two related operations were planned. One group of Indians was to march under Lieutenant Colonel Barry St. Leger through the Mohawk Valley, while another group was to serve with Burgoyne's main force on the march against Ticonderoga and Albany.

Some 400 warriors joined Burgoyne's army, less than he had

hoped but enough to spread an alarm up and down the frontier and to convince the British commander of the usefulness of the Indians.[7] However, in this as in other affairs, Burgoyne lacked insight into the minds of the American frontiersmen, who were only led to greater resistance. Burgoyne's bombastic invasion proclamation of June 20, 1777, also was misconceived. Burgoyne had written: "I have but to give stretch to the Indian forces under my direction (and they amount to thousands) to overtake the hardened enemies of Great Britain. . . . The messengers of justice and wrath await them in the field; and devastation, famine and every concomitant horror that a reluctant but indispensable prosecution of military duty must occasion."

If Burgoyne had expected to frighten the frontiersmen with these fine words, he was doomed to disappointment. Instead, a single killing involving his Indian warriors so inflamed the minds of the colonials that they rallied in large numbers from the farms and hamlets of New England. This incident was the murder and scalping of young Jane McCrea.

Miss McCrea, who lived in the Hudson Valley north of Albany, was the daughter of a New Jersey Presbyterian minister and was engaged to marry an American loyalist who had fled to Canada to join Burgoyne's army. Instead of leaving the troubled area, the girl decided to go to Fort Edward (south of Ticonderoga), hoping to greet her lover there. But the fort was abandoned and so she stayed at the home of a Mrs. McNeil. On July 27, 1777 — several days before Burgoyne's advancing army took over the fort — a scouting party of Indians came upon it, seized Mrs. McNeil and Jane and started back towards the army. A dispute soon arose between two of the savages over who should be the girl's guard. One of the angry Indians finally shot her, scalped her and stripped her clothing from her body.

Prior to this incident Burgoyne had tried to avoid such killings by issuing strict orders to the savages to spare aged men, women, children, and prisoners. On June 24 he had announced his "rules" for the campaign as follows:

> I positively forbid bloodshed when you are not opposed in arms.
>
> Aged men, women, children and prisoners must be held

sacred from the knife or hatchet, even in the time of actual conflict.

You shall receive compensation for the prisoners you take, but you shall be called to account for scalps.

In conformity and indulgence of your customs, which have affixed an idea of honor to such badges of victory, you shall be allowed to take the scalps of the dead, when killed by your fire and in fair opposition; but on no account or pretence, or subtility, or prevarication, are they to be taken from the wounded or even dying.

Now, only a few days after Burgoyne had laid down his rules, the British camp was startled to see a woman's scalp dangling from the hands of her murderer. Burgoyne immediately ordered the Indian's arrest; but when advised that all the other savages would defect if the man was punished, he was forced to pardon him.

News of the killing soon spread up and down the New York-New England frontier. And as the story travelled, Jane McCrea grew in beauty as the crime grew in horror. Murder of frontiersmen and women was a common occurrence, but that of Jane McCrea captured the people's imaginations. To the Americans the choice was to wait quietly in their homes for the impending onslaught, or to march together against the enemy on a distant battlefield. They chose to march, and soon hundreds of farmers and militiamen were trekking through the countryside to join General Gates' army.

Gates also played a significant role in spreading the story of Jane McCrea. In a letter to Burgoyne, which received wide publicity, Gates attacked the policy of using the Indians.

That the savages of America [said Gates] should in their warfare mangle and scalp the unhappy prisoners who should fall into their hands is neither new nor extraordinary; but that the famous Lieutenant General Burgoyne . . . should hire the savages of America to scalp Europeans and the descendants of Europeans, nay more, that he should pay a price for each scalp so barbarously taken, is more than will be believed in England until authenticated facts shall in every gazette convince mankind of the truth of this horrid tale. Miss McCrea, a young lady lovely to the sight, of virtuous character and amiable disposition, engaged to be married to an officer in your army, was with other women and children taken out of a house near Fort Edward, carried into the woods, and there scalped and mangled in the most shocking manner.

The facts thus exaggerated somewhat by the Americans, the growing patriot legend of Jane McCrea proved to be but the forerunner of Burgoyne's troubles. In the weeks that followed came the disasters to British arms at Bennington and Fort Stanwix, and Burgoyne was left alone to march his army to its defeat at Saratoga.

+

The failure of the British to take Fort Stanwix was the culmination of a series of events which saw the use of one of the most effective planted rumors of the entire war. The instigator of this operation was Major General Benedict Arnold.

It will be recalled that Burgoyne had planned to send a column under St. Leger from Oswego, travelling east into the Mohawk Valley with the mission of meeting the main army at Albany. The force that began this march included between 800 and 1,000 Indians under the famous Mohawk chief, Joseph Brant, and about 800 white men — British, American loyalists, and German mercenaries. St. Leger had received information that Fort Stanwix had only a weak garrison of about sixty men, and he did not anticipate trouble in seizing the fort. However, just before he arrived, the Americans received reinforcements which brought the garrison to a total of 750 men. St. Leger immediately invested the fort, paraded his mixed troops up and down before the palisades, and demanded its surrender. But the garrison, under the leadership of Colonel Peter Gansevoort, was determined to fight, and the sight of the painted savages only strengthened their resolve.

News of the arrival of the British column in the Mohawk Valley, and the investiture of Fort Stanwix, began to spread panic among the settlers. Some who had been adherents of the patriot cause began to think of saving themselves by going over to the British. There were other patriots, however, who were determined not to let the enemy pass. A force of 800 patriots, under Nicholas Herkimer, a brigadier general in the Tryon County Militia, was hastily recruited and, on August 4, 1777, they marched west with the intention of relieving Fort Stanwix.

While the battle raged at Oriskany Creek, 250 Americans suddenly thundered out of Fort Stanwix in a surprise raid on the lightly guarded British camps outside. The raid was a complete success. Before returning to the fort, these Americans thoroughly looted the camps, taking everything they could carry away including most of the belongings of the Indians.

These unexpected mishaps caused much discontent among the Indians who were, in the best of times, as Washington put it, "a not very persevering people . . . apt to be discouraged by the most trifling miscarriages."[8] On this occasion the miscarriages were serious. Instead of marching with a victorious army as they had believed, the Indians had found themselves in one of the bloodiest battles of the northern campaign. When, on returning to camp to tend their wounded and dead, they found most of their possessions gone, their morale sank even further.

It was in these circumstances that Benedict Arnold entered the scene. Arnold had been sent into the Mohawk Valley with a relief column of about 900 troops. As he marched towards Fort Stanwix, he learned of the efforts of the British to frighten the people into joining the royal standard. Whereupon on August 20, 1777, he issued some American counterpropaganda, modelled after one of the British broadsides. Arnold proclaimed:

> Whereas a certain Barry St. Leger, a British general in the service of the — George of Great Britain, at the head of a banditti of robbers, murderers and traitors, composed of savages of America and more savage Britons . . . have lately appeared on the frontiers of this state and have threatened ruin and destruction of all the inhabitants of the United States.
>
> They have also, by artifice and misrepresentation, induced many of the ignorant and unwary subjects of these states to forfeit their allegiance to the same, and join

them in their atrocious crimes and parties of treachery and parricide. Humanity to these poor deluded wretches, who are hastening blindfold to destruction, induces me to offer them and all others concerned, whether savages, Germans, Americans or Britons, pardon; provided they do within ten days of the date hereof, come and lay down their arms, sue for protection and swear allegiance to the United States of America. But, if still blind to their own safety, they obstinately persist in their wicked courses, determined to draw on themselves the just vengeance of Heaven, and of this exasperated country, they must expect no mercy from either.

This bold proclamation must have heartened the patriots almost as much as the Arnold proclamation of a later date outraged them. But Arnold was not yet finished with his psychological gambit. He also decided to spread a rumor in St. Leger's camp at Fort Stanwix that he was on the march with a great American army.

To carry this rumor into the enemy camp Arnold employed a mentally retarded Dutchman named Hon Yost Schuyler, who had been arrested within American lines with a British propaganda agent, trying to persuade the people to join the British. Both men were tried as spies, convicted and sentenced to death. Hon Yost's mother and brother, however, on hearing of the sentence hurried to Arnold and pleaded for his life.

Arnold learned, meanwhile, that Hon Yost was held in great awe by the Indians for the very reason of his mental backwardness. He now agreed to spare the Dutchman's life but only if he would go to St. Leger's camp and spread a false story regarding the number of Americans on the march. To assure good faith Arnold said he would retain the brother as hostage. The family agreed that Hon Yost would go. To give plausibility to the deception, Hon Yost's coat was shot through with several bullets to support his story that he had escaped. In addition, Arnold called upon a friendly Oneida Indian to follow Hon Yost to verify the story to the British.

Thus it was that on August 22, 1777, around noon, Hon Yost suddenly appeared in St. Leger's camp with an excited story. He exhibited his bullet-riddled garments to the Indians, and

babbled of the approach of a great American army whose soldiers numbered as the leaves of the trees. Then the Oneida
entered the camp and verified Hon Yost's tale. As the story
spread through the camp, the discouraged savages gathered the
remainder of their belongings, looted some of the white men's
and the whole Indian body fled the scene. St. Leger tried to stop
them, but panic leaped from red men to white and soon the
English, Germans, and loyalists all took to their heels, not tarry-
ing long enough to pack their tents and equipment. Arnold's
rumormongering had succeeded beyond his wildest dreams.

The siege of Fort Stanwix lifted with such unexpected
suddenness that the surprised Americans did not understand it.
At 11:00 that morning the enemy had responded to a bombardment from the fort with an answering fire. At 3:00 P.M. several
deserters approached the fort and told the defenders that
"General St. Leger and his army was retreating with the utmost
precipitation." Colonel Gansevoort sent out a party of sixty
men who soon confirmed the account. It was not until 7:00
P.M. that the puzzle was solved, when Hon Yost slipped into
the fort and related that Arnold was on his way "with two
thousand men" (even then Hon Yost was exaggerating Arnold's
force).[9] When Arnold's 900 troops did arrive, they were met by
the cheers of the garrison.

So a simple rumor, striking minds at the perfect psychological
moment, had sent the enemy flying.

+

The bloody events in the north during 1777 had their
counterpart on the Pennsylvania-Virginia frontier, where the
British government also activated the tribes of the western con-
federacy. In May 1777 General Carleton received a London
directive: "It is the King's command that you should direct
Lieutenant Governor Hamilton to assemble as many of the Indians of his district as he conveniently can, and placing proper
persons at their head . . . employ them in making a diversion
and exciting an alarm upon the frontiers of Virginia and
Pennsylvania." It was also suggested that Hamilton make a

propaganda offer to the "considerable numbers of loyal subjects in those parts" to join his forces. He was authorized to promise 200 acres of free land to any American who came over. "These offers," said the directive, "it is hoped will induce many persons to engage in the King's service; which may enable Lieutenant Governor Hamilton to extend his operations so as to divide the attention of the rebels, and oblige them to collect a considerable force to oppose him, which cannot fail of weakening their main army and facilitating the operations . . . to be carried on against them in other quarters."

Hamilton received his instructions at Detroit on June 16, and the following day he assembled a council meeting attended by members of the Ottawa, Huron, Chippewa, Potawatomi, Miami, Shawnee, and Delaware tribes. In the next two weeks Hamilton harangued the Indians, showed them "the hatchet," sang war songs, and described the methods they should use in making war on the frontier. As Burgoyne had done, Hamilton tried to impress upon the Indians that "they were men and were desired to make war against men, and not against women or children."[10] But, like Burgoyne, Hamilton was to learn that the savages had their own rules of warfare.

Hamilton also followed the suggestion to try to persuade some of the frontiersmen to come over. On June 24 he published a propaganda missive in which he invited the Americans to join his forces at Detroit. "I do assure all such as are inclined to withdraw themselves from the tyranny and oppression of the rebel committees," Hamilton wrote, "and take refuge in this settlement or any of the posts commanded by his Majesty's officers, shall be humanely treated, shall be lodged and victualled, and such as come off in arms and shall use them in defence of his Majesty against rebels and traitors, 'till the extinction of this rebellion, shall receive pay adequate to their former stations in the rebel service, and all common men who shall serve during that period, shall receive his Majesty's bounty of two hundred acres of land."

To distribute this interesting appeal, Hamilton employed his Indian raiders. By August 1777 the proclamations began to appear on the Pennsylvania-Virginia frontier, left by the Indians on the doorsteps of abandoned homes or on the bodies of scalped settlers. This mixture of terror with an offer of salvation seemed to have some effect; and American officers in several frontier forts tried to suppress the propaganda sheets whenever they were found.

By November Hamilton's offer had been brought to the attention of Congress, along with other reports which noted "a dangerous spirit of disaffection has been excited and fomented among some worthless and evil-disposed persons on the . . . frontiers, who lost to all sentiments of virtue, honor, or regard for their country, have been induced to aid our remorseless enemy."[11]

But by this time, important events elsewhere served to counteract the effects of the Hamilton-directed Indian raids. The news of the failure of St. Leger's expedition, for example, was diligently spread by the Americans among the western Indians. General Edward Hand addressed the Delawares at Fort Pitt: "Brothers, the news papers will give you a full account of the great battles our armies have gained. The Indians who were so foolish as to join our enemies have found their mistake and those who have not run away are quite sick of their conduct. . . . The Oneidas and Tuscaroras have joined our army and are now in pursuit of the enemy. . . . What I have told you is true but do not . . . depend on words alone. If you send to the northward your messengers may see with their own eyes."[12]

News of the surrender of Burgoyne's army also was spread in the Indian territories. In particular, Congress in December 1777 delivered an address to the Six Nations, a strong statement which reminded the Indians how the patriots had entreated them "to remain neuter" instead of listening "to the voice of our enemies." The result of their "unprovoked treachery," said Congress, was nothing but shame and disgrace. "Your foolish warriors and their new allies have been defeated and driven back in every quarter; and many of them justly paid the price of their rashness with their lives."

In this address Congress spoke with an especially fierce voice to those of the Iroquois confederation who had most strongly supported the British — the Cayugas, Senecas, and Mohawks.

Mark well what we now tell you, [said Congress], let it sink deep as the bottom of the sea, and never be forgotten by you or your children. If ever again you take up the hatchet to strike us; if you join our enemies in battle or council; if you give them intelligence, or encourage them or permit them to pass through your country to molest or hurt any of our people, we shall look upon you as our enemies, and treat you as the worst of enemies. . . . The hand of the thirteen United States is not short. It will reach to the farthest extent of the country of the Six Nations.

This address was dispatched to the northern commissioners with instructions to communicate it to the different Iroquois tribes. Congress seemed to be of two opinions concerning the defeated Indians. At first its hopes were raised so high by Burgoyne's surrender that it believed it might be possible to bring over the Six Nations en masse to the American side. But on second thought, Congress decided to try to restore friendship with them, and to induce them to return to neutrality.[13]

Early in 1778 the commissioners sent word to the Indians that a conference would be held at Johnstown. This meeting took place on March 9, 1778, and one of the commissioners later reported: "The number of Indians was something above 700 consisting of Oneidas, Tuscaroras, Onondagas, a few Mohawks, and three or four Cayugas but not a single Seneca attended. The latter had the insolence even to effect their surprise that while our tomahawks stuck in their heads, their wounds were bleeding and their eyes streaming with tears . . . we should think of inviting them to a treaty!"[14]

About all that the Johnstown meeting accomplished was a reaffirmation by the Oneidas and Tuscaroras of allegiance to the patriot side. The main body of the Iroquois remained anti-American. In a letter on the subject to Congress in May 1778, Washington offered his opinion that there was "very little prospect" of winning them over. "The advantage which the enemy possesses over us in having the means of making presents more liberally than we can," Washington wrote, "has made a strong impression upon their minds, and seems to be more than a counter-balance for any arguments we can offer to conciliate their attachment."

By June, Congress reconciled itself to the fact that it had failed to win over the hostile tribes and, perhaps, had "confirmed the savages in an opinion industriously inculcated in them by the enemy that the forbearance of these states proceeds from their inability to revenge the outrages committed against them." The Board of War subsequently recommended to Congress that an expedition be organized to march against the center of Indian agitation, British Detroit.[15] However, an expedition into Indian country was to await the passage of another year.

+

During the first six months of 1778 Hamilton had continued the hit-and-run raids on the frontier, and both American prisoners and scalps began to flow into Detroit. In January alone (according to Hamilton's report to Carleton), the Indians brought in 73 prisoners and 129 scalps. Despite this, that very month Hamilton distributed another propaganda paper on the frontier which emphasized the "kind and humane treatment" theme. Dated January 5, this propaganda paper was in the form of a circular letter to the frontiersmen and contained a statement by eight American captives who assured their countrymen that they were receiving good treatment from both Indians and white captors. The letter offered "safe conduct" to all Americans on the frontier who would come to Detroit.

This appeal was weakened by the very evidence of the scalps which came into Detroit, and eyewitness reports of them which filtered back to the American settlements only stirred the frontiersmen to greater resistance. Indeed, one of the British leaders at Detroit, Edward Abbott, came around to the view that the use of the Indians was doing the King's cause more harm than good. In a letter to Carleton on June 8, Abbott complained that "the employing Indians on the rebel frontiers has been of great hurt to the cause. . . .These poor unhappy

91

people are forced to take up arms against their sovereign, or be pillaged and left to starve. . . ."

Hamilton's bloody activities did not continue unmolested, and, in fact, led directly to one of the most important American expeditions of the war. Under the leadership of George Rogers Clark, this expedition changed the history of the Ohio Valley and led to the capture of Hamilton himself.

Clark, a backwoodsman who was serving as Virginia's military commander in Kentucky, had reached the conclusion that the best way to relieve the frontier was to strike deep into enemy territory, specifically into the Illinois country. He believed it possible to conquer the region before the British knew what had happened. Residents of the area consisted largely of settlers of French origin and these people, Clark hoped, might be receptive to American appeals.

Late in 1777 Clark returned to Virginia where he laid his plan before Jefferson, George Mason, and Richard Henry Lee. These leaders adopted the idea and undertook to persuade Governor Patrick Henry to support the Illinois expedition. Henry was won over and, shortly thereafter, the Virginia Assembly authorized Clark to raise seven companies to be used ostensibly in defending Kentucky. In reality, secret orders were issued to him to attack and seize the town of Kaskaskia, Illinois, and perhaps Detroit.

So it was that in the summer of 1778 the frontier was startled by news that Clark and the Virginians were in Illinois country. On June 4, after a march across southern Illinois, Clark surprised and took Kaskaskia, not far from the Mississippi. To the startled French inhabitants, he proceeded to explain the causes of the war and to assure them they would be free men if they took the oath of allegiance to the United States. He clinched his arguments by announcing the news of the French-American alliance, and by assuring the people their Church would be protected by the new government. Clark's talk was persuasive and the people of Kaskaskia took the oath of loyalty.[16] Not long thereafter the French residents of Vincennes, across the territory to the east, were also talked into allegiance to the Americans.

When news of Clark's activities reached Hamilton at his Detroit headquarters, the British leader immediately grasped the implications of the American presence in Illinois. If nothing was done, rebel influence might spread north and east which would threaten the entire British position in the territory. Hamilton decided on a counterblow, which he would personally direct, and in late 1778 he ordered an expedition against Vincennes. His march on Vincennes, which he reached in December 1778, proved successful. The inhabitants quickly capitulated to his force of 175 white soldiers and 60 Indians and resumed their allegiance to Britain.

Hamilton sought to consolidate his victory in a propaganda letter addressed on December 29 to "the People of Illinois." In this letter he warned the French "of the misfortunes to which they will be exposed by withdrawing themselves from the dominion of the King of England." He painted a forbidding picture of a combined force of Chickasaws, Cherokees, and other Indian tribes and a regiment of British regulars marching in the spring against the rebels. He reminded them that "the nations inhabiting the shores of the Lakes will all be devoted to whatever service I shall recommend to them." He concluded that it was up to the French inhabitants of Illinois: "If they suffer themselves any longer to be so far blinded by the promises of the Americans (hitherto so badly fulfilled) as to range themselves under their standard, they must prepare to abide by the consequences."

While Hamilton devoted himself to consolidating his position, Clark at Kaskaskia reached a daring decision to undertake a winter march against the British at Vincennes. On February 6, 1779, rellying the French of Kaskaskia and the surrounding territory, Clark began a 180-mile trek across Illinois. His force, consisting of about 120 men, half of them French, reached the vicinity of Vincennes on February 22, their presence still unknown to the enemy. Near the town Clark picked up a number of French inhabitants and learned from them that Hamilton's strength included a force of 200 Indians.

Knowing his own strength was not one-fourth that of the combined British, Indians, and French of Vincennes, but also aware of the lukewarm allegiance of the French to Britain, Clark decided upon a bluff to neutralize the latter. Several of the Frenchmen he had picked up, unaware of his strength, were dispatched to Vincennes to deliver the following note to the people:

> Gentlemen, Being now within two miles of your village with my army determined to take your fort this night and not being willing to surprise you, I take this step to request of such of you as are true citizens and willing to enjoy the liberty I bring you to remain still in your house, and those (if any there be) that are friends to the King, will instantly repair to the fort and join the hair buyer General and fight like men. And if any such as do not go to the fort shall be discovered afterwards, they may depend on being well treated and I once more request they shall keep out of the streets, for every [one] I find in arms on my arrival I shall treat him as an enemy.

Clark's bluff succeeded. The people who gathered in the public square to hear the message were so surprised and fearful that none dared to go to the fort to tell Hamilton. Clark gave further play to their imaginations by ordering his men to begin their advance with colors flying. By marching them to and fro behind a slight elevation of land, which allowed only the flags to be seen from the town, he created the impression that a force of about 1,000 men was approaching.

At 8:00 that evening, under cover of darkness and led by five of his French prisoners, Clark's column entered the town. The surprise was complete. Before Hamilton knew what had happened, the Americans were in control of Vincennes and he and his troops were besieged in the fort. Clark wasted no time with preliminaries and immediately sent a threatening surrender demand to Hamilton.

The British leader found himself in a very weak position. A large part of his Indian allies had fled into the woods, while inside the fort half of his defending force consisted of Frenchmen. Although he and the British soldiers were determined "to fight to the last extremity," the French "hung their heads," Hamilton later wrote, "and their sergeants first turned round and muttered with their men. Some said it was hard they should fight against their own friends and relations who they could see had joined the Americans and fired against the fort."[17] Faced with the probable defection of half his troops, Hamilton decided to surrender. The capitulation took place on February 24, 1779.

Hamilton's surrender was one of the most important blows struck against British prestige in Indian country in the entire war. Few events had more propaganda value for the Americans. That Hamilton, the proud English leader who had been almost deified by the western Indians, should be caught and placed in chains (as he was later on order of the Virginia Assembly) was an astounding fact to the savage mind. Now the name of George Rogers Clark of the Big Knives (Virginians) was spread up and down the frontier. Clark clearly understood that everything he said to the Indians would carry great weight, and in conferences with the Chippewas and other savages who had accompanied Hamilton, he threatened extermination to any who would not lay down their arms at once.

Clark also sent a strong speech to the tribes in the north in which he played to the hilt the role of conqueror. This speech deserves to be recalled in all its original flavor. Said Clark to the Indians (excerpts):

> Its as you will I dont care whether you are for peace or war; as I glory in war and want enemies to fight us, as the English cant fight us any longer, and are become like Young Children begging the Big Knives for mercy and a little bread to eat; this is the last speech you may ever expect from the Big Knives, the next thing will be the Tomahawk. And you may expect in four moons to see your women & children given to the dogs to eat, while those nations that have kept their words with me will flourish and grow. . . .[18]

Clark's victory in the Ohio Valley had lasting effects, his conquest leaving the United States in possession of the Illinois country at war's end.

+

Congress, we have noted, had hoped the disaster to Burgoyne's army would bring the Iroquois over to the American side, or at least their return to neutrality. But by the spring of 1778 evidence mounted that the Indians were about to strike again. In July the uneasy quiet was finally shattered when a combined British-Indian partisan force of about 900 men slipped into the Wyoming Valley of Pennsylvania, defeated the American militia, and laid waste to the entire valley. More than 1,000 homes were destroyed, cattle and swine were driven away, and hundreds of scalps were taken.

The frontier inhabitants cried out for protection and petitions flowed into Philadelphia asking for help. Congress consulted Washington, who decided in early 1779 to send a force against the Six Nations and selected General Sullivan to lead it. Washington informed Sullivan that: "The immediate objects are the total destruction and devastation of their settlements and the capture of as many prisoners of every age and sex as possible. It will be essential to ruin their crops now in the ground and prevent their planting more." Planning for the expediton immediately got under way but it was not until May 1779 that the operation began.

Meanwhile, the British and Iroquois renewed their raids in the spring and summer of 1779; their target, the people of the Mohawk and Schoharie Valleys in the New York and Pennsylvania borderlands. The attacks were led by Chief Joseph Brant and Captain Walter Butler. A loyalist officer, Richard Cartwright, Jr., who accompanied the raiders, described the small parties of Indians as:

> so many bands of lurking assassins, seeking an opportunity to destroy the peaceful and industrious inhabitants and ready to glut their cruelty alike with the blood of friend and foe without distinction of sex or age . . . it is impossible to bring them to leave women and children unmolested, and as for the rest, it must be expected they will regard all

96

white people alike, and if they can bring off a prisoner or scalp 'tis all but one to them.

Cartwright further described the Indian raiders as consisting of warriors who "may exert themselves against defenceless people or an enemy taken at surprise with great fury, [but] they will soon give way when taken at equal terms in the field."[19]

A similar evaluation had been voiced earlier in the British Parliament by Edmund Burke, who denounced the use of "savage auxilliaries" as executioners. Indians, he said, "were the most useless, and the most expensive of all auxilliaries. Each of their so-called braves cost as much as five of the best European musketeers and, after eating double rations for so long as they lasted, they . . . deserted wholesale at the first appearance of ill-success."[20]

Indeed, this is what happened when Sullivan's expedition moved out in earnest in the summer of 1779 and, in a campaign that lasted through September, ravaged the Indian countryside. By October Washington was able to report that "General Sullivan has completed the entire destruction of the Six Nations; driven all the inhabitants, men, women and children out of it and is . . . on his return to join this army with the troops under his command." Washington hoped that this demonstration of American power — "to chastise them whenever their hostile conduct deserves it" — would produce good effect. But it did not succeed in ending the Indian ravages. The Iroquois were only driven back to the British post at Niagara, where they nursed their wounds and launched revengeful and bloody raids against the frontier in 1780 and 1781.

During this period there were a number of related propaganda incidents. One involved an address entitled "Letter of the Marquis de Lafayette to the savages of Canada," disseminated in December 1778. In this letter Lafayette had urged "his children" in the north to desert the British and join the Americans, France's new allies.

You know, [wrote Lafayette], that your fathers want to lead the thirteen states with one hand and Canada with the other in order to join them against our enemy, and the king has sent a declaration [Admiral d'Estaing's proclamation] to the Canadians to promise them his aid. But I realize that you would be very glad to receive confirmation of this news from me. . . . So my children, you will see us soon arrive in Canada with General Washington, the great war chief of the Americans, and we shall know who are our friends and who our enemies. . . .

To counter this propaganda about the French alliance, and the argument that Britain was unable to protect them, the British on a number of occasions put on a "show of force" for the benefit of the Indians. In June 1779, for example, General Haldimand invited some western savages, as well as the Iroquois, to visit Quebec where they could see with their own eyes that it was the *British* fleet sitting in the bay. Haldimand cautioned the Indians not to listen "to mischievous birds that whisper into your ears all manner of bad news and falsehoods to disturb your well-being and unanimity in order to bring you strife and trouble."

Nevertheless the British authorities were beset on all sides. From Nova Scotia the British agent there reported to General Clinton in August 1779 that the Indians were much alienated and he warned: "As their attachment to the French interest is yet very strong and their regard for the rebels much strengthened by their alliance with France, it requires the greatest attention and address to keep them quiet." He added he feared they might take up arms should "any French squadron or ship" appear on the coast.[21]

Besides taking advantage of the potent French alliance, the Americans invoked an old technique to insure the loyalty of certain of the tribes. This was to present the chiefs army commissions, which brought the Indians the same pay and subsistence as other American soldiers. At least one such commission was offered in the rank of major to a chief of the St. Francois tribe of Canada;[22] but usually these commissions went no higher than the rank of captain.

Throughout the war Washington followed a policy of paying every courtesy to Indian visitors to his army. This had as its purpose, he once explained to General Schuyler: "To give them an idea of our force and to do away with the false notions they might have embibed from the tales which had been propagated among them."[23] An account of such a visit was recorded by James Thacher in May 1779.

> Our brigade [wrote Thacher] was paraded for the pur-
> pose of being reviewed by General Washington and a num-
> ber of Indian chiefs. His Excellency, with his usual dignity,
> followed by his mulato servant Bill, riding a beautiful
> gray steed, passed in front of the line and received the
> salute. He was accompanied by a singular group of savages,
> whose appearance was beyond description ludicrous. Their
> horses were of the meanest kind, some of them destitute
> of saddles. . . . Their personal decorations were equally
> farcial. . . . But his excellency deems it good policy to pay
> some attention to this tribe of the wilderness, and to con-
> vince them of the strength and discipline of our army, that
> they may be encouraged to be friendly or deterred from
> aggression, if they should become hostile to our country.

In the summer of 1780, when the French expeditionary force under General Comte de Rochambeau arrived at Newport, Rhode Island, it also played host to visiting Indians. Rochambeau showed his visitors great hospitality and sent them away loaded with presents, to serve in the backcountry as willing volunteers for the dissemination of allied propaganda.

During the last years of the war the uncompromising attitude of the Americans toward the Indians was well illustrated by a directive Jefferson sent to Clark in January 1780. "We would have you," Jefferson wrote, "cultivate peace and cordial friendship with the several tribes of Indians (the Shawanese excepted). Endeavour that those who are in friendship with us live in peace with one another. Against those who are our enemies let loose the friendly tribes. The Kikapous should be encouraged against the hostile tribes of the Chickasaws and the Choctawas and the others against the Shawanese. . . ."

Both Englishmen and Americans understood by this time that the Indians were impressed solely by two factors: success in war and economic power. The patriots sent sufficient forces to the frontiers to prevent the Indian raids from having a significant effect on the main strategy of the war. However, Britain's economic advantages also continued to count for a great deal and it used its "presents" to the Indians to effectively retain and hold the loyalty of many of the tribes. In the end, however, since the British Army and Navy failed to crush the rebellion, the King's employment of Indians only widened the split between the colonists and the mother country.

☆ 4 ☆

The Incitement
of Negro Insurrection

T HERE WAS YET another important group of people in America whose possible aid in subduing the rebels caught the imagination of British officials — the large slave population, estimated at between 500,000 and 600,000 persons.[1] The presence of these "intestine enemies," the bulk of them in the southern colonies, seemed, as in the case of the red men, a potential weapon the British might well seize upon to bring the colonists "back to their senses."

The Americans were well aware of the threat. Thus, in November 1774 James Madison wrote to a friend about his concern that:

> if America & Britain should come to a hostile rupture I am afraid an insurrection among the slaves may & will be promoted. In one of our counties lately a few of those unhappy wretches met together & chose a leader who was to conduct them when the English troops should arrive — which they foolishly thought would be very soon & that by revolting to them they should be rewarded with their freedom. Their intentions were soon discovered & proper precautions taken to prevent the infection. . . .

The subject of a slave insurrection surfaced in a House of Commons debate on October 26, 1775, when one of the supporters of the ministry, Governor William Lyttelton, compared America to a chain, the upper part strong and the lower part weak. Governor Lyttelton "explained this by saying the northern colonies or upper part of the chain were strong, populous, and of course able to make resistance; the southern colonies, or lower part, were weak, on account of the large number of Negroes in them. He intimated if a few regiments were sent there the Negroes would rise, and imbrue their hands in the blood of their masters."

Earlier in 1775, Dr. Samuel Johnson had published his political tract, *Taxation No Tyranny*, in which he referred to a proposal that the slaves be set free, an act, he suggested, "which the lovers of liberty must surely commend." When these words reached America in the spring, the always present colonial fears of a slave uprising came alive. Indeed, on June 19 the North Carolina delegates in Congress, in a letter alerting their home committees of safety, cited the Johnson statement.

Even in the northern colonies — in New York, Pennsylvania, and New Jersey, where the slave population was relatively small — hints of concerted action by the slaves set nerves on edge during the first year of the war. In New York, for example, one Johannes Schoonmaker of Ulster County overheard two of his Negroes discussing the amount of powder they would need to support a slave uprising. It was to be initiated by setting fire to their owners' homes and killing them as they fled the flames. The two men were arrested along with seventeen or eighteen others. The incident reminded southerners that their slaves outnumbered whites by two to one and even higher percentages in certain areas. Indeed, two Georgia gentlemen told John Adams that if the British landed one thousand well-provisioned troops in the south, and proclaimed freedom to all slaves who joined them, "twenty thousand Negroes would join in a fortnight."[2]

In Charleston, South Carolina, in June 1775 the city took on "the appearance of a garrison town." A resident there wrote that "one company keeps guard all day, and two every night. In our situation we cannot be too watchful and may require much strength, for our Negroes have all high notions of their liberty. . . ."[3] Similar concerns in North Carolina led various committees to adopt a series of precautionary measures. In June and early July 1775 special armed patrols were organized to seek out any Negroes who might possess weapons. The "patrollers" of Pitt County were authorized to shoot any number of Negroes above four, "who are off their masters' plantations and will not submit."[4]

In June, Josiah Martin, the royal governor of North Carolina, fearing he would be seized by the rebels, fled aboard a British sloop in Cape Fear River. From this place of safety, Governor Martin wrote to his superiors in London. In his letter, he indignantly referred to "a most infamous report" being circulated that he had "formed a design of arming the Negroes and proclaiming freedom to all such as should resort to the King's standard." His denial, however, was weakened by his subsequent comments, in which he referred to the high proportion of blacks to whites in neighboring Virginia and Maryland, "a circumstance," he said, "that would facilitate the reduction of those colonies."

While Martin's thoughts lingered on that prospect, the Americans in Pitt County on July 8, 1775, "fortuitously discovered a deep laid, Horrid Tragik Plan" for a slave insurrection that very night. A full report on the plot, dated July 15, by the chairman of the County Committee of Safety, Colonel John Simpson, gave credit for its exposure to a slave belonging to a Mr. Bayner and another belonging to a Captain Thomas Respess. According to the testimony of these Negroes, the "intended insurrection" was to be put "into execution that night."

Immediately, the Committee of Safety sounded the alarm and appointed 100 men to patrol the countryside. The show of force was successful. The next day, July 9, the committee met and examined the evidence that had been gathered. This evidence, largely based on Negro testimony, named a Captain Johnson of White Haven as the leader of the movement, and a Negro slave named Merrick, who had "propagated the contagion." On July 10 the committee ordered several Negroes caught in the "patrollers' " net be given eighty lashes and have their ears "crap'd." Additional evidence was accumulated, in the form of arms and "considerable ammunition" seized from the Negroes.

In the days that followed, the committee was busy "examining and scourging" the slaves. According to Simpson's report, "from whichever part of the county they come they all confess nearly the same thing": that on the night of the eighth they were all to fall on and destroy the families where they lived, then to go from house to house burning as they went, and finally, they were to retreat into the backcountry where they would receive a welcome by persons appointed by the British.

Early in August, while news of the "horrid" plan was disseminated, a letter Governor Martin had written several weeks before came to the attention of the Committee of Safety at New Bern. In this letter, written to a Lewis DeRosset, the refugee governor denied that he had ever "conceived a thought" of encouraging the Negroes to revolt. "And," he said, "I will further add my opinion that nothing could ever justify the design, falsely imputed to me, of giving encouragement to the Negroes, but the actual and declared rebellion of the King's subjects, and the failure of all other means to maintain the King's government."

But the King's subjects were already in rebellion! Thus, in the opinion of the New Bern committee, the Governor's words contained, "in plain English, and in every construction of language, a justification of the design of encouraging the slaves to revolt." Whereupon, the committee ordered Martin's letter be published in the press to expose his "public avowal of a crime so horrid and truly black a complexion. . . ."

Governor Martin, who eventually retired from the scene, found himself abused for even thinking of tampering with the slaves. However, the true infamy in the eyes of the southerners in this connection was not to be Martin's. This honor was reserved for the King's governor of Virginia, John Murray, Earl of Dunmore, who issued an "emancipation proclamation" in November 1775 which set in motion the most threatening movement of all against the south.

+

The events which led to Dunmore's proclamation also were related to the patriot agitation in Virginia, which in April 1775 led him to seize twenty kegs of gunpowder from the public magazine at Williamsburg. When this action stirred Virginians to attempt the forcible return of the powder, he warned them that if any injury or insult was offered him, "by the living God" he would free and arm the slaves, and would not hesitate at burning rebels' houses to ashes and spreading devastation wherever he could reach.[5]

The threat to free the Negroes and put arms into their hands "startled the Insurgents," and everywhere the Virginians reached for their weapons. From Philadelphia Thomas Wharton wrote of Dunmore to his brother, Samuel: "Could he act so diabolical a part he is not fit to hold the reins of government." However, the leaders of Virginia, Washington, Edmond Pendleton, and Richard Henry Lee among them, urged moderation on their excited countrymen and succeeded in preventing any immediate movement. The lull they won was short-lived; early in May, when news was received from the north of the skirmishing outside Boston, Patrick Henry aroused his followers for a march to repossess the powder.

At this point Dunmore sought to pacify the King's unruly subjects, and he offered to pay for the seized powder, which agreement succeeded in halting the march. However, being uncertain of the outcome, Dunmore set cannon before the palace in Williamsburg, obtained reinforcements from a British man-of-war, the *Fowey*, and armed his own slaves and some Indians he had been holding hostage. This mixed crew settled down to defend the palace against the Virginians, who never came.

In June, when the atmosphere seemed calmer, Dunmore recalled the Virginia Assembly into session to transact some important public business. Immediately the body got out of hand. With the fever of rebellion rising, Dunmore, fearful that he might be seized, fled in the early morning hours of June 8 with

105

his wife and children to the *Fowey*, lying in the harbor at York.

From this refuge, Dunmore meditated how he might crush the rebel movement. As news reached him that the Virginians were forming military units and undertaking general war preparations, he pursued a plan long conceived to raise a combined force of Indians, loyalists and Negroes which, together with his small group of marines and soldiers, he hoped would be sufficient to restore the King's authority in the colony. His plan, broached to his superiors in London on May 1, was approved.[6]

The summer of 1775 saw both sides arming for battle. While the patriots strained to find weapons and powder to equip their militia units, Dunmore collected a small fleet of ships at Gosport, about a half-mile from Portsmouth, and began planning the campaign. The need for provisions for his growing force, however, increased apace and his British seamen, who formerly had been able to freely obtain supplies in the colonial ports, were forced into plundering expeditions. In the process they began to entice the slaves from the nearby plantations.

Although alerted and chagrined by these hit-and-run operations, when autumn came the Americans were still unprepared to confront Dunmore's forces. In October the rebels were startled when Dunmore's men swooped down on Norfolk and seized the American press there. Writing about this incident to Lord Dartmouth, Dunmore said he had taken the press because "the public prints of this little dirty borough of Norfolk has for some time past been wholly employed in exciting, in the minds of all ranks of people, the spirit of sedition and rebellion by the grossest misrepresentation of facts, both public and private." Now, he said, he was going to have "a press for the King" on board his ship.

If the Virginia rebels were upset by the conversion of their press into a King's newspaper, they were even more angered by successive raids on October 13, 17, 19, 20, and 21, during which the rampaging governor seized arms, cannon, and other supplies. The thoroughly alarmed Virginia Committee of Safety could no longer wait: it ordered a regiment to the Norfolk area, under William Woodford.

In the days that followed there were new clashes. During one significant skirmish on November 7, Dunmore's forces, 150 men and a small following of Negroes and loyalists, routed about 300 Virginians and captured a number of prisoners. This victory so stimulated the governor and his supporters, that he decided the moment had come to issue his "emancipation proclamation." That same day, November 7, he published a proclamation, establishing martial law in the colony, and calling upon "every person capable of bearing arms to resort to his Majesty's standard, or be looked upon as traitors to his Majesty's crown and government." The most important sentence, however, was his announcement offering freedom to "all indented servants, Negroes and others" who were able and willing to bear arms for the King.

In a subsequent letter to General William Howe, Dunmore reported that, as a result of his proclamation, the slaves were "flocking in from all quarters." Gathering them in as fast as he could, the Governor assigned them to a Negro corps (called Lord Dunmore's Ethiopian Regiment), under white officers. By the end of November he had nearly 300 black soldiers, all decked out in uniforms. To add insult to injury, and to mock the rebels' slogan, *Liberty or Death*, he had emblazoned across the breast of each Negro's uniform, the slogan *Liberty to Slaves*.[7]

These actions infuriated the Virginians. If any hopes had remained that Britain might yet win back the allegiance of influential southerners, the Dunmore proclamation killed them entirely. Wrote Richard Henry Lee: "Lord Dunmore's unparalleled conduct in Virginia has ... united every man in the colony. If administration had searched through the world for a person best fitted to ruin their cause, and procure union and success for these colonies, they could not have found a more complete agent than Lord Dunmore."[8]

Washington was both worried and outraged when news reached him at Cambridge of the activities of the "arch-traitor to the rights of humanity, Lord Dunmore." Writing to Lee, Washington warned: "If, my dear sir, that man is not crushed before spring, he will become the most formidable enemy

America has; his strength will increase as a snowball by rolling, and faster, if some expedient cannot be hit upon to convince the slaves and servants of the impotency of his designs." Washington suggested that simply forcing Dunmore back aboard his ships was not sufficient: "Nothing less than depriving him of life or liberty will secure peace to Virginia."

A propaganda effort along the lines Washington suggested had already been made. In an article in the *Virginia Gazette* on November 25, an anonymous rebel writer, after attacking Dunmore, addressed himself directly to the Negroes and warned they would probably be sold in the West Indies and perish either "by the inclemency of the weather, or the cruelty of barbarous masters." The writer added:

> Be not then, ye negroes, tempted by this proclamation to ruin yourselves. We have given you a faithful view of what you are to expect; and declare before God in doing it, we have considered your welfare as well as that of the country. Whether you will profit by the advice, we cannot tell; but this we know, that whether we suffer or not, if you desert us, *you* most certainly will.

Still reports were heard of "great numbers" of slaves joining Dunmore. The English tenders, reported one writer, were "plying up the rivers, plundering plantations and using every art to seduce the Negroes."[9] In an attempt to halt this defection, the Virginia Assembly issued a warning of death to any Negro who joined the governor. To those slaves who immediately would forsake the governor, the Virginians offered a full pardon; and they also appealed to everyone "to explain and make known this offer of mercy to those unfortunate people."

The promise of punishment for slave fugitives was no idle threat. When two unlucky Negroes hailed a rebel vessel in the belief it was a British tender, and offered to aid the governor, they were brought in and sentenced to death as an example to others.[10]

In the meantime, the Virginia militia under Woodford had reached the vicinity of Great Bridge, several miles from Norfolk, where in December they began to dig in behind some earthworks. Dunmore, fearing the increase of rebel strength, ordered an attack, which took place on December 9. In a short but brisk exchange of fire at Great Bridge, the British lost sixty men killed or wounded, including some Negro soldiers. Forced to retire from the field, the British contingent retreated to Norfolk and back aboard Dunmore's fleet of ships.

For the Virginians this short battle proved decisive. The elated militia quickly followed up by occupying the all but abandoned town of Norfolk. Still, they were not yet rid of Dunmore. On January 1, 1776, his ships opened up a bombardment of the town, while landing parties began to set torches to waterside buildings. As this destruction got under way, the Virginia militiamen seemed to find the prospects of looting the town irresistible; they began to run amuck, setting fires of their own in the process. By the time the flames had subsided, two-thirds of Norfolk was in ashes, and another mark was chalked up against Great Britain. (Two years later an investigation by Virginia revealed that whereas Dunmore's forces had destroyed only 19 buildings, the Americans were responsible for the destruction of 863!)[11]

Meeting in convention in Williamsburg in late January 1776, the Virginians denounced Dunmore's offer of freedom to the slaves if they joined the British army. The Americans threatened death to "all Negroes or other slaves conspiring to rebel or make insurrection. . . ." To avoid such punishment, the Virginia convention offered the defecting slaves a "pardon" if they returned to their duty. However, the contagion of freedom had gone too far among the slaves. Meanwhile, Dunmore lingered off the coast, still hoping for success in raising a winning force. In March 1776, in another letter to Lord Dartmouth, he wrote: "Your lordship will observe by my [earlier] letter . . . that I have been endeavouring to raise two regiments here – one of white people, the other of black. The former goes on very slowly, but the latter very well, and would have been in great forwardness had not a fever crept in amongst them, which carried off a great many very fine fellows."

Spring came and still the governor lingered, his small navy trying various means to bring over more Negroes. Thus an

American captive aboard one of Dunmore's ships later reported that when three Negroes in a canoe rowed out to the vessel, the British captain, seeking their aid, promised them freedom "when this disturbance was over, which he expected would be very soon, and then each of them should have a plantation of the rebels' land."[12] These offers continued to have great effect. Thus, on June 26, 1776, Colonel Landon Carter of the Sabine Hall plantation recorded in his diary the defection to the British of ten of his Negroes:

> Last night after going to bed, Moses, my son's man, Joe, Billy, Postillion, John, Mullato, Peter, Tom, Panticove, Manuel & Lancasster Sam, ran away, to be sure, to Ld. Dunmore, for they got privately into Beale's room before dark & took out my son's gun & one I had there, took out of his drawer in my passage all his ammunition furniture, Landon's bag of bullets and all the Powder, and went off in my Petty Auger [pettiauger] new trimmed, and it is supposed that Mr. Robinson's People are gone with them, for a skow they came down in is, it seems, at my landing. These accursed villains have stolen Landon's silver buckles, George's shirts, Tom Parker's new waistcoat & breeches.

In an effort to prevent and hinder these defections, the Virginia Committee of Safety ordered that all Negroes above the age of thirteen be removed from the eastern counties of Norfolk and Princess Anne further inland, away from the British forces.

For many of the slaves who had earlier fled to Dunmore, the only reward was sickness and death. In June the governor again reported to London that the fever was proving "a very malignant one," and had carried off many of his troops, "especially the blacks." Had it not been "for this horrid disaster," he insisted, "I am satisfied I should have had two thousand blacks, with whom I should have had no doubt of penetrating into the heart of this colony."

The game had finally ended for Dunmore, and he sailed away to join the main British force converging on New York. Behind him, however, he left many bitter memories which continued to fester in the minds of the Virginians. Thus it was that in their convention in May 1776, the Virginia rebels approved the historic recommendation to their delegates in Congress to seek separation and independence from Great Britain. Among the reasons cited for this perhaps inevitable motion was Dunmore's "piratical and savage war against us," including his "tempting our slaves by every artifice to resort to him, and training and employing them against their masters."

Dunmore's activities also became an indictment of King George in June, when the Virginia Assembly adopted a new constitution and government. The preamble to the constitution, written by Jefferson, charged the King with encouraging the Negroes "to rise in arms among us." In Philadelphia this issue also was on Jefferson's mind when the young Virginian sat down to write the Declaration of Independence. In the rough draft of the Declaration he submitted to Congress, Jefferson attacked the King for "captivating & carrying" the Negroes into slavery; for opposing attempts to end the "execrable commerce," and finally for "exciting those very people to rise in arms among us, and to purchase that liberty of which he has deprived them, by murdering the people on whom he also obtruded them: thus paying off former crimes committed against the liberties of one people, with crimes which he urges them to commit against the lives of another."

This political attack against the throne on the grounds of supporting slavery did not stand in the final version of the Declaration, since too many Americans were involved in that "execrable commerce." When the delegates of South Carolina and Georgia objected to the statement, Congress struck out the entire paragraph.

+

As a result of Dunmore's debacle the threat of a general Negro insurrection receded, although fear of it remained. General Charles Lee, while on his way south in the spring of 1776, wrote to Robert Morris and recommended Congress have three or four regiments from the middle colonies on the alert, ready to reinforce the southern front in case a slave revolt should materialize.

As the situation remained stable, both sides turned their attention to the recruitment of small numbers of Negro soldiers. On Long Island the British organized a regiment of Negroes totalling about 200 men, while at the siege of Newport in August 1777, a newly raised Rhode Island all-Negro regiment under Colonel Christopher Greene distinguished itself in repelling three successive attacks by Hessian troops.[13] By August 1778, according to a special return by Alexander Scammell, Adjutant General of the Continental army, 755 Negroes were serving in uniform, the largest troop in New England detachments.[14]

This comparatively small number was an indication of the general American reluctance to use slave recruits. As early as 1775, when the Continental army was forming, Washington had asked a council of general officers whether they should "enlist any Negroes in the new army" or whether there should be a distinction "between such as are slaves and those that are free?" The council had agreed unanimously "to reject all slaves, and, by a great majority, to reject Negroes altogether."

This decision, announced shortly thereafter in general orders to the army, discriminated against some able free Negroes who had already fought bravely in early battles around Boston. In reconsidering the question, Washington on December 31, 1775 wrote to Congress: "It has been represented to me that the free Negroes who have served in this Army, are very much dissatisfied at being discarded. As it is to be apprehended that they may seek employ in the Ministerial Army, I have . . . given license for their being re-enlisted. If this is disapproved by Congress, I shall put a stop to it."

In Congress the southern delegates earlier had opposed, and they continued to oppose, the use of any Negroes in the army, whether slave or free. Congress supported Washington in this particular instance, however, and resolved on January 16, 1776: "That the free Negroes who have served faithfully in the army at Cambridge may be re-enlisted therein, but no others." Subsequently, Congress gave the responsibility to the states whether they should enroll Negroes in their militia and, as the war

112

dragged on and recruitment of white Americans became more difficult, the Negroes began to appear more frequently in the ranks. According to one estimate, at least 4,000 Negroes eventually served on the American side,[15] most of them north of the Potomac and mostly in New England.

+

Although British hopes of precipitating a general slave insurrection were not fulfilled, large numbers of Negroes did flee the southern plantations. On August 14, 1776, Henry Laurens reported from Charleston that many hundreds of Negroes "have been stolen and decoyed by the servants of George the Third. Captains of British ships of war and noble lords have busied themselves in such inglorious pilferage, to the disgrace of their master and . . . cause. . . . The British Parliament now employ their men-of-war to steal those Negroes from the Americans to whom they had sold them, pretending to set the poor wretches free but basely . . . sell them into tenfold worse slavery in the West Indies, where probably they will become the property of Englishmen again, and of some who sit in parliament. . . ."

But the British view, as it was expressed by Joseph Galloway, was that: "The Negroes may all be deemed so many intestine enemies, being all slaves and desirous of freedom, and would, was an opportunity offered them, take up arms against their masters." Even without a general uprising, he saw the large slave population as aiding the British cause "by reason of the great proportion of [southern] citizens necessary to remain at home to prevent insurrections among the Negroes," and to prevent their desertion to the royal standard.

In the year 1779, the entire problem of the slaves became more pressing following the entry of British forces into Georgia, their capture of Savannah, and the subsequently complete surrender of that state to Great Britain. To the north, South Carolina officials, correctly surmising they were the next target on the British schedule, hurriedly dispatched a call for help to Congress.

The enemy's success in Georgia and the threat facing the

113

Carolinas caused a change of attitude in the minds of some southerners toward employing the Negroes to fight on the patriot side. It gave impetus to a plan proposed in 1779 by Lieutenant Colonel John Laurens of South Carolina to free and arm the slaves for defense of the south. As early as 1776 this young southern liberal, who detested slavery, urged that the Negroes be permitted to earn their freedom by joining the patriot side.

With the entire area in danger, he recommended action to his father, Henry Laurens, a former president of Congress. The elder Laurens, although doubtful it would be accepted, agreed to push his son's plan in Congress. To his surprise, he found that the emergency had brought him the support of General Isaac Huger, who had been dispatched from South Carolina to get northern aid, and that of the other South Carolina delegate, William Henry Drayton.

Henry Laurens sought the opinion of Washington. In a letter to the Commander in Chief on March 16, Laurens wrote: "Had we arms for 3,000 black men as I could select in Carolina, I should have no doubt of success in driving the British out of Georgia and subduing East Florida before the end of July." But Washington disliked the plan. "The policy of arming our slaves," he wrote to Laurens, "is, in my opinion, a moot point, unless the enemy set the example; for should we begin to form battalions of them, I have not the smallest doubt . . . of their following us in it, and justifying the measure upon our own ground. The upshot then must be, who can arm fastest, and where are our arms?" He added that if only a few slaves were freed to fight, and the others left in slavery, the latter might become greatly dissatisfied with their status.

A member of Washington's staff, however, threw his support behind the Laurens plan. In a letter to John Jay on March 14, 1779, Alexander Hamilton wrote to the then President of Congress that he did not see how a sufficient force could be raised in the south without the Negroes. He argued that the Negroes would make excellent soldiers and that, "if we do not make use of them in this way, the enemy probably will. . . . An

114

George Washington

A propaganda symbol for the American colonists.

Major General Baron von Steuben

The German drillmaster who helped overcome the continentals' fear of the bayonet.

Brigadier General Daniel Morgan

American commander in the battle of Cowpens.

Commodore John Paul Jones

Intrepid commander of the Bonhomme Richard.

Colonel Benedict Arnold

Hero and then traitor.

BY
Brigadier-General ARNOLD,
A PROCLAMATION.

To the Officers and Soldiers of the Continental Army who have the real Interest of their Country at Heart, and who are determined to be no longer the Tools and Dupes of Congress, or of France.

HAVING reason to believe that the principles I have avowed, in my address to the public of the 7th instant, animated the greatest part of this continent, I rejoice in the opportunity I have of inviting you to join His Majesty's Arms.

His Excellency Sir *Henry Clinton* has authorized me to raise a corps of cavalry and infantry, who are to be clothed, subsisted, and paid as the other troops are in the British service, and those who bring in horses, arms, or accoutrements, are to be paid their value, or have liberty to sell them: To every non-commissioned officer and private a bounty of THREE GUINEAS will be given, and as the Commander in Chief is pleased to allow me to nominate the officers, I shall with infinite satisfaction embrace this opportunity of advancing men whose valour I have witnessed, and whose principles are favourable to an union with *Britain*, and TRUE AMERICAN LIBERTY.

The rank they obtain in the King's service will bear a proportion to their former rank, and the number of men they bring with them.

It is expected that a Lieutenant-Colonel of cavalry will bring with him, or recruit in a reasonable time, 75 men.

Major of HORSE - 50 men.	Lieut. Col. of INFANTRY - 75 men.
Captain of ditto - - - 30	Major of ditto - - - - - - - - - - 50
Lieutenant of ditto - 15	Captain of ditto - - - - - - - - - 30
Cornet of ditto - - - 12	Lieutenant of ditto - - - - - - - 15
Serjeant of ditto - - - 6	Ensign of ditto - - - - - - - - - - 12
	Serjeant of ditto - - - - - - - - - 6

N. B. Each Field Officer will have a Company.

Great as this encouragement must appear to such as have suffered every distress of want of pay, hunger and nakedness, from the neglect, contempt, and corruption of Congress, they are nothing to the motives which I expect will influence the brave and generous minds I hope to have the honour to command.

I wish to lead a chosen band of Americans to the attainment of peace, liberty, and safety (that first object in taking the field) and with them to share in the glory of rescuing our native country from the grasping hand of *France*, as well as from the ambitious and interested views of a desperate party among ourselves, who, in listening to *French* overtures, and rejecting those from *Great-Britain*, have brought the colonies to the very brink of destruction.

Friends, fellow soldiers, and citizens, arouse, and judge for yourselves,—reflect on what you have lost,—consider to what you are reduced, and by your courage repel the ruin that still threatens you.

Your country once was happy, and had the proffered peace been embraced, your last two years of misery had been spent in peace and plenty, and repairing the desolations of a quarrel that would have set the interest of *Great-Britain* and *America* in its true light, and cemented their friendship; whereas, you are now the prey of avarice, the scorn of your enemies, and the pity of your friends.

You were promised LIBERTY by the leaders of your affairs; but is there an individual in the enjoyment of it, saving your oppressors? Who among you dare speak, or write what he thinks, against the tyranny which has robbed you of your property, imprisons your persons, drags you to the field of battle, and is daily deluging your country with your blood?

You are flattered with independency as preferable to a redress of grievances, and for that shadow, instead of real felicity, are sunk into all the wretchedness of poverty by the rapacity of your own rulers. Already are you disqualified to support the pride of character they taught you to aim at, and must inevitably shortly belong to one or other of the great powers their folly and wickedness have drawn into conflict. Happy for you that you may still become the fellow-subjects of *Great-Britain*, if you nobly disdain to be the vassals of *France*.

What is *America* now but a land of widows, orphans, and beggars?—and should the parent nation cease her exertions to deliver you, what security remains to you even for the enjoyment of the consolations of that religion for which your fathers braved the ocean, the heathen, and the wilderness? Do you know that the eye which guides this pen lately saw your mean and profligate Congress at mass for the soul of a Roman Catholic in Purgatory, and participating in the rites of a Church, against whose antichristian corruptions your pious ancestors would have witnessed with their blood?

As to you who have been soldiers in the continental army, can you at this day want evidence that the funds of your country are exhausted, or that the managers have applied them to their own private uses? In either case you surely can no longer continue in their service with honour or advantage; yet you have hitherto been their supporters of that cruelty, which, with an equal indifference to your, as well as to the labour and blood of others, is devouring a country, which, from the moment you quit their colours, will be redeemed from their tyranny.

But what need of arguments to such as feel infinitely more misery than tongue can express, I therefore only add my promise of the most affectionate welcome and attention to all who are disposed to join me in the measures necessary to close the scene of our afflictions, which, intolerable as they are, must continue to increase until we have the wisdom (shewn of late by *Ireland*) in being contented with the liberality of the Parent country, who still offers her protection, with the immediate restoration of our ancient privileges, civil and religious, and a perpetual exemption from all taxes, but such as we shall think fit to impose on ourselves.

B. ARNOLD.

Benedict Arnold's broadside to the officers and soldiers of the Continental Army.

Major General "Gentleman
Johnny" Burgoyne

Major General Lord Charles Cornwallis

SOUTH-CAROLINA.

By Sir *HENRY CLINTON*, *Knight of the Bath, General of His Majesty's Forces, and MARIOT ARBUTHNOT, Esquire, Vice-Admiral of the Blue, His Majesty's Commissioners to restore Peace and good Government in the several Colonies in Rebellion in North-America.*

PROCLAMATION.

HIS MAJESTY having been pleased, by His Letters Patent, under the Great Seal of Great-Britain, to appoint us to be his Commissioners, to restore the Blessings of Peace and Liberty to the several Colonies in Rebellion in America, WE do hereby make public his most gracious Intentions, and in Obedience to his Commands, DO DECLARE, to such of his deluded Subjects, as have been perverted from their Duty by the Factious Arts of self-interested and ambitious Men, That they will still be received with Mercy and Forgiveness, if they immediately return to their Allegiance, and a due Obedience to those Laws and that Government which they formerly boasted was their best Birthright and noblest Inheritance, and upon a due Experience of the Sincerity of their Professions, a full and free Pardon will be granted for the treasonable Offences which they have heretofore committed, in such Manner and Form as his Majesty's Commission doth direct.

NEVERTHELESS, it is only to those, who, convinced of their Errors, are firmly resolved to return to and support that Government under which they were formerly so happy and free, that these gracious Offers are once more renewed, and therefore those Persons are excepted, who, notwithstanding their present hopeless Situation, and regardless of the accumulating Pressure of the Miseries of the People, which their infatuated Conduct must contribute to increase, are nevertheless still so hardened in their Guilt, as to endeavour to keep alive the Flame of Rebellion in this Province, which will otherwise soon be reinstated in its former Prosperity, Security, and Peace:

Nor can we at present resolve to extend the Royal Clemency to those who are poluted with the Blood of their Fellow Citizens, most wantonly and inhumanly shed under the mock Forms of Justice, because they refused Submission to an Usurpation which they abhorred, and would not oppose that Government with which they deemed themselves inseparably connected: And in order to give Quiet and Content to the Minds of his Majesty's faithful and well affected Subjects, WE do again assure them, that they shall have effectual Countenance, Protection and Support, and as soon as the Situation of the Province will admit, the Inhabitants will be reinstated in the Possession of all those Rights and Immunities which they heretofore enjoyed under a free British Government, exempt from Taxation, except by their own Legislature: And we do hereby call upon all his Majesty's faithful Subjects to be aiding with their Endeavours, in order that a Measure, so conducive to their own Happiness, and the Welfare and Prosperity of the Province, may be the more speedily and easily attained.

GIVEN under our Hands and Seals, at Charles-Town, the First Day of June, in the Twentieth Year of His Majesty's Reign and in the Year of Our Lord One Thousand Seven Hundred and Eighty.

HENRY CLINTON,

MARIOT ARBUTHNOT.

By their EXCELLENCY's Command,

JAMES SIMPSON, *Secretary.*

CHARLES-TOWN: Printed by ROBERTSON, MACDONALD & CAMERON, in Broad-Street, the Corner of Church-Street.

Sir Henry Clinton's broadside offering pardons to repentent South Carolinians

A view of Lord Cornwallis's surrender at Yorktown

essential part of the plan is to give them their freedom with their swords. This will secure their fidelity, animate their courage, and, I believe, will have a good influence upon those who remain, by opening a door to their emancipation." These views, of course, were opposed to those of Washington.

Since the need for a decision was urgent, Congress appointed a committee to consider the matter and it received arguments, including a "representation" made by young Laurens. In his arguments, Laurens referred to the strength of the British force in the south (3,500 regular troops, 1,500 others expected) which, he said, constituted more than South Carolina could handle, even if they did not arm the Negroes.

With only six "very weak" battalions in Carolina for defense and no possibility of obtaining reinforcements from neighboring states, the "only resource" left to the patriots, said Laurens, was the Negroes. Therefore, he recommended that Congress purchase these people from their owners (at $1,000 per slave) and place them into service, the condition of that service to be "emancipation at the end of the war." Laurens further argued:

> It is well known that in times of invasion a large body of slaves is generally regarded as a mass of internal enemies. But commotions on their part are always less to be apprehended in proportion as the military force of the country is more respectable and the successes of the invaders become more doubtful. Besides, a reinforcement of such troops as are here proposed would give a decided turn to affairs, change the nature of the war from defensive to offensive, and in all human probability enable us to expel the enemy from Georgia in the course of the campaign.[16]

The formal proposal, made to the committee by the delegates of South Carolina, was that Congress pay for the release of 3,000 slaves in South Carolina and Georgia, and help arrange for putting them into military service. On March 29, 1779, the committee, noting the fact the southerners themselves were behind the measure and in view of the critical situation in the South, approved the Laurens plan. Congress also unanimously endorsed it, declaring: "That every Negro who shall well and faithfully serve as a soldier to the end of the present war, and shall then return his arms, be emancipated and receive the sum of fifty dollars."

Having adopted a plan with such far-reaching implications for the institution of slavery, Congress further ordered that it should not go into effect without the consent of the two states concerned. Shortly thereafter, Colonel Laurens hurried to Charleston to present the proposal to the South Carolina Assembly. His reception was cold. Most of the southerners there were bitterly opposed to any plan so hostile to slavery and it was defeated.

In the meantime, the British devised an intriguing propaganda plan aimed at bringing the Negro slaves over en masse to the British camp. On June 30, 1779, the British Commander in Chief, General Clinton, issued the following proclamation:

> Whereas the enemy have adopted a practice of enrolling Negroes among their troops, I do hereby give notice that all Negroes taken in America, or upon any military duty, shall be purchased for a stated price, the money to be paid to the captors.
>
> But I do most strictly forbid any person to sell or claim right over any Negro, the property of a rebel, who may take refuge with any part of this army: and I do promise to every Negro who shall desert the rebel standard, full security to follow within these lines any occupation which he shall think proper.

This well-conceived proclamation, calculated to make "fair game" of all Negroes in America except those who joined the British, brought a round of denunciation from the Americans, who denounced Clinton as a "brutish tyrant" and a fitting companion of "the noted Negro thief, *Lord Dunmore.*"[17]

But with British forces operating successfully in the south between 1779 and 1781, the proclamation seems to have played an important part in bringing thousands of slaves over to the British camp.[18] Some of the Negroes were promptly organized into military units, and in Georgia at least one group of British-trained fugitive slaves, calling themselves the "King of England's Soldiers," continued to harass the people living on the Savannah River even after the end of the war.[19] The final total of

slaves who fled the plantations will never be known; one estimate is that South Carolina lost 25,000 slaves, and that seven-
eighths of the Negroes of Georgia went over to the British.[20]
Jefferson believed that during Cornwallis' invasion of Virginia in
1781, the state lost 30,000 slaves.

But with the world turned upside down by the surrender of
Cornwallis at Yorktown, the game ended for Britain. In May
1782 General Carleton succeeded Clinton as Commander in
Chief at New York. His mission was to liquidate the war and
arrange an evacuation of the city. But the issue of the Negroes
who had joined the British continued to trouble both sides.
Under terms of the provisional treaty signed in Paris by the two
parties, all Negroes were supposed to be given up to the Americans. However, since many slaves had joined the British "in
consequence of royal proclamations promising them protection
and liberty," General Carleton decided it would be "inhuman to
the last degree and a base violation of public faith to send those
Negroes back to their masters who would beat them with the
utmost cruelty." Accordingly, he refused to turn them over to
the Americans.

Thus, when the British evacuated Charleston on December 14,
1782, they carried with them 5,327 Negroes, who soon found
themselves scattered in a variety of places, including Jamaica,
East Florida, St. Lucia, Halifax, England, and New York. When
British forces departed New York City in November 1783,
they also took away 3,010 Negroes — 1,336 men, 914 women,
and 760 children.[21] Other blacks found themselves scattered
hither and yon, some becoming once more part of the execrable commerce," resold for profit in the West Indies.

Once again, when the final military decisions were evaluated,
the British appeal to these "intestine enemies" had done the
King's cause little good. Like the employment of the Indians,
the involvement of the Negroes only served to embitter the
conflict and strengthen the determination of patriots north and
south to stand together.

☆ **5** ☆

The Campaign
to Subvert the Hessians

IF ONE OF the results of Dunmore's proclamation of Negro "emancipation," and the ministry's agitation of the Indian tribes had been to push the Americans faster down the road towards independence, the King's decision in 1775 to hire foreign troops also strengthened patriot conviction that reconciliation with the mother country was impossible. At the time of the King's decision, few British officials questioned the desirability of using foreign mercenaries to reinforce the British army, and the government almost routinely approved the recommendation of General Gage, made in October 1774, that: "If force is to be used at length, it must be a considerable one, and foreign troops must be hired."

The practice of hiring mercenaries was an ancient and honorable one in the eighteenth century, and therefore it was not strange that the royal court turned to the powers of Europe in an effort to find reinforcements. The King's representatives first tried to obtain the services of 20,000 Russians from Catherine the Great. When she declined, and efforts to obtain a regiment from Holland also failed, the British government turned to the principalities of Germany, whose rulers were more than glad to trade German manpower for English sterling.

Rumors that Britain was seeking mercenaries from Russia and the German states soon reached America. In besieged Boston the then Major General Henry Clinton, on hearing of the negotiations, recommended that Russian soldiers be obtained rather than Germans. In a letter of explanation to the Adjutant General of the British army in 1775, Clinton argued that the German soldiers would desert, whereas the Russians would not because "they have no language but their own; they cannot desert." Clinton clearly foresaw an American campaign to subvert the mercenaries, since a large number of Germans had settled in the colonies, particularly in Pennsylvania, who could make direct appeals to the Hessians to desert.

If this important factor was given serious consideration by the British government, it failed to deter it from bringing in German troops. Between January 9 and February 5, 1776, the British negotiated three treaties with the Duke of Brunswick, the Landgrave of Hesse Cassel, and the Hereditary Prince of Hesse Cassel for about 17,000 troops. Later treaties were signed with other German principalities which brought the total number of foreign troops to just under 30,000 men.

On February 29, 1776, the first treaties were submitted to Parliament. A member of the Whig opposition, Captain James Luttrell, promptly pointed to the same weakness which Clinton had detected. In a speech in Parliament, Luttrell noted that there were some 150,000 Germans then living in the colonies and that Britain, by employing German mercenaries, was simply providing "an excellent opportunity for our hired troops to desert, because they most likely will be offered lands and protection." Several months later Ambrose Serle, secretary to Admiral Howe, also commented on the adverse effect the use of foreign troops would have in tending "to irritate and inflame the Americans infinitely more than two or three British armies upon such an occasion."[1] These misgivings, however, did not halt Parliament's approval of the treaties.

+

During the spring of 1776 several important documents crossed the Atlantic to the colonies. One was a letter from Lord George Germain, who informed the new British Commander in Chief, General William Howe, of the impending arrival of

German reinforcements, some of whom were destined for Canadian service.[2] Other documents came from "several eminent gentlemen" in London, who advised their American friends as follows: "If offers of settlement &c., are prepared to fling into the camp in German, when the Germans arrive it must have a great effect." This suggestion from the Whigs of England was adopted by the Americans and became one of the central techniques used in the ensuing patriot propaganda campaign.

The documents from the eminent gentlemen of London were carried to Boston by one George Merchant, an American who had been captured by the British at Quebec, taken to England, and then released there. Apparently contacted by the English Whigs, Merchant took immediate return passage to America, carrying hidden in his clothing copies of the British treaties for the German troops. These papers, which confirmed the rumors of the hiring of mercenaries, moved Benjamin Franklin to comment: "The German auxiliaries are certainly coming. It is our business to prevent their returning."[3]

On May 21, 1776, Congress, after studying the treaties, created a five-man committee which was ordered to extract and publish the papers. It was also directed to recommend a suitable reward for Merchant and to prepare an address "to the foreign mercenaries who are coming to invade America." Named to the committee were John Adams, William Livingston, Thomas Jefferson, Richard Henry Lee, and Roger Sherman. For some unknown reason, the committee completed only the first two assignments. No action was taken on the address, although a draft of an eloquent appeal to the invaders was prepared by a non-committee member, George Wythe.[4]

Not until August, when the Hessian troops had already arrived aboard British transports off Staten Island, did Congress take further action. It directed a new committee, composed of Jefferson, James Wilson, and Richard Stockton "to devise a plan for encouraging the Hessians, and other foreigners [other Germans] employed by the King of Great Britain, and sent to America for the purpose of subjugating these states, to quit that iniquitous service." On August 14 the committee brought in its report. Congress adopted it in the form of a resolution which became the first American propaganda broadside directed to the German troops.

In this broadside Congress explained to the Germans that American policy had long been to provide protection to all who were willing to settle in the country, regardless of background or religion, and that such a policy would be continued. In view of the "cruel and unprovoked war," said Congress, in which Britain had applied for help to "certain foreign princes who are in the habit of selling the blood of their people for money," Americans had thought that the German troops "would choose to accept of lands, liberty, safety and a communion of good laws and mild government, in a country where many of their friends and relations are already happily settled," rather than to fight an unjust war against an innocent people. Thus Congress announced that:

> these states will receive all such foreigners who shall leave the armies of his Britannic majesty in America, and shall choose to become members of any of these states; that they shall be protected in the free exercise of their respective religions, and be invested with the rights, privileges and immunities of natives, as established by the laws of these states; and, moreover, that this Congress will provide for every such person 50 acres of unappropriated lands in some of these states, to be held by him and his heirs in absolute property.

Translated into German, copies of this resolution were dispatched to Washington at his New York headquarters. The General was much impressed with these propaganda papers. "I am persuaded," he wrote, "[that it] would produce salutary effects if it can be properly circulated among them. I fear it will be a matter of difficulty." The next day, in order to insure their better dissemination, he requested Congress supply him with a larger quantity of the papers.

The problem of disseminating these propaganda broadsides to the German troops was resolved by Washington through the use of agents, one of whom apparently was a fifty-six-year-old German immigrant named Christopher Ludwick, who later became "Superintendent of Bakers" in the Continental army.

On August 26 Washington wrote to Congress: "The papers designed for the foreign troops have been put into several channels, in order that they might be conveyed to them, and from the information I had yesterday, I have reason to believe may have fallen into their hands."

The papers indeed had come into the hands of the Germans. Major Carl Baurmeister of the Hessian forces, in a confidential letter to the Landgrave dated September 2, 1776, reported that: "Congress intended to distribute in the Hessian camp several thousand printed leaflets, dated August 14th, informing us in high-sounding phrases of their just cause and promising property to deserters. A few came into the possession of the brigade on Staten Island. . . . So far I have been unable to obtain one of these handbills; if I do I shall enclose it in some future letter."

This first propaganda appeal to the Germans was soon followed up with a second broadside. The new appeal resulted from a suggestion made by an American colonel, James Wilson, who had seen the first broadside in the American camp at Amboy. Wilson wrote to John Hancock, President of Congress, expressing surprise that no distinction had been made between the German officers and privates. He said several persons — "one of them a German well acquainted with the manner and disposition of his countrymen" — had expressed concern on this account and he wondered whether "it is not yet too late to offer additional rewards to officers in proportion to their rank and pay."

Congress agreed Wilson's suggestion was pertinent. On August 27 a three-man committee composed of Jefferson, John Adams, and Franklin brought in another report which Congress subsequently adopted. In this second broadside, Congress offered the following new incentive to German officers who would defect: "To a colonel, 1,000 acres; to a lieutenant colonel, 800 acres; to a major, 600 acres; to an ensign, 200 acres; to every non-commissioned officer, 100 acres." Any officers who brought off a number of soldiers with them were promised additional rewards.

The next day Franklin sent copies "of both sorts" of broadsides to General Gates for distribution. "Some of them," wrote Franklin, "have tobacco marks on the back so that tobacco being put in them in small quantities, as the tobacconists use, and suffered to fall into the hands of these people, they might divide the papers as plunder before their officers could come to the knowledge of their contents, and prevent their being read by the men."[5]

Franklin well understood that in a propaganda operation of this type, the officers would be more difficult to subvert. The real targets were the enlisted men.

+

It was unreasonable to hope for immediate results from these early propaganda efforts, especially after the combined British-German forces easily cleared the Americans from the field in the battle on Long Island on August 27. However, the Americans received the encouraging news from Canada that the German troops serving with Carleton's forces were desertion-minded. On August 4, 1776, two Canadian militia captains told General Gates that "great numbers" of the Germans were deserting daily, and they claimed on one occasion seventy Brunswickers had made off together.

This report was verified several weeks later by a twenty-two-year-old deserter, one Anthony Hasselaband, who went over to the Americans and reported that he and nineteen others had fled Montreal on June 24.[6] Among the reasons Hasselaband cited were the great dissatisfaction among the Germans over the lack of pay and failure of the British to provide provisions promised them.

There was, however, a more important reason why many of the German enlisted men were dissatisfied, stemming from the manner in which they had been "recruited" for the British service. A typical instance was that of Johan Gottfried Seume, a theological student who had been travelling through Germany on his way to Paris when recruiting officers of the Landgrave of Cassel placed him under arrest. Seume later wrote that he found himself among other miserable "companions in misfortune," strangers of all kinds who, he said, "were arrested, imprisoned, sent off. They tore up my academic matriculation papers, as

being the only instrument by which I could prove my identity."[7]
Thus, dissatisfactions were created in these German soldiers
that would prove fertile soil for American propaganda.

Some of the Germans captured by Washington's scouting
parties in the New York area verified the story that they had
been taken from their country by force. On October 26, 1776,
after twelve Waldeckers were captured near White Plains, these
men expressed a willingness to join the American side. Wrote
Washington's aide, Tench Tilghman: "They say if their fellow-
soldiers knew how kindly they would be treated, and how
plentifully and happily they might live, they would lay down
their arms and come among us. We shall contrive to make good
use of these fellows."

The use of such prisoners of war to spread American propaganda had been on Washington's mind for some time. As early
as May 1776 he had toyed with the idea of raising some companies of American Germans "to send among them when they
arrive" in order to stir up a spirit of disaffection and desertion.
But in October, with the German prisoners in his hands,
Washington decided to use them to carry patriot propaganda
into the enemy camp.

The first step was to turn the new prisoners over to
Christopher Ludwick, who escorted them to Philadelphia where
they were treated with great hospitality as an informal
prisoner "reeducation" program began. The next step was to
send the now-enlightened Germans back to the British camp in
exchange for American prisoners. To disguise his purpose,
Washington suggested to the Board of War that it send him all
British prisoners it could spare, to be exchanged with the
Germans. "The return of the latter," he said, "I think will be
attended with many salutary consequences, but should it be
made without that of a large proportion of other troops, it will
carry the marks of a design and occasion precautions to be
taken to prevent the ends we have in view."[8]

However, the British were not unaware of American intentions. Frederic Mackenzie, a British officer, wrote on November
11: "General [Archibald] Robertson is of opinion that the men
have been gained over by the rebels, whose intention it is now

to send them among their countrymen, that they may endeavour to persuade them to desert. . . . Should they come back, it will be prudent to keep a strict watch upon them in order to discover if they attempt to corrupt their fellow soldiers."

Despite this, the American strategy of treating German prisoners well and returning them to the British camp proved successful. Baurmeister took note in his journal of two German jaegers (riflemen) who had been captured on October 23 and then released: "They could not praise enough the good treatment they had received. They had even been given companions who could speak German and who promised them great rewards if they would enter the rebel service and urge their countrymen to do likewise."

Unfortunately for the American cause, the overall military picture had darkened so considerably by November 1776 that few Germans deserted. Instead, on the sixteenth the German forces captured Fort Washington, and four days later Fort Lee also fell. Washington's army fled into New Jersey with the King's army close behind. During these unhappy hours Congress, seeking to invigorate its propaganda program, appointed a committee to translate into German one of the treaties between London and Hesse. It was hoped that a dispersion of copies of this document, with its blood money provisions (for soldiers killed or wounded), might work for the American interest.[9]

The most important American propaganda during this period was, however, Washington's blow against the Hessians at Trenton. This desperate action on December 25 not only brought to a halt the disastrous succession of American defeats, but it also placed in American hands some 948 Hessian prisoners. Now indeed the patriots could undertake a large-scale indoctrination program.

On December 28, a Congressional committee, in a letter of congratulations to Washington on his victory, suggested to the general that the capture of the Hessians was a favorable opportunity to acquaint them "with the situation and circumstances of many of their countrymen, who came here without a farthing of property and have, by care and industry, acquired plentiful fortunes." The committee also suggested that the officers be separated from enlisted men, and the latter be turned over to the Pennsylvania Council of Safety for further disposition.

Washington immediately wrote to the Council of Safety, urging that the German prisoners be well treated and suggesting that the various Congressional propaganda broadsides be distributed among them. The prisoners, meanwhile, were marched to Philadelphia where they were paraded through the streets on December 30, 1776, for the edification and encouragement of the populace.

The following day the Council addressed the public concerning the prisoners.

There arrived yesterday in this city [said the Council] near one thousand Hessian prisoners, taken by his Excellency, Gen. Washington in his late fortunate and successful expedition to New Jersey. The General has recommended to this Council to provide suitable quarters for them, and it is his earnest wish that they may be well treated, and have such principles instilled in them whilst they remain prisoners, that when they return on being exchanged they may fully open the eyes of their countrymen in the service of the king of Great Britain, who at present are not a little jealous of their English fellow soldiers.

These miserable creatures now justly excite our compassion. They have no enmity with us. According to the arbitrary customs of the tyrannical German princes, they were dragged from their native country and sold to a foreign monarch, without either consulting their inclinations or informing them of the place they were destined for, or the enemy they were to contend with. Their pay a mere pittance, they were necessitated and encouraged to plunder. It is therefore nothing strange that they have been guilty of great irregularities, tho' inferior to the brutal behaviour of the British troops. But from the moment they are rescued from the authority of the British officers, we ought no longer to regard them as our enemies, at least whilst their conduct will justify our favorable opinion. 'Tis Britain alone that is our enemy. . . . The most favorable opportunity now offers to weaken the force of our

127

enemies, by making their auxiliaries our friends and we earnestly entreat you to embrace it by suppressing any resentment that might naturally arise on recollecting their late hostility, and treating the much injured and deceived Hessians now in our power in the most friendly manner as a people we would wish to unite with ourselves in improving the fertile forests of America, extending its manufacture and commerce, and maintaining its liberty and independency against all attacks of foreign and arbitrary power.

The Council, in another letter to the committee at Lancaster, Pennsylvania, where many of the prisoners were to be sent, repeated Washington's recommendations "to have them well informed of the reasons for the war, and good principles instilled in them."

On January 1, 1777, Washington also recommended to a Congressional committee that the Council of Safety separate Hessian enlisted personnel from their officers, and send them to the German counties. He said that: "If proper pains are taken to convince them how preferable the situation of their countrymen, the inhabitants of those counties, is to theirs, I think they may be sent back in the spring, so fraught with love of liberty and property too, that they may create a disgust to the service for the remainder of the foreign troops and widen that breach which is already opened between them and the British."

After they were marched to Lancaster, the Hessians were imprisoned and a census taken to determine who were skilled in various trades. More than 300 were found to be skilled tailors, millers, bakers, carpenters, smiths, etc. Since skilled labor was in short supply, the Council on March 3, 1777, authorized the parole of the Germans to trustworthy Americans for employment. In indenturing them to various persons, Congress agreed to pay for their rations. Those who employed the Hessians were made responsible for them and liable for $200 if a prisoner deserted.

The Germans were put to work in a variety of activities. They helped to make shot and cannon for Washington's army, worked as hired farmhands, and cut wood to build barracks, etc. An especially popular group of prisoners captured at

Trenton were members of the Hessian band. They were in great demand for parties and balls. On the first anniversary of the adoption of the Declaration of Independence, they serenaded Congress at a dinner in Philadelphia. When Congress temporarily evacuated the city, the band traveled with it.

In the months that followed, a new situation arose which, to Washington, seemed to threaten the American propaganda effort aimed at subverting the German mercenaries. This problem involved the captivity of General Charles Lee, second in command under Washington, who had been captured by the British on December 13, 1776. The British considered Lee, who had held a commission as a lieutenant colonel in the British Army, a deserter. He was kept under close guard and plans were made to send him to England to stand trial for treason.

Congress, which considered Lee to be one of America's top military leaders, ordered Washington to obtain his immediate exchange as a prisoner of war, by returning five Hessian officers captured at Trenton and a British lieutenant colonel. It further directed that if the British persisted in considering Lee a deserter and refused to give him up, the five Hessian field officers and the lieutenant colonel should be detained "and sacrificed as an atonement for his blood should the matter be carried to that extremity."[10] Washington was to notify General Howe of this American policy.

The Commander in Chief saw many things wrong with Congress' order, and on March 2, in a letter to Robert Morris, Washington complained: "Does Congress know how much the balance of prisoners is against us? That the enemy have, at least, 300 officers of ours in their possession, and we not fifty of theirs. . . . Do they know that every artifice is now practicing to prepossess the Hessians with an idea of our mal-treatment of their countrymen (in our possession), that we are treating of them as slaves; nay, that we mean to sell them? And will not the close confinement of their . . . officers be adduced as strong evidence of this? Congress, therefore, should be cautious how they adopt measures."

Congress, however, reiterated its instructions that the Hessian officers and British lieutenant colonel be exchanged only if "the

enemy will relax in their treatment of Genl. Lee and acknowledge him to be a prisoner of war."[11] On the British side,
General Howe was as worried over the question as was General
Washington. He feared that if Lee was sent to England to stand
trial, Congress would carry out its threats against the Hessians
and this, in turn, "would occasion much discontent" among the
German mercenaries. In September 1777, unwilling to make a
decision, Howe passed the problem along to London, which
finally agreed to designate Lee as a legitimate prisoner of
war.[12] Still, Lee was not released in a prisoner exchange until
March 1778.

+

Although the British had driven the Americans from Philadelphia in September 1777, the war dragged on with no sign of
victory. Discouragement set in, even among the formerly
exuberant German officers, one of whom now wrote: "It is
truly to be desired that this miserable war will soon end."[13]

As the winter of 1777-1778 began, the Americans received a
number of reports to the effect that certain German officers
were willing to change sides if enough inducements were held
out. One such report reached Washington's ears in January 1778.
Whether these stories were responsible for the renewed propaganda offer made by Congress in April is uncertain; but in that
month a new promise was held out "To the officers and soldiers
in the service of the King of Great Britain, not subjects of the
said King."

This was the longest message yet addressed to the Germans.
Congress again emphasized that Americans were fighting "a just
and necessary war," and that they were certain the Germans
were reluctant soldiers. "We not only forgive the injuries which
you have been constrained to offer us," said Congress, "but we
hold out to your acceptance a participation in the privilege of
free and independent states. Large and fertile tracts of country
invite and will amply reward your industry."

These free lands, continued Congress, amounted to 20,000 to
30,000 acres, set aside specifically for men who defected from

the British side. Every German captain who came over with forty men, before the first day of September 1778, was promised 800 acres of good woodland, "also four oxen, one bull, three cows, and four hogs." If he came over with his lieutenant, the latter would receive 400 acres of woodland, two oxen, two cows, and four hogs. A sergeant who accompanied his captain would receive 200 acres, and his share of livestock, while each private who also defected would get 50 acres and livestock.

Officers or noncommissioned officers who came off together or separately were also promised rewards. Congress further announced:

> Such of the officers and non-commissioned officers as choose to enter into the military line, shall receive an additional rank in detached corps, which shall be formed of native Germans of those who now reside in America; which corps shall not be employed but with their own consent in any service than that of guards at a distance from the enemy, or in garrison upon the western frontiers.

One thousand copies of this appeal were published in German. A printer at Lancaster, Francis Bailey, produced the broadsides, 500 copies of which were immediately dispatched to Washington for distribution.[14]

This new broadside was disseminated just before the British evacuation of Philadelphia, an evacuation forced upon them in June 1778 by France's entrance into the war. Howe's successor as Commander in Chief, General Sir Henry Clinton, decided to make the withdrawal to New York by land. Although the retreat was generally successful, the British-German forces suffered hundreds of desertions during the march. Lieutenant General Wilhelm von Knyphausen recorded on July 6, 1778, that the Hessian corps alone (that is, excluding other German mercenaries) had lost 236 men to desertion during the march across Jersey. Their defection was attributed by Adjutant General Baurmeister "to our long stay in Philadelphia and the many kinds of temptations, which need not be very alluring to blind the common soldier and make him break his oath." These temptations included American girls with whom many had fallen in love. During the British retreat Washington voiced the opinion that the enemy might lose "near one thousand men" through desertions, but the final figure was closer to 600.[15]

+

Several weeks later, Congress' propaganda offer of April 1778 brought in the first two officers known to defect from the German regiments — Lieutenants Carl Frederick Fuhrer and Carl Wilhelm Kleinschmidt. These two men appeared at Washington's new camp at White Plains, New York. In an interview with the Commander in Chief, they said they had served as first lieutenants in the Hessian corps, that they had been among the prisoners taken at Trenton, and had been lately exchanged.

Washington wrote to Congress about the two defectors on August 9. He reported they had asked to enter the American service and had claimed there were a number of other German officers of the same disposition. "It appears to me," said Washington, "that important advantage may attend the encouraging a disposition of this nature if it really exists, which is far from impossible, from the influence it will necessarily have on the soldiery by increasing that spirit of desertion and discontent which already prevails among them."

Washington suggested Congress authorize the two officers to raise a corps for themselves, "by inlisting such German inhabitants, and such of the prisoners and deserters from the foreign troops as may be willing to engage." This corps could be a kind of experiment, he said, that might be increased as circumstances dictated. Washington added that the two Germans had expressed confidence such a plan would succeed, but that they expected some "augmentation of rank." He recommended this be granted, but that it not be carried too far.

While waiting for Congress' reaction, a week later Washington received a letter from General von Knyphausen (Lieutenant Fuhrer was of his regiment), apparently containing derogatory information concerning the two men. Kleinschmidt, according to another report, had deserted "on account of his debts."[16]

Congress sent Washington's letter to the Board of War, which brought in a recommendation on August 29, 1778, that "a new corps of troops be raised by the name of German Volunteers, to consist of such deserters from the foreign troops which have been or shall be in the service of the king of Great Britain." The Board suggested the corps be enlisted for three years, or the duration of the war, and that its personnel receive the same bounty and clothing given regular army troops. It further recommended that Fuhrer and Kleinschmidt be raised to the rank of captain, dependent on their success in enlisting at least thirty men in a three-month period beginning September 3, 1778. Congress quickly approved the plan.

The two new captains seemed to have entered their work with great enthusiasm and within several months the British camp became aware that "the light-minded officers, Fuhrer and Kleinschmidt, are persuading many to take service" with the Americans.[17] One of these new recruits may have been Lieutenant Charles Juliat, a third German officer, who showed up within the American lines and also asked to serve with Washington's army.

Juliat's petition was sent to the Board of War. The Board, apparently feeling that Fuhrer and Kleinschmidt were sufficient personnel to get the new corps started, recommended that he be permitted to serve as an infantry volunteer with Count Casimir Pulaski's legion.[18] However, it soon became clear the new deserter was undependable. Although he accepted the Board's recommendation, Juliat found his position and circumstances not to his liking. In early November 1778 he defected back to the British camp.

If Juliat had been a deliberate British plant, he could not have more effectively torpedoed the activities of Fuhrer and Kleinschmidt. The Americans began to have second thoughts about the corps of German volunteers and, early in December, concluded it would be "impolitic to trust them." Thereupon, the Board of War recommended to Congress that the plan for the new German corps be set aside. Congress accepted the recommendation on January 9, 1779, and ordered that Fuhrer and Kleinschmidt be informed "that it is inexpedient to employ them at this time." The auditors at Philadelphia were ordered to pay them their expenses, plus one month's extra pay and subsistence, a total of $397.[19]

The two officers were in an unenviable position. No longer trusted by the Americans and facing drastic punishment if they returned to the British side, they must have found their prospects discouraging. In the next few years they made several appeals to their old German commanders (one in February 1779 and one in October 1780) asking for reinstatement. On this latter occasion, Baurmeister wrote: "The pitiable deserted Lieutenants Fuhrer and Kleinschmidt . . . have sent in very humble requests to be pardoned and received in our lines again." However, unlike Juliat, who was pardoned and served again with the British forces during the war, the two men seem to have become permanent displaced persons. On October 1, 1781, according to Von Krafft, portraits of the two men, and that of a third German officer deserter, Von Masco, were affixed to a gallows in New York as deserters. (After 1781, the two names vanished from the record.)

They were, however, not the only German officers who deserted. At least three others, including a chaplain, changed sides during the war.[20]

+

One of the important tactics adopted by the patriots in their propaganda campaign — an "illegal" tactic — was to try to cause desertions from among prisoners of war. This applied in particular to Burgoyne's "Convention Army,"[21] whose 2,700 German soldiers became a tempting target for American propaganda.

When Burgoyne surrendered in October 1777, the prisoners were marched to Massachusetts. The German prisoners were segregated in barracks on Winter Hill, near Cambridge, while the English prisoners occupied nearby Prospect Hill, in barracks built by the Americans during the siege of Boston. During their year's stay in Massachusetts (before the prisoners were marched to Virginia to sit out the war), the soldiers of the "Convention Army" were encouraged to flee their captivity and join the Americans.

134

To counter American propaganda in the camps, the German commander, General Friedrich Adolph von Riedesel, harangued the enlisted men in an effort to prevent desertion. On April 4, 1778, in a circular letter read to the men, he posed the question:

> Which is better, to be false now and desert and, after the war, be a slave, or to live here with the officers and soldiers for a short time in misery, and return afterward as an honored and brave soldier to his own people, and be able in peace and quiet to recall one's good actions? I therefore exhort all the brave soldiers, considering them my comrades and loving them as my children, to reflect and act as becomes a good soldier and give up all thoughts of desertion; and should there be evil disposed men in the corps, I hereby admonish all the good ones to keep a vigilant eye on these, in order that the already achieved glory of the whole corps may not be dimmed by such shameful desertions.

Riedesel was struggling against formidable odds. The Americans had pressed into their service "good for nothing Germans" (i.e., German-Americans) who were able to talk many a Convention soldier into defecting. Late in April 1778, according to historian Von Eelking, "the presumption of the Americans soon degenerated into impudence." This presumption was the distribution of copies of Congress' latest offer of lands and livestock to any who would desert. Wrote Von Eelking: "They not only busily circulated the proclamation, dressing it up in the most tempting language, but they posted it on houses by the roadside, and even in the camp upon the barracks and the houses of the sentinels."

Both the German and English officers protested against this "illegal" activity and Riedesel ordered the broadsides be removed from the barracks. The following month, the Americans came up with a new propaganda leaflet to counter British arguments that all deserters were being forced to enter state militias. Published in German, this leaflet contained a resolution of Congress dated May 22 which recommended to the various states that "all those who have deserted, or shall desert during the present war from the English army or navy, shall be free from militia service." All these efforts produced many deser-

135

tions, both English and German, from the "Convention Army," with one writer listing the latter at 160 men as of April 1.[22]

While some Americans were eager to enroll these deserters in the militia service, Washington had learned from bitter experience that they rarely could be trusted. A typical Washington comment was contained in a letter to Colonel Theodore Bland in July 1779. "With respect to the deserters from the Convention Army," Washington wrote, "I must entreat that you will use every possible means to have them recovered, and to prevent any farther desertions. There is not the smallest confidence to be placed in the professions of the soldiery and let them be as solemn as they will, and even sanctified by an oath, they will seize the first opportunity to escape to the enemy." Such men not only redefected, but often carried off with them American arms and other expensive pieces of equipment.

Several years later, however, when some Hessian deserters approached the French minister in Philadelphia in July 1780 and asked to join the French expeditionary army in America, both Washington and Congress agreed to this step. As the war neared its end, and as recruiting of Americans for the Continental army became extremely difficult, Washington changed his mind about using German prisoners of war. In April 1782 he agreed that ten of these men might be profitably incorporated into every American company.[23]

Washington made his recommendation to the Secretary of War, and the plan was approved by Congress. Soon thereafter the German prisoners at Lancaster and Reading were visited by a German-speaking clergyman who announced to them that the King of Great Britain had refused to pay their subsistence any longer as prisoners of war, and that their own princes had abandoned them. Therefore, he said, Congress was now offering them a choice: either enlist in the American army or pay for their past maintenance. If they had no money to pay (and they had none), various farmers were willing to advance the sum if they bound themselves to labor for such farmers for three years. In any event, they must take the oath of allegiance to the United States.[24]

The clergyman advised the Germans to enter into military service rather than to submit to the farmers. He pointed out that every man who enlisted would receive eight dollars bounty, "and one hundred acres of good land in America after the war."[25] However, this combination of threats and promises did not produce any immediate results. On August 8, 1782, two American officers appeared and repeated the proposition, and this time they laid down an ultimatum: The Germans *must* accept one or the other choice — indent themselves over to the farmers, or serve with the American forces. On this occasion there were some results; some men went off to the army and at least thirty-nine men signed to serve on the American frigate, the *South Carolina* (subsequently captured by the British).[26]

Additionally, the propaganda war against the Germans still serving in the field was renewed by various southern governors. In Virginia, Governor Thomas Jefferson, who entertained some of the German officer prisoners in his home and used those occasions to spread American doctrines, renewed the original offer of Congress on February 2, 1781. In a proclamation which reproduced almost the identical language of the 1776 appeal, Jefferson added the following statement:

> I have therefore thought fit by and with the advice of the Council of State to issue this my proclamation hereby notifying more generally the said engagement of Congress, and further promising to all such foreigners who shall leave the armies of his Britannic majesty while in this state and repair forthwith to me at this place, that they shall receive from this Commonwealth a further donation of two cows, and an exemption during the present war from all taxes . . . and from all militia and military service: and moreover that they shall receive a full compensation for any arms and accoutrements which they shall bring with them, and deliver to the commanding officer or any of the posts holden by our forces, taking his receipt for the same.

In Georgia, where Savannah was still held by British and German troops, Governor John Martin also issued a proclamation in German. In February 1782, he offered 200 acres of land, a cow, and two swine to every noncommissioned officer or private who would desert the British service.[27]

The American propaganda campaign continued into the last days of the war. Following the peace treaty of 1783, there was an increase in the numbers of Germans who fled the British side, especially from the regiments captured at Yorktown. During the march northward, an estimated 752 Germans defected (plus hundreds of British soldiers) from those regiments. "These desertions," wrote Baurmeister, "are due only to the scattering of printed invitations and previous persuasion on the part of the inhabitants, who have resorted to every possible inducement."[28]

In July 1783, several months before the British evacuated New York, Baurmeister received American permission to travel to Lancaster and Reading to seek out his countrymen and explain that a general pardon and amnesty had been issued by their commanders. He found many former prisoners in various situations: some were living on farms, were married and had children; others were indented for three years and working in iron mines and small manufacturing shops. Of 162 Brunswickers he located in one area, only 39 professed any desire to return to Germany, while none of 13 Hesse-Hanauers he talked to wanted to return. In Philadelphia he discovered 52 Hessian deserters but could do "no more than let them read a copy of the general pardon, and even in doing this I had to be cautious."[29]

+

The American psychological warfare campaign against the mercenaries was the most successful one of the Revolution. Of the 29,867 German soldiers hired by King George during the war, only 17,313 or about fifty-eight percent returned to Germany.[30] That left 12,554 unaccounted for. Of that number, approximately 1,200 were killed in battle or died of wounds, 6,354 died of illness and accidents, and about 5,000 deserted to join in improving "the fertile forests of America, extending its manufacturing and commerce, and maintaining its liberty and independency."

138

☆ **6** ☆

Kidnappings, Rumors and Bribery

IN ADDITION TO the American and English propaganda campaigns, a number of other subversive operations were undertaken during the Revolution. These included attempts by both sides to kidnap each other's leaders, the planting of false rumors and other deceptions, and British efforts to bribe a number of leading Americans.

+

The kidnapping attempts in particular caused sleepless nights on both sides. Washington was a party to several American plots to carry off from their beds high-ranking British generals, and it is clear the British authorities encouraged similar attempts against key civilian and military personnel on the American side.

This phase of the war was stimulated by the seizure of Major General Charles Lee, reportedly in his nightshirt, in December 1776 by a British scouting party. The news of Lee's capture was a great shock to the patriots, many of whom considered him to be their best military man. Even Washington, before becoming disillusioned with Lee during the Battle of Monmouth, accepted this evaluation of his subordinate and considered his captivity a great loss.

On the other hand, in the British camp there was much rejoicing and the incident gave birth to several plans by loyalist elements to try to carry off Washington and other leaders of the Revolution. In this connection, Thomas Nelson reported to Jefferson on January 2, 1777: "The general was informed a few nights ago that a conspiracy was formed by some people in Bucks county near his camp to kidnap him as poor Lee was, but he has more prudence than to be caught in this manner."

The following summer it was the rebels who were rejoicing over a similar exploit — the successful kidnapping of a British major general, Richard Prescott, the commanding officer of the English garrison at Newport. Late one night in July 1777, forty Rhode Island militiamen, led by Lieutenant Colonel William Barton, slipped past the British sentries, and seized Prescott in his bed, which was also occupied by a young lady. He and his aide-de-camp were hustled away.

With a note of admiration a British officer later commented: "It is certainly a most extraordinary circumstance that a General commanding a body of 4,000 men, encamped on an island surrounded by a squadron of ships of war, should be carried off from his quarters in the night by a small party of the enemy from without, and without a shot being fired."[1] In reporting the incident to London, General Howe described the kidnapping "as distressing as it was unexpected."

In rebel quarters the event was received, James Thacher wrote, "with great joy and exultation, as it puts in our possession an officer of equal rank with General Lee." That this was one of the main aims of the American exploit was openly admitted to the British officers who contacted the Americans under a flag of truce to inquire about General Prescott's needs.[2] A Providence newspaper described the exploit in detail, boasting that whereas it had taken a British lieutenant colonel and seventy soldiers to seize Lee, "a lieutenant colonel. . . . with only thirty-eight privates and six officers has taken a Commander in Chief, when almost encircled by an army and navy."[3] The *London Chronicle* commented on the episode with the following rhyme:

On General Prescot being carried off naked,

"unanoited, unanealed"
What various lures there are to ruin man;
Woman, the first and foremost all bewitches!
A nymph thus spoil'd a General's mighty plan,
And gave him to the foe — without his breeches.[4]

Congress was so pleased by the affair that on July 25 it voted to present Barton a sword; on December 24 it recommended he be promoted to the rank of full colonel. It also recommended to Washington that Barton be used in such service as best adapted "to his genius." With Prescott in his hands, Washington had leverage in obtaining an exchange for his second in command, General Lee. This success led to other attempts to seize high-ranking enemy officials. Thus, several months later, when Washington learned that there was "a Hessian general quartered at one Fisher's, covered only be a small guard," he informed Brigadier General William Maxwell that this might be "a glorious opportunity for a partisan exploit." The attempt, however, seems never to have been made.

In the case of the British side, following the defeat of the American army at Brandywine, General Howe sent out patrols to gather up the spoils, including any rebels they could lay their hands on. During the course of their sweep, they seized the chief executive of Delaware, President John McKinly, who was imprisoned aboard the warship *Solebay*. When British forces occupied Philadelphia, he was taken there in prisoner status, although allowed to seek private lodgings. When the British evacuated the city in July 1778, McKinly made the trek with them to Long Island. He was finally exchanged in September 1778 for William Franklin, the royal governor of New Jersey, who had been seized by the patriots in the summer of 1776.

Raids launched in the dead of night with the mission of seizing American officials, military and civilian, also were repeatedly undertaken by loyalist troops, with only infrequent moves by the British Army itself. In the first instance, Joseph Galloway was one of the leading plotters; on one occasion he concocted a plan to seize Governor William Livingston of New Jersey, along

141

with members of the assembly and other government bodies, but it was never carried out.

More typical of loyalist kidnapping operations was one which came to light in British-occupied Philadelphia in March 1778. One William Hamet, described by a loyalist gazette as "an intrepid young man who had suffered much by the rebel plunderers," learned that two American officers were billeted in nearby Jersey and he organized a party to take them. In the dead of night they crossed the Delaware, approached the house where the officers were asleep, broke in, and seized them in their beds. Their weapons were confiscated and they were carried off to Philadelphia as prisoners.

The unhappy effects of such operations were described by Caesar Rodney, who complained to the delegates of Delaware in Congress that: "We are constantly alarmed in this place by the enemy and refugees, and seldom a day passes but some man in this and the neighbouring counties is taken off by these villains, so that many near the bay, who I know to be hearty in the cause, dare neither act or speak lest they should be taken away and their houses plundered." Rodney appealed for American troops to be sent to protect the area.

On February 27, 1778, Congress took official notice of these operations and, in a formal resolution, denounced the loyalists who were banded together "for the purpose of seizing and secretly conveying to places in possession of the British forces, such of the loyal citizens, officers, and soldiers of these states as may fall into their hands." Congress declared that any such person was to be put to death "as a traitor, assassin and spy," if the offence was committed within seventy miles of the headquarters of any American army. Handbills of this resolution were printed and were distributed behind British lines.

+

It was another matter, however, if Britons and Americans seized each other and, in 1778, Washington came up with a plan to lay hands on General Clinton at his New York headquarters. Washington sent the plan to Brigadier General Samuel Parsons,

142

assuring him "that taking of Clinton in this manner" was not only practical but also desirable and "honorable." The Commander in Chief gave detailed instructions on how to carry out the exploit, including the following deception: "Namely to let the officers and soldiers in the enterprise be dressed in red and much in the taste of the British soldiery."[5]

For reasons unknown, the attempt on Clinton did not occur. It may, however, have planted a seed in the British commander's mind, because in February 1779 Clinton authorized a secret expedition of 1,000 soldiers to try to seize Governor William Livingston in his home near Elizabeth Town, New Jersey. The soldiers, landing under cover of darkness, took possession of Livingston's house at 5:00 in the morning of February 25, only to discover that the Governor had stayed away that night at a friend's house. However, the Governor's two young daughters, the only occupants of the house, were roused from their beds and forced to turn over the Governor's papers to the raiding party's commander, who then ordered a withdrawal.

This raid was but one of several abortive attempts by the British and Tory officers to capture Mr. Livingston, who had become a target for being too energetic in denouncing the enemy, providing militia troops to Washington's army, and wielding a caustic pen. Concerning his literary efforts, for example, Livingston in December 1777 published an article in the *New Jersey Gazette,* in which he observed that at the opening of every campaign in the spring, the British "plunderers, and their Tory emissaries," predicted:

> the total reduction of America before the winter. In the fall they find themselves as remote from their purpose as they were in the spring; and then we are threatened with innumerable hosts from Russia and Germany, who will utterly extirpate us the ensuing summer, or reduce us to the most abject submission. They have so beat this beaten track that for mere sake of variety, I would advise them to explore a new road; and not compel us to nauseate a false-hood, not only because we know it to be one, but for its perpetual repetition without the least variety or alternity. . . . The utmost they can do, they have already done; and

are at this moment as far from any prospect of subjecting us to the dominion of Britain, as they were in the ridiculous hour in which General Gage first arrived in Boston. . . .

Several weeks after this incident, Livingston sent a letter of complaint to Clinton. It was not the kidnapping attempt, said the Governor, which troubled him but the fact that he had in his possession "the most authentic proofs of a general officer under your command having offered a large sum of money to an inhabitant of this state to assassinate me, in case he could not take me alive." This was such a repugnant plan, Livingston commented, that he was sure the British commander would not be a party "to a design so sanguinary and disgraceful." The Governor said he would give Clinton an opportunity to disavow "such dark proceedings." He added that if the British Commander in Chief had approved such a plot, he should beware since "your person is more in my power than I have reason to think you imagine."

Clinton's answer came in a brief statement published in a New York paper, in which he denied he had "a soul capable of harboring so infamous an idea as assassination." Clinton concluded: "Sensible of the power you boast of being able to dispose of my life by means of intimates of yours, ready to murder at your command, I can only congratulate you on your able connections." Livingston responded with a second missive on April 15, in which he attacked Clinton's reasoning powers and denied he had ever threatened or said anything about murder.

But some sixteen months later, in August 1780, Clinton concluded he had actually been the target of attempted murder while aboard his ship in Huntington Bay. One night, while dining with two members of his staff, all three men became violently sick "with convulsive spasms and other strong symptoms of poison." A British army physician at hand tended the sick men, and they quickly recovered. Clinton concluded that poison had been placed into their wine, each man having drunk a glass. After examining the residue, the physician pronounced it was "strongly impregnated with arsenic." Clinton needed no other evidence to conclude that someone had tried to kill him and the logical man was William Livingston.[6]

Throughout the last years of the war, other sporadic kidnapping attempts were made by both sides. An American one involved a plan conceived by Washington in October 1780 to seize the traitor, Benedict Arnold, following his defection to the British. Washington authorized Major Henry Lee of Virginia, a daring cavalry officer, to kidnap Arnold in New York and return him to American control. He emphasized that he wanted Arnold alive "to make a public example of him." Lee selected two men to make the attempt, Sergeant John Champe, of Virginia, a member of his corps, and an undercover "inhabitant of Newark" to help him. Champe's difficult role called for him to pretend to follow Arnold's example, that is, to defect to the British side.

His "desertion" took place on the night of October 20-21. But as he attempted to quietly slip away from Lee's camp, Champe was detected by American guards who gave close chase. He barely made it to the banks of the Hudson and dashed aboard a boat heading for the New York side. Taken to British headquarters, he was interviewed there by Sir Henry Clinton himself. After expressing his admiration for Arnold and proclaiming his loyalties to the King, he was accepted for enrollment in Arnold's recently formed Legion. A day or so later, according to a report which Lee passed on to Washington, Champe "accidentally met Colonel Arnold in the street which has paved a natural way for further acquaintance."

Shortly after, Champe and his anonymous New Jersey assistant prepared a tentative plan to go to Arnold's house one night, overpower him, and carry him off by boat to Jersey. Unfortunately, just before they were about to make their move, Arnold's Legion was ordered aboard British transports and sailed off on a punitive expedition to Virginia. At his first opportunity, Champe slipped away from Arnold's forces and made his way back to Major Lee.

Washington was greatly disappointed by the failure to seize Arnold. Perhaps as an alternative, in December 1780 Washington directed Lieutenant Colonel David Humphrey to "surprise and bring off Genl. Knyphausen from Morris's house on York island, or Sir Henry Clinton from Kennedy's house in the city."

With either of these men his prisoners, Washington would be in a good position to exchange them for the detested Arnold. This attempt was made on the night of December 25 but failed when high winds drove the landing boats below the city. "As such incidents always do," a Hessian officer wrote, "it made us take more precautions."[7]

Early in the new year, however, another American raiding party slipped across Lower Bay to New York and headed inland to New Utrecht, where some Hessians were quartered. The Americans managed to seize two Hessians, Major von Maybaum and his nephew, Lieutenant von Maybaum, in their beds and carried them off to Amboy. This incident upset the Germans, particularly General Friedrich Riedesel and his wife, who were quartered on Long Island. Riedesel, it will be recalled, had been captured with Burgoyne's army at Saratoga and not released in a prisoner exchange until 1779. Mrs. Riedesel wrote after the Maybaum kidnappings:

> we knew they intended to do the same thing for my husband, since our house was quite isolated and stood near the river. Had they surprised the watch, they could have carried him off without anyone noticing the deed. For this reason the slightest noise he might hear at night set him on the alert, thus making him lose sleep. I, too, grew so accustomed to staying awake that often daylight surprised me, and only then would I sleep a few hours, for my husband would only sleep when he thought I was awake, so dreadful to him was the thought of becoming a prisoner again.

During this same year, 1781, the British made two attempts to seize Thomas Jefferson. One occurred in January when Arnold led a 2,000-man raiding party into Virginia, reportedly carrying with him a pair of silver handcuffs to clap on the young Governor. Jefferson, trying desperately to raise militia troops to oppose Arnold, was alerted and fled Richmond, taking with him some stores and state papers. The second effort was made in June, when Cornwallis dispatched a cavalry force under Lieutenant Colonel Tarleton to seize Jefferson and other members of the Virginia Assembly, then meeting at Charlottesville. Tarleton managed to seize seven of the assemblymen. Fortunately for Jefferson, he again received advance notice and fled Monticello minutes before a column of hard-riding British horsemen reached the premises.

In 1782 the Americans brewed a plan to kidnap King George's heir, Prince William Henry, who was visiting New York City with Admiral Robert Digby. Washington approved this operation but, in a letter to Colonel Matthias Ogden, he warned "against offering insult or indignity to the person of the Prince, or Admiral, should you be so fortunate as to capture them." The operation failed to take place. Years later the United States ambassador to Britain, Louis McLane, is reported to have shown Washington's letter of instructions to the King (formerly Prince William Henry and then William IV of Great Britain), who remarked: "I am obliged to General Washington for his humanity, but I'm damned glad I did not give him an opportunity of exercising it towards me."

From the viewpoint of the overall strategy of the war, these little incidents were not very important. Nevertheless, they forced each side to take measures to prevent losses and thus contributed in a general way to the war of nerves.

+

Another aspect of the psychological war was played out by rumors, deliberately planted or otherwise. The American Revolution was no exception to the general rule of wartime that, when there is a lack of hard authoritative news about "what's happening," rumors will sprout profusely. For example, in June 1777 such a rumor arose following the American retreat from Ticonderoga. According to this fantastic story, General Schuyler, the northern commander, and Major General Arthur St. Clair had turned traitors, being paid for their treason "in *silver balls*, shot from Burgoyne's guns into our camp," and collected by St. Clair to divide up with Schuyler.[8] In this situation there was enough American shock and disappointment at the retreats in the north for Congress to launch a special investigation of the two men, who were subsequently cleared.

Another rumor, which Washington could "hardly give credit

to," stated that the British in besieged Boston in December 1775 were resorting to "germ warfare"; that is, sending out innoculated persons "with design of spreading smallpox through" the American camp and countryside. Later, on March 13, 1776, as the British army prepared to evacuate Boston, Washington warned his troops in his general orders against going into the city without permission, "as the enemy with a malicious assiduity, have spread the infection of the smallpox through all parts of the town." However, there was no evidence this was anything but a general outbreak of that pernicious disease.

The origin of the planted rumor sometimes is more easily determined. In August 1777 one of the most successful of this type was the rumor disseminated by the then American general, Benedict Arnold, in the enemy camp outside besieged Fort Stanwix in August 1777. In a different context, a planted rumor was spread by British agents in 1777 in an effort to disrupt American recruiting in the southern states. Concerning this, Richard Henry Lee complained to Jefferson that "some evil disposed persons (no doubt hired for the purpose) have industriously propagated among the N. Carolina troops, and among the recruits of Virginia in the upper parts, *that the plague rages in our Army*. In consequence of which, it is said, the recruiting business stops and desertions are frequent. There never was a more infamous and groundless falsehood. The Army is extremely healthy, and the wisest methods are pursued to keep them so. I mention this, dear sir, that some adequate plan may be adopted to stop the progress of such wicked lies as are now, with industry, circulated through the country."

Another planted rumor of American origin, disseminated among the British and German soldiers in Charleston in 1782, purported to know that the entire British garrison was to be sent to the West Indies. Despite British efforts to deny the rumor, the story caused a great deal of desertion.

A special type of falsehood spread on numerous occasions dealt with the supposed deaths of prominent leaders of the Revolution. In 1776 John Adams was reportedly poisoned in New York City; while two years later a story was spread — and caused much depression among Americans until it was proved false — that Franklin had been mortally wounded in France by a knife-wielding assassin. In 1780 the loyalist publisher, James Rivington, also printed a rumor that the French minister, Chevalier de la Luzerne, had died by violence during a visit to Washington's camp.

The setting into motion of tales — true, false, or simply exaggerated — also played a role in military deceptions, and was a practice to which Washington applied himself on several occasions. In 1777, for example, in getting ready to dispatch Morgan's riflemen to reinforce the northern army, Washington wrote Governor George Clinton that "it would be well, even before their arrival, to begin to circulate . . . ideas [about their ability as Indian fighters] with proper embellishments throughout the country, and in the army, and to take pains to communicate them to the enemy. It would not be amiss, among other things, to magnify numbers."

In November 1777, Washington approved a plan conceived by Major General Philemon Dickinson to try to persuade the British that an attack on New York was imminent. In a letter to Dickinson, Washington also suggested the following devices: "A great show of preparatives on your side, boats collected, troops assembled, your expectation of the approach of Generals Gates and Putnam entrusted as a secret to persons who you are sure will divulge and disseminate it in New York; in a word, such measures taken for effectually striking an alarm in that city."

Similarly, in March 1779 Washington wrote to General Sullivan, as the latter prepared for his punitive expedition against the Iroquois:

> Nothing will contribute more to our success in the quarter where we really intend to strike, than alarming the enemy to a contrary one, and drawing their attention that way. To do this you may drop hints of an expedition to Canada. . . . You may also speak of the probability of a French fleet making its appearance in the spring in the river St. Lawrence, to cooperate with us. It will be a great point gained, if we can, by false alarms, keep the force

already in Canada from affording any timely assistance to the savages, refugees and those people against whom the blow is levelled.

As we noted in Chapter 2, alarms were set off in Canada during this period and defensive measures were taken, which may have played a role in allowing Sullivan's expedition to march largely unopposed against the Indians.

In June 1780, American partisans spread a rumor throughout the Carolinas that the British were seizing all young men and sending them "to the prince of Hesse." Lieutenant Colonel George Turnbull of the New York Volunteers wrote to General Cornwallis exclaiming: "It is inconceivable the damage such a report has done," in halting a movement among many southerners to make peace with the King's men.

+

It would be very strange if Britain and her American adherents had not tried to persuade or bribe rebel leaders to defect, and they did so on several occasions, their prime targets including Franklin, Joseph Reed, and Generals Washington, Sullivan, and Lee. The British attitude in these situations was best stated by Germain in secret instructions sent to Clinton in 1779. "The gaining over some of the most respectable members of the Congress," wrote Germain, "or officers of influence and reputation among their troops, would, next to the destruction of Washington's army, be the speediest means of subduing the rebellion and restoring the tranquillity of America."

The first such attempt at "gaining over" came in response to an American effort to get the patriot viewpoint across to a British officer — General Burgoyne — and influence his actions. The instigator of this very wordy affair was Major General Charles Lee, who wrote to Burgoyne at Boston with the approval of several members of Congress. As a former British officer who had served under Burgoyne in Spain and distinguished himself against the enemy, Lee hoped to convince his old commander of the correctness of the patriot cause.

Lee's letter, dated June 7, 1775, was a long, American attack

150

on the ministry and British policies. Addressing Burgoyne as an old friend, Lee expressed the fear that "the avenues of truth" would be shut to him with regards to the American position. "I assert, sir," wrote Lee, "that even General Gage will deceive you, as he has deceived himself. I do not say he will do it designedly; I do not think him capable. But his mind is so totally poisoned, and his understanding so totally blinded by the society of fools and knaves, that he no longer is capable of discerning facts as manifest as the noon-day sun."

What was the truth concerning the American Revolution? According to Lee, the truth was that Britain could not possibly succeed in stopping it, in conquering America. All the colonists, he said, "from the first estated gentlemen to the lowest planters and farmers," were animated by the same spirit and no less than 150,000 men in arms were determined "to preserve their liberties or perish."

Lee's letter was dispatched northward to Burgoyne, who did not respond until July 8, 1775 — several weeks after the crucial Battle of Bunker Hill. Burgoyne's answering letter, "painfully polite and even more painfully pompous,"[9] argued the government's side. In particular, he tried to emphasize that the British constitution was the best safeguard of the public liberty, that the vital principle of that constitution was "the supremacy of the King and Parliament," a supremacy which the colonists were rebelling against.

According to Burgoyne, America's arguments for taking up arms were weak and implausible. "Is it the weight of taxes imposed," he asked, "and the impossibility of relief after a due representation of her burden, that has induced her to take arms? Or is it a denial of the rights of British legislation to impose them, and consequently a struggle for total independency? For the idea of power that can tax externally and not internally . . . though it may catch the weakness and the prejudice of the multitude in a speech or pamphlet, it is too preposterous to weigh seriously with a man of your understanding."

After proceeding in this manner, Burgoyne proposed to Lee that they meet in order that further explanations might clear the air and lead the way to peace. He added: "I know Great

151

Britain is ready to open her arms upon the first overture of accommodation; I know she is equally resolute to maintain her original rights; and if the war proceeds, your one hundred and fifty thousand men will not be a match for her power."

Lee, who saw himself as a peace negotiator as well as military genius, prudently consulted the Provincial Congress of Massachusetts concerning the proposed interview. He told that body he was prepared to attend if it approved and if he was accompanied by one of its members. However, the Provincial Congress was suspicious of British motives and, while it did not come out flatly against the meeting, it suggested to Lee "whether such an interview might not have a tendency to lessen the influence which the Congress would wish to extend to the utmost of their power to facilitate and succeed the operations of war."[10] Lee took the hint and, in a short note passed through British lines, he rejected Burgoyne's invitation.

The incident did not end there. Both sides took advantage of the correspondence to have their own arguments published to the world. Lee's was printed in the American press, whereas Burgoyne's letter was published in broadsides which were scattered around the Boston area. Of these broadsides, General Gage wrote on July 24: "It's hoped General Burgoyne's letter will open people's eyes, who are blinded to an astonishing degree by the leaders of the rebellion."

So a private correspondence − which began with both sides hoping they could quietly persuade a key enemy officer of the correctness of their cause − ended in the realm of open propaganda to the people.

+

The next British effort to win over "an officer of influence" in the American army took place in June 1777. The target was Major General John Sullivan, second in command of the northern army. The propagandist was Peter Livius, an acquaintance of Sullivan and former chief justice of New Hampshire, who had fled to Canada to become chief justice of

152

the province of Quebec. Livius' attempt on Sullivan was in the form of a "seductive" letter, obviously written with the approval of British authorities in Canada. Their hope seems to have been to cause a major American defection in coordination with Burgoyne's invasion of the colonies.

The Livius letter was dated June 2. "I have long desired," he began, "to write my mind to you on a matter of the very greatest importance." But circumstances, he said, had made delivery of a letter uncertain until he had found his present messenger. "You know better than I do the situation of your Congress," Livius continued, "and the confusion there is among you, and the ruin that impends; you have felt how unequal the forces of your own people are to withstand the power of Great Britain; and for foreign assistance, I need not tell you how precarious and deceitful it must be."

Proceeding in this vein, Livius painted a dark and dreadful future for the colonists, with Sullivan being "one of the first sacrifices to the resentment and justice of government. Your family will be ruined and you must die in ignominy." But there was an alternative fate. Said Livius: "Now, Sullivan, I have a method to propose to you, if you have the resolution and courage for it, that will save you and your family and estate from this imminent destruction, it is in plain English to tread back the steps you have already taken, and to do a real essential service to your King and country, in assisting to re-establish public tranquillity and lawful government. You know I will not deceive you. Every one who will exert himself for government will be received, and I do assure you firmly upon my honour I am empowered to engage particularly with you."

He was not being asked, Livius continued, to declare himself immediately, or at all, "until you can dispose matters so as to bring the province [of New Hampshire] with you." To accomplish this end, Livius suggested the General might send from the colony all those who were opposed to British rule, and to keep at home those who were favorable. At the same time, Sullivan should send "all the material intelligence you can collect" to Livius himself, or to General Burgoyne, "using my name."

153

Livius assured Sullivan that if he did these things, he would not only receive a pardon and security for his property, but that he also would be further "amply rewarded."

The Livius letter was dispatched from Canada by a messenger who, unfortunately for Livius, was soon stopped by an American scouting party, and who revealed he was carrying a secret paper hidden in the false bottom of a canteen. Sullivan was not present when the canteen was opened at Fort Edward on June 16, 1777, by General Schuyler, in the presence of four staff officers.[11]

From this point the situation became slightly complicated. Schuyler, having read Livius' letter to Sullivan, thought it might be an opportunity to obtain intelligence about Burgoyne's plans. Without waiting for Sullivan to return from the field, Schuyler had a letter composed in which he himself posed as General Sullivan. As Sullivan he announced himself ready to return to allegiance to the King, and he declared to Livius that he no longer was a supporter of independence, which he had from the beginning "abhorred from my soul." He also casually announced himself ready to receive Burgoyne's orders regarding the impending campaign.

The fake Sullivan letter was approved by a council of general officers at Ticonderoga on June 20, and sent north by messenger. General Sullivan himself did not learn of the Livius letter and Schuyler's counterplot until the next day, June 21, and then he expressed an opinion that the plan would fail. He explained that he feared Livius, who knew him very well, would detect the deception. He also wished an opportunity to answer the letter himself, but, in the interests of the plot, he remained silent — until August 1777. By that date Burgoyne's invasion of New York was well under way and the entire affair seemed quite useless. Whereupon, Sullivan published Livius' offer and his own rejection to the world.[12]

+

The effect on public opinion of the attempt on Sullivan was mild compared to the excitement several months later when it

154

was revealed that Washington had been the target for a similar attempt. The propagandist on this occasion was a man who had been a fervent and early supporter of the patriot cause, the Reverend Jacob Duché, a Philadelphia minister. Duché not only had read the opening prayers for both the First and Second Continental Congresses, but his words had so inspired the assembly that he was offered (and served for a short time) the post of First Chaplain of Congress.

Apparently the influence which caused Duché to send his subversive letter to Washington was General Howe's seizure of Philadelphia in late 1777. As a well-known patriot clergyman, rector of Christ Church and St. Peter's, Duché was promptly arrested by the British. His release, however, followed within one day. It remains a mystery what happened to Duché in the days and weeks that followed, what influence or pressure may have been brought to bear upon him. All that is known is that on October 8 Duché sat down and wrote a 3,000-word appeal to Washington, asking him to use his influence to end the resistance to Britain.

Duché began on a cautious note. If his letter should happen to find Washington in a meeting or in the field, he said, "before you read another sentence I beg you to take the first opportunity of retiring and weighing well its important contents." Duché then proceeded to a description of his political views, which were, he said, that he had never really believed in "armed opposition" to Britain, nor had he held any ideas of independence or separation from the mother country. In flattering tones, he suggested that Washington surely must have felt the same way.

What, he asked, have been the consequences of independence? "A degeneracy of representation, confusion of councils, blunders without number. The most respectable characters have withdrawn themselves, and are succeeded by a great majority of illiberal and violent men." These men, said Duché contemptuously, were nothing but bankrupts, attorneys, men of desperate fortune — "the dregs" of Congress — with few gentlemen among them of the caliber of a Washington.

"After this view of Congress," he continued, "turn to the army. The whole world knows that its very existence depends

155

upon you, that your death or captivity disperse it in a moment, and that there is not a man on that side of the question in America capable of succeeding you. As to the army, itself, what have you to expect from them? Have they not frequently abandoned even yourself in the hour of extremity? Have you, can you have the least confidence in a set of undisciplined men and officers, many of whom have been taken from the lowest of people, without principle, without courage. Take away those that surround your person, how very few are there that you can ask to sit at your table?"

Having concluded this snobbish note, Duché proceeded to strike down American arguments and expectations of foreign aid, or hopes for help from the Whig opposition in England. The patriots simply had no chance, he said, in the face of the power of Britain. Under such discouraging circumstances, Duché continued, Washington could play a crucial role in bringing about an accommodation, by recommending to Congress "the indispensable necessity of rescinding the hasty and ill-advised declaration of independency," by recommending "an immediate cessation of hostilities."

Duché assured the American leader: "I write not this under the eye of any British officer, or person connected with the British army or ministry. The sentiments I have expressed are the real sentiments of my own heart, such as I have long held." Duché said he was sure the weight of Washington's influence would succeed with Congress but: "If it should not, you have one infallible resource still left. Negotiate for America at the head of your army."

To deliver this subversive document, Duché enrolled as messenger (to her future misfortune) Mrs. Elizabeth Graeme Ferguson, a lady of Philadelphia society with a minor reputation for literary attainments, who was married to a loyalist. On October 15, 1777, Mrs. Ferguson appeared at Washington's camp outside Philadelphia and requested an interview. Washington, who knew of her, had her ushered in and she handed over the bulky Duché letter of fourteen folio pages. The General opened the letter and began to read.

Washington must have been greatly surprised by Duché's appeal. The next day, in forwarding the letter to Congress, he reported his reaction: "To this ridiculous, illiberal performance I made a short reply by desiring the bearer of it, if she should hereafter by any accident meet Mr. Duché, to tell him I should have returned it unopened if I had any idea of the contents." Washington added that, despite Duché's assertion that no British official was involved: "I cannot but suspect that the measure did not originate with him, and that he was induced to it by the hope of establishing his interest and peace more effectually with the enemy."

Several weeks later Washington wrote of the incident in a letter to Francis Hopkinson, Duché's brother-in-law. He said he had sent the letter to Congress in order to protect himself, "for had any accident happened to the army entrusted to my command, and it had ever afterwards appeared that such a letter had been written and received by me, might it not have been said that I betrayed my country?"

Congress, which had been assailed in such uncomplimentary terms by Duché, was angered by the letter. The former Chaplain of Congress became a "Judas," and "apostate" and "the first of villains." The members of Congress also were convinced "that the letter he wrote to our worthy General must have been dictated by a Howe."[13] From the British viewpoint, the entire affair was badly mismanaged and hurt their cause. In the subsequent excitement after the public disclosure, the poor, would-be propagandist sailed for England.

Duché did not return to America and to Philadelphia until many years later, in 1792, when the incident was almost forgotten. At that time there took place "the interesting incident of his visit to President Washington; who had been apprised of and consented to it, and manifested generous sensibility on observing the limbs of Mr. Duché, the effects of a slight stroke of paralysis sustained by him in England."[14] Duché lived on for six more years, and died in America.

+

The failure of these "seductive" letters seems not to have discouraged the British and, in the following year, 1778, several new attempts were undertaken to win over influential Americans. The leading planner on this occasion was George Johnstone, a member of the commission sent to America in connection with the "conciliatory bills." A member of Parliament and a former British governor of Florida, Johnstone tried to smooth the path for the commission by making contact in England with friends of several Americans. Two of the patriots Johnstone hoped to reach were Robert Morris and Joseph Reed, both members of Congress.

In searching for letters of introduction, Johnstone approached Reed's brother-in-law in England, Dennis DeBerdt, who in the spring of 1776 had also written a letter on behalf of Lord Howe's abortive peace mission. DeBerdt, still hopeful of a reconciliation between the two countries, agreed in 1778 to write a letter of recommendation for Governor Johnstone, whom he described to Reed as "a steady proved friend of America and its just rights." But along with these kind words for Johnstone, DeBerdt voiced the general English dismay and disbelief that the Americans were allying themselves with the French, "the sworn enemies of British liberty and the Protestant religion." To accompany DeBerdt's cover letter, Johnstone prepared his own letter to Joseph Reed, in which he assured the latter of his friendship and explained that the commission was authorized to resolve all the differences between England and America "short of a total separation of interests."[15]

After the commissioners reached British-held Philadelphia early in June 1778, Johnstone dispatched the letters to Valley Forge, where Reed was serving on Washington's staff. Reed received his brother-in-law's letter with displeasure, unhappy that DeBerdt had allowed himself to be "used" for a second time by the British government. As for Johnstone's letter, Reed decided to reveal it to Congress. His view of the entire plan of the new commissioners was similar to Washington's: that it was

158

another "insidious" maneuver to distract and divide the patriots. After consulting with Washington on the matter, Reed prepared an answering letter to Johnstone.

However, Johnstone never received Reed's response because of the confusion and excitement attending the British evacuation of Philadelphia. Before leaving the city Johnstone made one last effort to get in touch with Reed. He approached the same lady who carried Duché's letter to Washington, Mrs. Ferguson. In his talk with her Johnstone suggested that Reed, if he would exert his influence to settle the war, might command "ten thousand guineas and the best post in the government, and if you should see him, I could wish you would convey that idea to him." Mrs. Ferguson said later she was "hurt and shocked" at this suggestion, and that she asked Johnstone if he did not think "that Mr. Reed will look upon such a mode of obtaining his influence as a bribe?" To which Johnstone replied: "By no means, madam. This mode of proceeding is customary in all negotiations, and one may very honorably make it a man's interest to step forth in a cause."[16]

When Reed returned to Philadelphia with the American army on June 18, he found a message from Mrs. Ferguson asking for an interview. Their meeting took place three days later, at which time Mrs. Ferguson repeated Johnstone's offer to which Reed made his famous reply to the effect that he was not worth purchasing, but such as he was, the King of England was not rich enough to buy him.[17]

For several weeks after this incident, Reed was silent about it, presumably to protect Mrs. Ferguson.[18] Not until Morris and Francis Dana publicly revealed approaches to them by Johnstone, and Congress ordered all letters received by its members be placed before the body, did Reed speak up. His news in July 1778 caused the greatest sensation, and Congress ordered all the Johnstone letters published. On August 11 it further adopted a resolution which cited portions of the letters and Reed's meetings with an unidentified lady, and declared such activities were nothing less than "direct attempts to corrupt and bribe the Congress of the United States of America."

159

So once again, Britain's efforts to win over "some of the most respectable members of Congress" had ended in exposure and failure. At British headquarters in New York, Johnstone became an obvious handicap to the work of the commission and a decision was made that he return to England. He sailed a few months before the other commissioners also gave up the struggle. A year later, in September 1779, the full story of Johnstone's enterprise and Mrs. Ferguson's role was revealed when Reed published a pamphlet which contained most of the letters dealing with the affair.

There was one more such attempt made by Britain, aimed at persuading one of the most famous men of the Revolution, Benjamin Franklin, to use his influence to bring about an accommodation. This strange episode took the form of the bizarre "Weissenstein" letter, flung into the grate at Franklin's home outside Paris. Marked "secret and confidential," the letter was similar to Duché's letter to Washington, in that the following warning to Franklin was on the outside cover: "Read this in private, before you look at the other papers – but don't be imprudent enough to let any one see it before you have considered it thoroughly."[19]

Signed with an obvious pseudonym, "Charles de Weissenstein," the document was dated June 16, 1778, Brussels. It contained two enclosures: (1) "Project for allaying the present ferments in North America" and (2) "Great outline of the future government in North America." Who was its mysterious author? "It is an Englishman," the writer began, "who addresses you, but an Englishman neither a partisan of mere obstructive faction tending to confound all order of government, nor yet one who is an idolatrous worshipper of passive obedience to the *divine right of Kings.*"

Continuing in this manner, with an attack on the past actions of both the Parliament and the ministry, the author patently strove to establish himself in Franklin's eyes as a friend of America. But, at the same time, he did not let the opportunity pass to assail France, America's new ally. "The progress of the new alliance," he assured Franklin, "is easily foreseen and to be traced out – For the present, and for a year or two to come, you will obtain the most ample promises, and ready acquiescence [by France]. Then will come evasions to your applications, contemptuous delays, and of a sudden declaration that you must shift for yourselves. England has been just served thus in the hopes of her present inability to resent the treatment — in that there may probably be a great mistake — but with respect to America there can be no such error, for when will she be able to combat France and compel her to adhere to treaties?"

From this argument "Weissenstein" proceeded to the question of whether America had the power or resources to stand alone "as an independent empire." No, he answered his own question, America could not, since the costs of a standing army and the creation of a regular navy were not within the ability of the country. "Yet without these, your rising state will neither be in a capacity to secure itself from hostile ravages, acquire new alliances, or preserve any beneficial purpose. . . . Your sea port towns at the mercy of an enemy, will be too insecure a deposit for the constituent stores of your commerce and the navigation so precarious as to sink almost all the profit."

In view of these unhappy circumstances (but recognizing American suspicions of the British administration and its representatives), the writer then posed the following question to Franklin: "Why not offer some conditions directly to the King himself?" The writer said he was assuming that America "is willing to treat" and he was prepared to transmit "into the King's own hands any proposals on your part, which are not couched in offensive terms."

To facilitate the handling of Franklin's proposals, "Weissenstein" recommended a secret rendezvous. He suggested that Franklin deposit his reply at a certain spot in the Cathedral of Notre Dame, there to be picked up by a British agent who would have a paper in his hand "as if drawing or taking notes." For more positive identification, the agent also would wear a rose in his hat or in the lapel of his coat.

With what must have been raised eyebrows, Franklin turned from this remarkable letter to the enclosures. There he found further enlightenment in a paragraph which dealt with the British "Indemnity to the principal American leaders." Named

161

to receive "offices or pensions for life at their option, according to the sums opposite their names," were Adams, Hancock, Washington, Franklin, etc. The sums were not listed, but the blank spaces next to the names invited filling in by the recipients. It was further stated that if the King should ever create American peerages, the persons named and their descendants would be among the first to receive them, and in addition: "Mr. Washington to have immediately brevet of Lieutenant General" in the British Army.

Franklin's first reactions to these amazing proposals are not known. John Adams, who was living with the Pennsylvania philosopher at the time, later reported that Franklin consulted with him, that it was agreed they would do nothing without informing the French, and that Franklin would prepare an answer. Adams said Franklin seemed convinced that the proposals had come directly from the King.[20]

In his reply to "Weissenstein," Franklin began calmly enough, first disputing the point that France would cheat the United States, or fail to support her. He also took exception to the statement that America could not defend itself without Britain's help. "Our militia," he said dryly, "you find by experience are sufficient to defend our lands from invasion; and the commerce with us will be defended by all the nations who find an advantage in it. We, therefore, have not the occasion you imagine of fleets or standing armies, but may leave those expensive machines to be maintained for the pomp of princes, and the wealth of ancient states. We propose, if possible, to live in peace with all mankind."

The main drift of "Weissenstein's" letter, continued Franklin, seemed to be "to impress me with an idea of your impartiality, by just censures of your ministers and measures, and to draw from me propositions of peace. . . . You yourself, sir, are quite unknown to me. You have not trusted me with your true name. . . . I may be indiscreet enough in many things, but certainly, if I were disposed to make propositions (which I cannot do, having none committed to me to make) I should never think of delivering them to the Lord knows who, to be carried to the Lord knows where, to serve no one knows what purposes."

Warming to his reply, Franklin said that he found the present approach to him "as insidious as that of your conciliatory bills. Your true way to obtain peace, if your ministers desire it, is to propose openly to the Congress fair and equal terms." Further, the offer of places, peerages, and pensions was enough to stamp the author. "This offer to corrupt us, sir, is with me your credentials, and convinces me that you are not a private volunteer in your application. It bears the stamp of British court character. It is even the signature of your King."[21]

According to Adams, the original "Weissenstein" documents and Franklin's reply were sent to the French foreign minister, Vergennes, who turned the matter over to the Paris police. The police surveillance report was later sent to Franklin. It said that a gentleman had appeared, at the day, hour, and place appointed. The man had wandered around the cathedral, gazing at the statues and pictures, but always keeping an eye out for the spot where Franklin was to deposit his reply. After some time the gentleman left and was followed to his hotel. The name he had assumed, said Adams, "was Colonel Fitz-something – an Irish name that I have forgotten." His real name, according to the French police, was M. Jennings, a former captain of the King's guard in England.[22]

In any event, this attempt to persuade or bribe an important leader of the Revolution to desert his cause ended in failure, as had those in America. The irony of all these efforts was that the one major defection from the rebel side during the war – Benedict Arnold's – resulted not from any direct approach to him, but was initiated by the "base traitor" himself.

☆ 7 ☆

Overseas Propaganda

THE PROPAGANDA WAR of the Revolution was not confined to the territory of the United States and Canada. Very early in the struggle the Americans realized that they would need outside help if they were to succeed in their war with Britain, and that such aid, economic and military, could only come from Europe. Whereupon, they invoked the instrument of propaganda in the effort to win friends among the European powers.

The American overseas propaganda campaign did not officially begin until July 4, 1776, the date of adoption of the Declaration of Independence. In the very first sentence of that famous document, Jefferson said it was "a decent respect to the opinions of mankind" which had called forth the Declaration. In reality, however, he was appealing to the one country which had shown more than passing interest in the North American convulsions – to France, which six months earlier had sent a secret emissary to Philadelphia to hint to the colonists that they must first declare their independence of Britain before aid would be forthcoming. The American leaders came to realize that until the thirteen colonies announced a formal state of belligerency, no European power would risk interfering in England's "internal affairs."

The issuance of the Declaration was the real beginning of America's campaign to woo the friendly and unfriendly nations of Europe. In charge of the overseas propaganda program (in

165

the informal sense) was Doctor Franklin, working in coordination with the French. Congress had dispatched the seventy-year-old philosopher to Paris late in 1776 as one of three commissioners charged with the mission of obtaining formal recognition of the United States, and economic assistance. The other Americans, who were already in Europe, were Silas Deane and Arthur Lee.

Although Franklin was well known in Europe for his scientific, literary, and philosophical achievements, his arrival in France in December 1776 made an unexpected and tremendous impression on the French public. "No one," wrote Carl Van Doren, "could have foreseen the outburst of enthusiasm which made Franklin overnight the most famous man in the world in French opinion." There were various reasons for this, but undoubtedly the most important was the fact that France had been dreaming of revenge against Britain ever since her humiliation in the Seven Years' War. When, to their pleasure, the famed Benjamin Franklin stood on their soil, the French acclaimed him as being not only "a rational sage" like Voltaire, and "a child of nature" like Rousseau,[1] but also as the man who (rumor said) had single-handedly created the American Revolution.

The adulation Franklin received was to be of great use to him, not only in his diplomatic efforts but also in the propaganda campaign he immediately embarked upon. In time, in fact, his own image was to become an American propaganda symbol, reproduced by the enthusiastic French in dozens of portraits, in miniatures, medallions, statuettes, drawings and prints; and on rings, handkerchiefs, and snuffboxes.

Prior to Franklin's arrival, the French themselves had given publicity to two important American propaganda documents – Paine's *Common Sense* and Jefferson's Declaration of Independence. Both were published by government order in *Affaires de l'Angleterre et de l'Amérique,* a periodical printed covertly by the French foreign office under a faked Antwerp dateline. Because its sponsorship was hidden, *Affaires* was considered a safe publication in which the still neutral French could counter British propaganda on the Continent. (The British had a number of propaganda outlets in Europe, one of which was a paper called the *Courrier de l'Europe,* published in Holland but with a wide circulation in France.)[2]

Writing from Paris about *Common Sense* in August 1776, Silas Deane informed Congress that the French version had had "a greater run, if possible, here than in America," and had stirred the enthusiasm of France for the American cause. In December Deane also reported that the Declaration had become "an old story in every part of Europe" and was "well received." In both instances, however, the French had edited each document in an effort to tone down some of the antimonarchial sentiments expressed in them, and they also added certain "explanatory" notes. Some months later copies of the original Declaration reached Europe, and these unexpurgated versions were scattered throughout the continent by the American agents.

Franklin's first significant propaganda activity came shortly after his arrival in Paris, when he obtained the translation and publication of an early draft of the Articles of Confederation, and also the publication of the thirteen constitutions of the American states. In January 1777, while dining with the young duc de La Rochefoucauld d'Enville, Franklin either persuaded Rochefoucauld or the latter volunteered to make the translations of the constitutions.[3] They appeared separately in *Affaires,* and were later published together in a compilation edited by Rochefoucauld.

+

That the Pennsylvania philosopher clearly understood the role of political propaganda was revealed in a letter he wrote to Richard Price towards the end of the war. Speaking of the limitations of the ancient Greek and Roman orators, who could reach but a limited audience assembled within hearing of their voices, Franklin remarked:

> Now by the press we can speak to nations; and good books and well written pamphlets have great and general influence. The facility with which the same truths may be repeatedly enforced by placing them daily in different

167

lights in *newspapers,* which are everywhere read, gives a great chance of establishing them. And we now find, that it is not only right to strike while the iron is hot but that it may be very practicable to heat it by continually striking.[4]

In Paris Franklin was able to strike repeatedly in the ready-made platforms offered him by the French papers, covert or otherwise. *Affaires* in particular served as a vehicle for numerous Franklinian articles. Very early Franklin made contact with the editor, Edmund-Charles Genet (who also was translator for the French foreign office), and began sending in propaganda items. During the four years of *Affaires'* existence (it stopped publication in December 1779), the paper reprinted a number of famous Franklin essays, including his *Edict of the King of Prussia*, a parody of the English King's claim to arbitrary rule over America, and his *Rules by Which a Great Empire May Be Reduced to a Small One.*

In addition to these original contributions, Franklin sent Genet many extracts taken from American newspapers relating to the war in America and pro-American propaganda writings by his English friend, Richard Price. Letters from colleagues in America concerning political-military events also provided items for the French gazettes. These sources assured a full hearing for the American viewpoint in France.

It was much more difficult, however, to get rebel propaganda into other European newspapers. Yet even here the distinguished American's reputation served him well; certain liberal European publishers wrote to Franklin and asked for American news to counterbalance the flood of British propaganda. For example, one such writer, Reinier Arrenberg, introduced himself in a letter to Franklin on March 31, 1777, as second secretary of the Physical Society of Rotterdam as well as publisher of the *Gazeteer Française de Liede.* Arrenberg announced his willingness to pay for any news Franklin could send.[5]

Franklin took advantage of this opportunity and started a flow of American propaganda to Arrenberg which continued for several years. For assistance in operating this "news service," Franklin called upon the American agent in Holland, Charles William Frederick Dumas (see below). Among the stories

Arrenberg published was one dealing with the cruel treatment meted out to American prisoners by the English – a theme which was well exploited by the American propagandists during the war.

Besides Arrenberg, a number of other volunteer publishers offered their services. In December 1777, one C.S. Peuch of Utrecht wrote to Franklin requesting prompt and authentic news of America for his *Gazette*. From Germany a Baron De Hupsch, publisher of the *Universal Gazette* in Cologne, begged Franklin in June 1778, to make contributions from time to time to counter, he said, the pro-English propaganda being disseminated by paid journals of the various German states.

All these European volunteers helped Franklin in his job of spreading American views and doctrines throughout the Continent. His most important assistance, however, came from Charles Dumas, his friend at The Hague. A native of Switzerland and an active pro-American, Dumas had been recommended to Congress by Franklin as a man who might gather intelligence in Europe and serve in related capacities. An offer to be an American agent was made to Dumas in December 1775, which he accepted.

As a writer and man of deep learning, Dumas was acquainted with many of the professors and other western European intelligentsia who were active in publishing various Dutch- and French-language newspapers. He soon became involved in feeding rebel news items to such liberal papers as the *Gazette de Leide* and the *Courrier du Bas-Rhin*, as well as supplying information to Franklin and Congress' Committee of Secret Correspondence.

In the early years, Dumas' letters to the Secret Committee often contained appeals "for news." For example, in a letter on June 14, 1777, Dumas reported that Europeans "complain everywhere of knowing nothing of your affairs but what the English wish Europe should know." On this subject, he said, "we have often to wait some months before the truth is unfolded from a heap of impostures, which do not fail sometimes to answer the malice of your enemies in leaving false impressions on minds."

169

The Committee attempted to send American newspapers and letters regularly to Europe, but the British Navy was very active, and many a packet of rebel papers ended up in a watery grave, or in London instead of Paris or Amsterdam. In this connection, Franklin wrote to Congress suggesting they investigate the possibility of dispatching once a month "little light vessels" to keep up a more regular correspondence. "Even the receiving letters of a certain date," Franklin said, "though otherwise of no importance, might serve to refute the false news of our adversaries on both sides of the water." However, little seems to have been done by Congress, and communications across the Atlantic continued in haphazard fashion.

Operating as best he could under these limitations, Dumas spread the American message in the Dutch provinces, and performed numerous outstanding services to the United States. Francis P. Renaut has written that without his activities, "insurgent propaganda" in the Netherlands would have been insignificant or snuffed out at an early date by the wide-ranging activities of the British ambassador. For five years Dumas filled the breach, until John Adams arrived in Amsterdam and took over personal direction of America's propaganda campaign in that country.

+

In the year 1777 a striking propaganda document — a form of black propaganda[6] — began circulating in France. It was called *The Sale of the Hessians*, was written originally in French, and is attributed to Franklin.[7] The text centered on the treaties between Great Britain and the German princes for the hire of the mercenaries. Most of these treaties contained a "blood money" provision — that is, the prince would receive levy money for each man killed amounting to about seven pounds per man, with three wounded men reckoned as one killed. Franklin, of course, was well acquainted with these treaties, having served on one of the Congressional propaganda

170

committees which prepared an appeal to the German soldiers. The American philosopher was particularly appalled by and contemptuous of the German rulers who, he charged, had "sold the blood of their people."

The Sale probably came from Franklin's pen shortly after news reached Europe (in March 1777) of Washington's victory over the Hessians at Trenton. The document was in the form of a letter, dated February 18, 1777, from Count de Schaumbergh to "Baron Hohendorf, Commanding the Hessian Troops in America" (both names were fakes). In the letter, the Count spoke of his great joy at learning that "of the 1,950 Hessians engaged in the fight, but 345 escaped. There were just 1,605 men killed, and I cannot sufficiently commend your prudence in sending an exact list of the dead to my minister in London. This precaution was the more necessary, as the report sent to the English ministry does not give but 1,455 dead. This would make 483,450 florins instead of the 643,500 florins which I am entitled to demand under our convention."[8]

The supposed Count de Schaumbergh continued his letter, attributing the differences between British and German casualty lists to a dispute over the listing of wounded men. Regarding the wounded, the Count expressed confidence that Baron Hohendorf would not try "by human succor to recall the life of the unfortunates whose days could not be lengthened but by the loss of a leg or an arm. That would be making them a pernicious present, and I am sure they would rather die than live in a condition no longer fit for my service. I do not mean by this that you should assassinate them. We should be humane, my dear Baron, but you may insinuate to the surgeons with entire propriety that a crippled man is a reproach to their profession, and that there is no wiser course than to let every one of them die when he ceases to be fit to fight."

The Sale of the Hessians was first circulated in manuscript form in France, and later reprinted in support of the growing European protests against the sale of German manpower to England. To the British and German leaders the furor was, at least, embarrassing.

171

+

"All Europe is on our side of the question, as far as applause and good wishes can carry them," Franklin wrote in May 1777 to Samuel Cooper. The British government, finding European opinion favoring the underdog rebels, and noting a growing anti-English attitude, was disturbed, especially so after the Americans gained new prestige with their success at Trenton. In an attempt to halt and reverse this trend, British propagandists appear to have resorted to numerous false reports and rumors. One such report, for example, claimed Franklin was only a deserter who had had a terrible quarrel with Congress and really wished to submit to England. Another claimed the Americans, in talks with the Howe brothers, had already agreed to reconciliation with England.

Until this latter report in particular could be refuted, doubts were created in European minds as to the American cause. In late 1777, when Congress received word from Paris of this story, it quickly adopted a resolution denouncing "the insidious enemies of the United States of America" who had "endeavoured to propagate in Europe false and groundless reports" of a treaty between Congress and the King's commissioners. Congress directed Franklin and the other Americans overseas to inform the European powers "that no treaty whatever has been held between the King of Great Britain or any of his Commissioners and the said United States since their declaration of independence."

A month prior to this resolution's adoption, the momentous news of Burgoyne's surrender at Saratoga was sent speeding to Europe via several fast ships, including the *Ranger* under John Paul Jones. Jones reached Nantes on December 2, 1777, and hurried to Paris, only to learn he had been beaten by twelve hours by Jonathan Loring Austin of Boston, who had sailed aboard a French vessel.

No news received in Europe during the Revolutionary War had such tremendous impact on public opinion there, as did the British surrender at Saratoga. It was an event so completely unexpected, that it was, for that very reason, a huge American propaganda success in Europe. Franklin, his French allies, and Dumas saw to it that the story of Burgoyne and Saratoga was spread throughout the Continent. Dumas later wrote in a letter of congratulations to the Americans: "This news has made the greatest possible sensation in this country; a deep consternation among those who have all their interest in England, a marked joy among those who hate your enemies."

The three American commissioners, Franklin, Deane, and Lee, reported to Congress that the news of Saratoga had "occasioned as much general joy in France as if it had been a victory of their own troops over their own enemies." The commissioners added they had taken the opportunity to press the French ministry for conclusion of the long-sought-for recognition of American independence. Not long thereafter, on February 5, 1778, the treaty was finally concluded.

The one event during this period which Britain could point to with pride, although it was spoiled by Burgoyne's surrender, was the capture of Philadelphia. But the Americans disparaged the significance of that event. Richard Henry Lee, in a letter to his brother, Arthur Lee, offered suggestions on what to tell the French ministry about Howe's seizure of Philadelphia. The latter (Arthur Lee) sent an edited version of his brother's letter to Count de Vergennes on December 6, 1777:

> Suffer me here to observe a little upon the enemy's possession of Philadelphia. In Europe where our affairs are not so well understood perhaps it may make some noise. When first entered into this war we not only considered but openly declared, that we regarded our great towns as indefensible . . . that the possession of them would avail little toward the accomplishment of the views of our enemies. With us, therefore, the enemy's possession of Philadelphia is really of little importance. In truth our towns are only as spots upon the great map of our strength. But it is far from certain that Gen. Howe will retain Philadelphia two months. . . . Boston was once theirs. They have no reason to triumph on that.

+

The fourth year of the war saw Franklin's attention turn to what appeared to be a fertile field for American propaganda — across the Irish Sea. As early as July 1775, Congress had addressed itself to the people of Ireland, seeking support against England, and had suggested that the Irish themselves were not "without grievances." The Irish indeed had many complaints against Great Britain: English laws had nearly ruined their industry; Irish farmers felt exploited by landlords; and the Irish Parliament worked in England's interest by means of corruption.

In addition to their common grievances, America and Ireland were drawn together because the latter had played an important role in providing immigrants to America, many of whom were fighting in Washington's army. These things created a natural bond of sympathy between the Irish and Americans. Thus by 1778, when Ireland's disaffection reached a crisis stage, Franklin's interest was stimulated and, on October 4, 1778, he printed an address "To the Good People of Ireland."

In most sympathetic tones Franklin spoke of the "misery and distress which your ill-fated country has been so frequently exposed to." The British ministry, the Parliament, the King — all came in for Franklin's censure as he reviewed the events which had led the Americans to take up arms. "I have it in my commission," Franklin also said, "to repeat to you, my good friends, the cordial concern that Congress takes in everything that relates to the happiness of Ireland; they are sensibly affected by the load of oppressive pensions on your establishments; the arbitrary and illegal exactions of public money by King's letters; the profuse dissipation by sinecure appointments with large salaries, and the very arbitrary and impolitic restrictions of your trade and manufactures, which are beyond example in the history of the world."

Despite these circumstances, which might call for an Irish rebellion, Franklin urged Ireland to remain "peaceable and quiet" for the time being. But he added subversively, should the British government "whom you at this time acknowledge," not remove the restraints on Irish trade, commerce and manufacturing, "I am charged to assure you that means will be found to establish your freedom."

This appeal was printed on Franklin's press at Passy, and turned over to a "Dutch smuggler" at Brest to carry to Ireland. The vessel unfortunately was intercepted by an English privateer, and the papers confiscated and forwarded to the Admiralty. However, Franklin apparently had not put all his broadsides in one basket because other copies made their way into Irish hands. On November 4, 1778 — a month after it came off Franklin's press — the *Hibernian Journal*, an Irish Whig newspaper, reprinted the address.

Irish disaffection was encouraged further at this time by news of the activities of John Paul Jones. Sailing unmolested in the Irish Sea, in April and May 1778 Jones raided the English and Scottish coasts, partly in retaliation for the burning of American towns. The news of these raids, and the toll he took of British commerce, not only caused panic in the seaport towns of England, but sent insurance rates soaring on British shipping. Franklin, in addition, had commissioned several Irish-manned privateers, which were extremely active against English shipping, seizing dozens of vessels.[9]

Irish domestic agitation, John Paul Jones' successes, and American propaganda began to worry the British authorities. To the ministry it must have seemed that a rebellion in their backyard, in imitation of the American insurrection, was in the making; and that an Irish Washington and an Irish Congress would soon emerge. By late 1779, the Irish crisis reached a climax and, when it appeared almost too late to halt Ireland's drift to rebellion, the British moved quickly to stem the tide. In December the government announced an important program of concessions to the Irish — commercial and religious — which had the effect of turning Irish public opinion temporarily away from insurrection.

During the months preceding the height of Irish agitation, the psychological war against Britain threatened to turn into a real invasion by French and Spanish forces. A large portion of the French propaganda paper, *Affaires*, had been devoted to elaborate descriptions of plans for the invasion of England. *Affaires* reminded the British of the many past landings by invaders, and warned that the Channel did not constitute an insuperable barrier.

In the summer of 1779, following Spain's entrance into the war against England (in May), some 50,000 French troops were mustered along the coast of France while a French-Spanish armada moved towards England with the mission of clearing the seas of the British Navy. The invasion threat produced much excitement in London, and a royal proclamation dated July 9 directed that all horses, oxen, and cattle which might be used by the invading forces, be driven away from the coasts, or other steps taken so they would not fall into enemy hands.

The King's proclamation awakened the British people to their danger and with the awakening came many recriminations against the King's ministers, who were attacked for "obstinately persisting in affirming that the kingdom was in perfect safety" and for their "total want of preparation." The landings, how- ever, did not take place, apparently because of the indecision of the French commander, who tarried in the Channel until a typhoid epidemic among the crews and a storm so disrupted his fleet that he was forced back to Brest.

About this time, John Paul Jones sailed in search of prize ships, and in September, encountered the English vessels, *Serapis*, and the *Countess of Scarborough*. In the famous battle during which his own ship, the *Bonhomme Richard*, went down, Jones boarded and took the fifty-gun *Serapis*. This remarkable victory, the capture of a larger warship by a smaller one, was the talk of Europe for many months and enhanced the American cause. In a letter of congratulations to Jones, Frank- lin told the superb commander that "scarce any thing was talked of at Paris and Versailles but your cool conduct and persevering bravery during that terrrible conflict. You may believe that the impression on my mind was not less strong than on that of others."

Jones took his prizes into the Dutch port of Texel, where his presence gave Dumas and the French propagandists in Holland an opportunity to organize noisy demonstrations for the new

American hero, who was warmly received by the public. Speaking of Jones' activities in a letter to a friend, who had reported the British punitive raids in Connecticut, Franklin later wrote: "We have given them a little taste of this disturbance upon their own coasts this summer; and, though we have burnt none of their towns, we have occasioned a good deal of terror and bustle in many of them, as they imagined our Commodore Jones had four thousand troops with him for descents."[10]

+

In the sixth year of the war, the American propagandists in Europe suffered a setback which was a consequence of British victories in the southern states; in particular the capture of Charleston. Unaware that events were going against rebel arms in the south, the Americans set in motion a propaganda letter that boomeranged almost as soon as it appeared. The incident occurred in May 1780, when an American at Lorient forwarded to Franklin a copy of a letter that had been printed in a Philadelphia newspaper on April 8. The letter was supposedly written by the British commander in America, General Clinton, to Lord Germain. In it Clinton voiced doubts about his chances of success in the expedition against Charleston. The letter contained such premonitions of disaster, that it seemed Clinton was putting his reservations on record in order to be able to defend himself in case of failure.

Although Franklin said he had doubts "whether some parts" of the letter had really been written by Clinton, in forwarding it to Dumas, he commented: "I have no doubt of the facts stated, and think the piece valuable, as giving a true account of British and American affairs in that quarter." Franklin requested Dumas to publish the letter, and he also dispatched a copy to England, where he hoped his British friends would manage to reprint it there.

Dumas had misgivings about the letter's authenticity, but he delivered it to the editor of the *Courrier du Bas-Rhin*, who published it in June. Whereupon, the British ambassador to the

177

Netherlands, Sir Joseph Yorke, promptly denounced the document as a forgery. Within a few days Yorke's position was fully vindicated by the arrival of news from America of the capitulation of Charleston to the British. The *Courrier*'s chagrined editor, who had welcomed American news, felt he had been duped and in another article he promptly attacked the letter and its American instigators.

In this incident serious damage was done to the American reputation for writing, speaking, and disseminating "the truth." William Lee, who was in Brussels when the affair was exposed, wrote to John Adams to express his concern over it. "You must be sensible," he said, "of the injury it will bring to America and the cause of liberty, if the world is permitted to be impressed with the idea that Congress and its agents are base enough to be guilty of such a mean and pitiful conduct as to forge and publish the greatest falsehoods as solid truths."

This faux pas led Franklin and Adams to begin an investigation into the origins of the letter and, on July 20, Adams reported to Lee:

> Within a few days past I have seen a gentleman from America who says it was a mere *jeu d'esprit*, written by an officer in the army. . . . I have been all along afraid that our countrymen would at length imitate their enemies in this kind of imposition. . . . We have no need for such aids as political lies. Our character for truth, sincerity and candor is more real strength than ever can be derived from such impostures, however artfully performed.

Adams thus took a stand for a "campaign of truth," in which black propaganda would have little place. Such a policy, however, would have been very constricting indeed on that master of the hoax and faked letter, Benjamin Franklin.

The incident had been clumsily handled only because communications with America were so poor, and the Americans in Europe had no way of knowing how military events were progressing. Thus, in the summer of 1780, as British hopes revived with the great victory at Charleston, American supporters in Europe grew silent. On July 22 Dumas wrote plaintively to Congress: "It is to be wished that we may soon receive

178

news from America which will raise again the courage of friends of the United States, to whom the misfortune of Charleston has caused much pain, in proportion as it has reanimated those who favor your enemies. The latter, in the meantime, forge and utter every day rumors injurious to the United States, such as that they are about to submit."

Although no news of a decisive nature was received from America, by September Dumas was able to report that Dutch public opinion was slowly recovering from "the false notions" caused by the capture of Charleston. Meanwhile, Dumas was busy briefing his American guest, John Adams, who had arrived in Amsterdam the previous month.

+

Adams' role as an American propagandist in Europe is not as well known as that of Franklin, although he made a number of important contributions in both Holland and in France. The New Englander had first arrived in France in 1778 to replace Silas Deane. Prior to his return to America in August 1779, he became acquainted with Genet and was asked to contribute articles to *Affaires*.

It was not, however, until Adams' second trip to Europe in 1780 as Congress' "peace commissioner," that he became a full-fledged publicist for the American cause. By this time, *Affaires* had been dropped as a publication by the French foreign office. But, as Adams reported to Congress on February 23, "those political intelligences and speculations which were formerly published in *Affaires* were finding outlets in the *Mercure de France* and the *Gazette de France*, both published overtly by the French government under Genet's direction.

Soon after his second arrival in France, Adams wrote to Genet, offering himself as a regular contributor to his papers. The English news dispatches from New York, Adams complained, were entirely fabricated. "I see thousands of these things every day that might easily be counteracted," he wrote. "I do not wish you to publish anything against your rules; and if ever I propose anything of that sort, it will be from ignorance

179

or inattention; and I rely upon your knowledge and prudence to check it. But as I am likely to have a little more leisure than I have had for a long time, if you will give me leave, I will assist you a little in your labors for the public good."

Genet accepted Adams' offer and on May 17 he sat down to his first effort, a lengthy counterargument to a speech made several weeks earlier in the House of Commons by General Henry Conway. In his speech Conway had urged, among other things, that the alliance between France and America was unnatural. Adams, of course, took the opposite view in his letter to Genet, insisting that the two countries were "natural allies" because their interests were the same. Customs, languages, and religion were much less important in deciding the friendship and enmity of nations than other essential interests. In fact, Adams continued, the people of America were "universally of the opinion that, from the time they declared themselves independent, England became their natural enemy" and, since the latter had been for centuries the natural enemy of France, consequently America was "the natural friend of France."

Adams' initial contribution was translated into French and published in the *Mercure de France* on June 3, 1780. A copy of it also was dispatched to London, where friends of the United States managed to get it reprinted in the *General Advertiser.*

On May 28, Adams completed another counterargument, which also was published in the two newspapers above. This essay was a point-by-point refutation of a speech made by Lord Germain, which also had attacked the French-American alliance. Adams argued that:

> every step of Congress, every proceeding of every assembly upon the continent, every prayer that is made in the pulpit, and every speculation in the newspapers demonstrates the high sense they have of the importance of this alliance. It is said that this alliance has been of little utility. Has it not employed the British army? has it not cut out work enough for the British navy? has it not wasted for England her annual twenty millions? has it not

180

prevented these from being employed against America? has it not given scope to American privateers? has it not protected the American trade? has it not hurt that of Great Britain?

These arguments were irrefutable and, when published in the London press, must have made sad reading in ministerial circles.

+

When Adams reached Amsterdam in the summer of 1780 in pursuit of a Dutch loan and recognition of the United States, the Netherlands was in a state of political transition. An established maritime nation, the Netherlands had come into conflict with England for conducting a clandestine trade with the Americans, and for trading in naval supplies with the French. To protect their commerce from British seizure, the Dutch began to explore the idea of joining the newly formed Armed Neutrality, an agreement of the small naval powers of Europe (led by Russia) which aimed at protecting their shipping against all belligerents.

This was the political situation when Adams arrived in Amsterdam. He soon contacted the "indefatigable" Dumas, who became his aide, translator, and contact man, and within a few weeks he learned some of the problems facing an American propagandist in that conservative country. Writing of this to Franklin in October, Adams exclaimed: "It is necessary for America to have agents in different parts of Europe, to give some information concerning our affairs, and to refute the abominable lies that the hired emissaries of Great Britain circulate in every corner of Europe, by which they keep up their own credit and ruin ours. I have been more convinced of this, since my peregrinations in this country, than ever. The universal and profound ignorance of America here has astonished me. It will require time and a great deal of prudence and delicacy to undeceive them."

To enlighten the Dutch, Adams turned to his writing table and his productions soon were going out to such editors as John Luzac of the *Leyden Gazette* and A.M. Cerisier, of the *Lettres*

Hollandois, the latter being a paper originating in the French legation at The Hague. These publications, Adams later wrote to Robert Livingston, "have a vast influence in forming ... public opinion."

One of the most interesting of Adams' propaganda feats during this period followed a conversation with one Hendrik Calkoen, whom he later described as "the first gentleman of the bar at Amsterdam; a man of letters, well read in law and history, and an elegant writer." Calkoen asked for information on American affairs and, Adams recalled: "I gave him a collection of our constitutions, and a number of pamphlets and papers, and desired him to commit to writing his questions."[11]

Calkoen had many questions, twenty-six in all, and during the month of October 1780 Adams applied himself to answering them. The Dutch lawyer's questions covered military, political, and economic topics and were in the form of challenges to Adams to prove certain points. For example, Calkoen asked Adams to "show that America, notwithstanding the war, daily increases in strength and force."

To this Adams replied (excerpts):

It has been found by calculations that America has doubled her numbers, even by natural generation alone, upon an average about once in eighteen years. This war has now lasted six years; in the course of it we commonly compute in America that we have lost by sickness and the sword and captivity about five-and-thirty thousand men. But the numbers of people have not increased less than seven hundred and fifty thousand souls, which gives at least a hundred thousand fighting men. We have not less, probably, than seventy thousand fighting men in America more than we had on the day that hostilities were first commenced on the 19th of April 1775. There are near twenty thousand fighting men added to the numbers in America every year. Is this the case of our enemy, Great Britain? Which then can maintain the war the longest?

Calkoen also challenged Adams to prove that no single person in America had so much power and influence "that his death, or corruption by English money" could have any significant effect on the American struggle. Here Adams insisted with much fervor that the Revolution's success was not dependent upon any man. "If there ever was a war that could be called *the people's war*," Adams wrote, "it is this of America against Great Britain; it having been determined on by the people, and pursued by the people in every step of its progress."

The British government, Adams continued, had repeatedly deluded itself by hopefully seeking and seeing in such individuals as Hancock, Dickinson, Franklin, Samuel Adams, and himself, "the soul" of the Revolution. But, said Adams, all these men had been absent from the central fulcrum of the Revolution, the Congress, for years, "yet Congress has been as active and as capable as before. . . . In short, sir, all these pretences are the most ridiculous imaginable. The American cause stands upon the essential, unalterable character of the whole body of the people." Not even the defection of such a famous man as General Washington, "which I know to be impossible," declared Adams, could subvert the American cause.

Throughout his discussions Adams sought to demonstrate to Calkoen that Britain could not conquer America, and to bolster his argument he called upon the words of two "unwilling witnesses and cruel enemies" — Generals Burgoyne and Howe. Both these retired British generals had published in 1780 separate statements in defense of their conduct in America: one being *The Narrative of Lieut. General Sir William Howe,* presented to a committee of the House of Commons on April 29, 1779, and the other, Burgoyne's *A State of the Expedition from Canada.*

Adams, citing the words of the two British commanders, demolished any doubts that might have remained about the fighting abilities of the colonists or America's chances of victory. Burgoyne had declared several times in his testimony that "the Americans possess the *quality* and *faculty* of fighting" and that it was absurd for English critics to continue to insist that the Americans were a rabble, who could not fight. General Howe also had enlightened a House of Commons committee on the many difficulties facing British military operations in North America. Almost every movement in the colonies, Howe had

183

said, "was an act of enterprise, clogged with innumerable difficulties. A knowledge of the country, intersected as it every-where is, by woods, mountains, waters, or morasses, cannot be obtained with any degree of precision necessary to foresee and guard against, the obstructions that may occur."

Adams' performance was unquestionably effective. He answered Calkoen's twenty-six questions in ten letters, written between October 4 and 27, 1780. Burgoyne's and Howe's pamphlets were translated into French (one into Dutch) for wider distribution. Calkoen not only became an adherent to the American cause (he later helped Adams draw up petitions to the merchants of Amsterdam favoring American independence), but he also undertook to spread American ideas among "a society of gentlemen of letters" which met regularly in Amsterdam.

During his continuing sojourn in Holland, Adams also became acquainted with Baron Jan Derck van der Capellen, one of the former regents of Amsterdam, who had been ousted for his liberal and anti-English views. Van der Capellen had begun a correspondence with several American patriots, including Livingston and Franklin, and was one of a number of Dutchmen who had quietly agitated against English influence in the Netherlands.

Adams later wrote of van der Capellen that he had "frequent and intimate conversations" with the Dutchman and that "he has been of the utmost service to our cause. . . . I dare not say in what a multitude of ways he has served us. Posterity will, perhaps, know them all." One of these services was van der Capellen's secret publication in September 1781 of an appeal *To the People of the Netherlands,* in which he attacked the conservative Dutch authorities who had deferred to Britain. The Baron had ended his appeal with the following cry: "Let all be ready, every man with his musket, bayonet and side arms, let them follow the example of the people of America where not a drop of blood was shed till the English struck the first blow, and Jehovah will support our righteous cause."

This inflammatory Dutch pamphlet had an effect reportedly like "an electric shock." Spread clandestinely through the principle cities of Holland, it led the Dutch authorities to offer a $2,500 reward for the arrest of the unknown author or printer.

It also was banned from being reprinted, published or circulated. However, the secret of van der Capellen's authorship was kept well hidden and was revealed only many years after the Revolution by a friend.[12]

What did all this agitation and propaganda mean on the political and diplomatic level? Together with British reprisals against Dutch commerce, American propaganda certainly played a role in the shift of public opinion in Holland away from Britain and towards the French-American alliance. By December 1780, when the Dutch began to seriously consider joining the Armed Neutrality, the worried London government concluded that it would be more convenient for the British Navy to have the Netherlands as a belligerent and she declared war on The Hague. Thus by January 1781 the conflict, which had begun with the American insurrection, had spread into a war encompassing France, Spain, Holland, and the Americans on one side, and Britain on the other.

It was under these circumstances that Adams succeeded in winning formal recognition of American independence from the Netherlands in April 1782, and shortly thereafter a substantial loan. Finally, in October of the same year, he concluded a treaty of amity and commerce – the second such treaty for the new American nation.

Adams was not bashful about claiming some credit for the American success in Holland. In a letter to Livingston in September 1782, he quoted the Spanish minister at The Hague as telling him: "Sir, you have struck the greatest blow of all Europe. It is the greatest blow that has been struck in the American cause, and the most decisive. It is you who have filled this nation with enthusiasm; it is you who have turned all their heads." Adams was delighted to record "things which were certainly said with deliberation," although he recognized that the charge of vanity might be flung afterwards at him, as it was.

+

In the spring of 1782, with the peace negotiations underway in Paris between Franklin and a British representative, another

185

item of black propaganda began to circulate in the salons of Europe. It was a brainchild of Franklin's and was in the form of the extraordinary *Supplement to the Boston Independent Chronicle*. Franklin's purpose in publishing this document was to stir public opinion against Britain during the peace talks, in hopes of gaining concessions.

Printed on his press at Passy, the *Supplement* had every appearance of an actual newspaper supplement, complete with advertisements. The main feature of the paper was a letter purportedly from a New England militia captain, who wrote that he had intercepted eight large packages containing the scalps of American frontiersmen, their women and children, and scalps of soldiers. Included with the packages was an address from the Seneca Indians to Governor Haldimand in Canada, asking that the scalps be forwarded to King George "that he may regard them and be refreshed; and that he may see our faithfulness in destroying his enemies."

Each package was further broken down into a complicated inventory, which listed in detail how the various scalps had been obtained. Package number one, for example, contained "43 scalps of Congress soldiers killed in different skirmishes; these are stretched on black hoops, 4 inches diameter; the inside of the skin painted red, with a small black spot to note their being killed by bullets. Also 62 of farmers killed in their houses; the hoops red; the skin painted brown, and marked with a hoe; and a black hatchet in the middle, signifying their being killed with that weapon." Other packages contained the scalps of women, some with no mark except "the short club," to show "they were knocked dead, or had their brains beat out."

Franklin forwarded a copy of this gruesome "masterpiece" to John Adams on April 22, and suggested: "If it were republished in England, it might make them a little ashamed of themselves." As was the proper procedure when issuing black propaganda, Franklin was silent about the authorship (as was the case with *The Sale of the Hessians*). To Adams he professed "some doubt" as to the truth of the form of the *Supplement* but none, he said, "as to the substance, for I believe the number of people actually scalped in this murdering war by the Indians to exceed what is mentioned in [the] invoice." The paper was subsequently reprinted in France and reached England, where Horace Walpole read it in an English gazette and immediately pronounced it as too good not to be by Franklin.[13]

The fact that a great deal of propaganda favorable to the American cause was published in England during the war, was partly the accomplishment of certain pro-American, antigovernment individuals in that country. These persons included the radical friends and correspondents of Franklin and other Americans, who by any strict interpretation of the law were "traitors" to King George's England.

They were not simply unorganzied and scattered individuals who happened to disagree with the foreign policy of the British government. There was a certain informal subversive "apparatus," centering on a number of English clubs which Franklin had organized or joined just prior to the outbreak of the war, in particular *The Society of 13* or *Deistic Society of 1774*. The members who had been brought together by common interests, included such English and foreign intellectuals as David Williams, Thomas Bentley, Joshua Wedgwood, R.E. Raspe, John Horne Tooke, and John Paradise. Associated with them, but apparently not members of the club, were such well-known writers and scientists as Joseph Priestly, Richard Price, Benjamin Vaughn, and J.R. Foster.[14] Some were members of Parliament.

From this handful of Whiggish intellectuals, many lines went out into British society so that their sum influence was far greater than their numbers would warrant. However, in the early years of the war, it was very dangerous for these men to openly preach their views. For a time the Habeas Corpus Act was revoked and at least one member, John Horne Tooke, was jailed for three years on a charge of libelling the King in a newspaper article. Yet even under these trying conditions, such men as Priestly and Price, too well known to be intimidated, continued their pro-American writings and agitation.

Shortly after Franklin's arrival in Paris in 1777, members of the society renewed their contacts with him, and a steady flow of mail — some in ciphers and code — went back and forth across the Channel, often carried by smugglers or European travellers sympathetic to the American cause. These operations sometimes became so conspiratorial that on one occasion, in September 1777, Franklin arranged to meet Benjamin Vaughn *au naturel* in a Paris steam bathhouse![15]

One of the devices for getting intelligence from England was revealed by Franklin in a letter to James Lovell in August 1780. "I have had several volunteer correspondents in England," Franklin explained, "who have in their letters for years together communicated to me secrets of state, extracted from the newspapers." It was with the help of these unpaid English volunteers that news and propaganda materials flowed both ways across the Channel. Towards the end of the war, these men, utilizing their various contacts, managed to slip many a pro-American story into the British press, thus providing an outlet in England for the voices of Franklin and Adams and the "voice of America."

☆ 8 ☆

EPILOGUE

Washington, Congress and the Declaration of Independence

Iᴛ ᴍᴀʏ ʜᴀᴠᴇ been true, as John Adams asserted, that the American Revolution was effected in the hearts and minds of the people "before the war commenced." However, the war was the real test and proof of the people's commitment. Although throughout the struggle the British government resorted to many devices to shake the rebelling colonists from their separatist notions, the stubborn Americans, as we have seen, clung to their Declaration. They clung also to one of the most important characters on the colonial scene, a man who became as much a propaganda symbol to the Americans as the words "liberty" and "independence." He was, of course, the enigmatic Virginian who became Commander in Chief of the American army, George Washington.

Washington was one of the indispensable figures of the Revolution, even as Congress was the movement's overall director. For eight long years Washington commanded the American army. During the same period the British government changed commanders four times. For eight years, even during the period of the so-called Conway cabal, when Washington's reputation had fallen, there was only one center of American resistance — Washington's army. As the years passed the name of Washington became a propaganda asset of first magnitude.

189

The reader who dips even briefly into the correspondence of the Revolution is struck by the eminent position Washington attained in the minds of his contemporaries. His physical presence alone seems to have stirred as much awe as his real achievements. Of this, Douglas Southall Freeman wrote: "Men caught their breath in admiration when they saw him on a spirited horse. Everything about him suggested the commander — height, bearing, flawless proportions, dignity of person, composure, and ability to create confidence by calmness and by unfailing, courteous dignity."

In the eyes of Abigail Adams, who met Washington for the first time in 1775, "the gentleman and soldier" were blended in him, and modesty seemed to mark "every line and feature of his face." To a Frenchman, Washington was "one of those master-pieces of nature," a born leader who inspired respect and confidence at first sight. "He was," wrote the Frenchman, "tall, his face was commanding, his eyes were kind, his language gracious, his gestures and words simple and above all a calm and firm behaviour harmonized all these qualities."[1]

Even before the war began, a London newspaper singled Washington out and recalled for Britons the Virginian's "very able, spirited and prudent conduct . . . when he covered and preserved the remains" of General Braddock's army during the French and Indian War a decade before. Washington's initiative during that debacle, it was observed, had "endeared him to every brave man, and stamped him with the name of being a most noble officer."[2]

A British officer who spent much of the war in American captivity, was impressed by the unique reputation Washington had among his countrymen. Everywhere, wrote Thomas Anburey, Washington's name was spoken with great respect. Patriot propaganda, it is true, cited his exploits in such great flights of language that another English observer could only record his amazement at the American claims after Trenton: "Alexander, Pompey and Hannibal were but pigmy Generals, in comparison with the magnanimous Washington." But Trenton *was* an important stroke and it made his reputation.

190

Horace Walpole, writing on April 3, 1777, described Washington's march through the British lines in New Jersey as "a prodigy of leadership." The English historian, George Otto Trevelyan, stated that from Trenton onward, "Washington was recognized as a far-sighted and skillful general all Europe over" – in Moscow, Potsdam, Madrid, Vienna, and London.

In dealing with his army, Washington demonstrated he was a master of most of the methods and techniques every successful commander must employ to steel men against hardship and to stimulate them on the battlefield. We have noted his use of general orders to pass along news that boosted the army's morale. Through his general orders he praised men and units when they performed well, or harangued them when discipline became lax. Understanding the importance of camp rumors, Washington also set them in motion to raise the army's spirits – through casual conversation.[3] He was, Allen Bowman wrote, the idol of the army: "A message from him could stir an entire corps to enthusiasm. His appearance in camp would produce general jubilation."

Towards the latter years of the war Washington had achieved an unassailable reputation overseas, even among the British. Thus, for example, a writer in the *London Chronicle* commented in July 1780:

> That nature has given General Washington extraordinary military talents, will hardly be controverted by his most bitter enemies. Having been early actuated with a warm passion to serve his country in the military line, he has greatly improved his talents by unwearied industry, a close application to the best writers upon tactics, and by a more than common method and exactness. In reality, when it comes to be considered that at first he only headed a body of men entirely unacquainted with military discipline or operations, somewhat ungovernable in temper, and who, at best, could only be styled an alert and good militia; acting under very short enlistments, unclothed, unaccoutred, and at all times very ill supplied with ammunition and artillery; and that with such an army he withstood the ravages and progress of near forty thousand veteran troops, plentifully

191

provided with every necessary article, commanded by the bravest officers in Europe, and supported by a very powerful navy, which effectually prevented all movements by water — when all this comes to be impartially considered, we may venture to pronounce that General Washington may be regarded as one of the greatest military ornaments of the present age. . . .

In Paris, Benjamin Franklin also praised Washington. In a letter to the General, he suggested that: "Should peace arrive after another campaign or two and afford us a little leisure, I should be happy to see your Excellency in Europe, and to accompany you if my age and strength would permit, in visiting some of its ancient and most famous kingdoms. You would on this side of the sea enjoy what posterity will say of Washington. For 1000 leagues have nearly the same effect with 1000 years. . . . At present I enjoy that pleasure for you, and I frequently hear the old generals of this martial country (who study the maps of America and mark upon them all your operations) speak with sincere approbation and great applause of your conduct; and join in giving you the character of one of the great captains of the age."

+

The Second Continental Congress was not the hero that Washington was to the people, it could not be; yet its role was even more crucial and significant than his. Of that organization, historian Claude Van Tyne wrote: "The audacity of the Continental Congress will ever be a matter of wonder. Without unity in instruction, with no power to form a government, without jurisdiction over an acre of territory, with no authority to administer government in any acre if they had it, with no money, no laws and no means to execute them, they entered upon the task of regulating a society in the state of revolution."

Indeed, a British newspaper, the *Middlesex Journal*, suggested that government officials in London "flatter themselves that, in the state to which things have come, the colonies will be easily conquered by force alone." It argued, in April 1776, that the members of the Continental Congress felt in themselves "a degree of importance, which, perhaps, the greatest subjects in Europe scarce feel." From shopkeepers, tradesmen, and attorneys, this anonymous newspaper writer noted, "they are become statesmen and legislators, and employed in contriving a new system of government for an extensive empire, which they flatter themselves will become, and which, indeed, seems very likely to become, one of the greatest and most formidable that ever was in the world." Under the Continental Congress, he pointed out, perhaps 500 people responded to it, and perhaps 500,000 "act under those five hundred," all of whom felt a proportional rise in their own importance. Further, a member of Congress filled a station superior not only to what he had ever filled before, but what he had ever expected to fill. Consequently, such an individual, "if he has the ordinary spirit of a man, will die in defence of that station."

The coming together of these highly literate individuals in Philadelphia, led the Congress into a number of fascinating propaganda ventures. Within that body of fifty to sixty men, there was, of course, no propaganda agency. They themselves, delegates of the thirteen colonies, created propaganda through the process of debate and the ballot. A key aspect of this policy-making procedure was the ad hoc committee, appointed to prepare the necessary supporting documents as well as to consider, investigate, and recommend policies.

It was in the Congressional committees that propaganda appeals were born and addressed to the Canadians, the orations to the Indians, the broadsides to the Hessians, etc. A useful and flexible system, the committee arrangement provided an outlet and opportunity for some of the best writers in Congress, such as Jefferson and John Dickinson, to put their skillful pens to work on the important policy papers that issued from that body.

The British and their German allies soon became aware of the central place Congress held in the conflict. Thus, Major Carl Baurmeister of the Hessian forces noted in January 1778:

> The Americans are bold, unyielding, and fearless. They have always lived in plenty, and we cannot block their resources, then their indomitable ideas of liberty, the main

193

springs of which are held and guided by every hand in Congress! Good for nothing and unimportant as most of these men may have been before these disturbances (because they were incompetent and without wealth) they now resort to every means, for more than one reason, to weaken the rich and the loyalists within and stubbornly resist the English without.

Baurmeister was quite correct. The members of the Continental Congress constituted a political directorate which played an essential role throughout the Revolution. During its course, it served both as legislature and executive in directing the struggle to a successful conclusion. It sent ambassadors to European countries which became America's allies, its Board of War was an executive agency which transmitted its policies and decisions to the commanders in the field and particularly to the Commander in Chief. In almost all that it did during the conflict, it propagandized the American cause.

Of all the great papers it produced, perhaps the greatest from the point of view of propaganda was Jefferson's Declaration of Independence. Its issuance was, of course, not an isolated event. Six months before, in January 1776, the long-smouldering issue of independence had burst into brilliant print with the appearance of Thomas Paine's pamphlet, *Common Sense,* in which the author levelled an attack on the monarchy and argued the merits of separation. Paine's pamphlet set off a great debate in the American press, a useful and important controversy which served in the months that followed to familiarize the American people with the idea of separation from Great Britain.[4]

The rush to independence began in earnest when the various delegations in Congress received instructions from their home states to vote for separation, beginning first with North Carolina on April 12 and Virginia on May 15. The climax to the march to the Declaration came on Friday, June 7, when Richard Henry Lee of Virginia arose in Congress and introduced the following historic resolutions:

> That these United Colonies are, and of right ought to be, free and independent states, that they are absolved from all allegiance to the British Crown, and that all political

connection between them and the State of Great Britain is, and ought to be, totally dissolved.

That it is expedient forthwith to take the most effectual measures for forming foreign alliances.

That a plan of confederation be prepared and transmitted to the respective Colonies for their consideration and approbation.

In the heated Congressional debate that followed, a conservative group led by Dickinson won a preliminary victory over the radicals by gaining postponement of a decision on the resolutions until July 1. In the meantime, however, they agreed to the appointment of a committee to prepare a declaration of independence — in the event Congress should arrive at a decision.

On June 11 a Committee of Five was elected to draw up the declaration. Those chosen were Jefferson, John Adams, Benjamin Franklin, Robert Livingston, and Roger Sherman. On the twelfth, members of the other committees were elected to prepare the plan of treaties and plan of confederation. Of the Committee of Five, Jefferson was the only member who was free from duties on the other committees, Adams and Franklin being chosen members of the treaties group, and Livingston and Sherman serving on the confederation body.

Subsequently, when the Committee of Five met to discuss the project, Jefferson was chosen to write the declaration. The true reasons for his selection have been the subject of some dispute, but certainly they included the general inclination on the part of the other delegates "to put Virginia at the head of everything" because of that colony's great influence in the South. Whereupon, the thirty-four-year-old Jefferson retired to write the paper.

In two days' time, as Jefferson later recalled, he completed a first draft, which he showed to Adams and Franklin. Both men made minor changes in wording. Jefferson revised the draft, making additional changes, before submitting it to the full committee, which reported it to Congress on June 28. It was not until July 2, when Congress officially voted for independence, that Jefferson's brainchild was examined paragraph by paragraph by the members. For three days — the second, third, and fourth — while the distressed young author sat by, Congress edited and, in Jefferson's eyes, mutilated the composition. Whole sections were shorn away. When the delegates had completed their editing, Jefferson's draft stood reduced by almost one fourth of its original length. Congress sent the final approved copy of the Declaration of the Representatives of the United States in General Congress Assembled to the printer on July 4th.

+

Although Jefferson in later years said he had "turned to neither book nor pamphlet" to write the Declaration, there was ample precedent for it in his earlier writings, in particular a pamphlet he published in 1774, *Summary Views of the Rights of British America,* and his preamble to the Virginia Constitution of a few weeks before, both of which contained a recital of grievances against the King. There also was an important precedent in the Virginia Declaration of Rights, penned by George Mason.

In detailing American grievances against the King (they constitute the bulk of the Declaration), Jefferson obviously had a persuasive intent. Joseph Barton of Delaware illuminated part of this intent in a letter written on July 9. "I could hardly own the King," Bardon wrote to a cousin, "and fight against him at the same time, but now these matters are cleared up. Heart and hand shall move together." Later generations of Americans, less involved in such matters and perhaps uncomfortable with polemics, have sought their inspiration in the famous phrases of Jefferson's second paragraph ("We hold these truths to be self evident, that all men are created equal . . . ."), rather than his list of grievances.

But Jefferson's great achievement in the Declaration was that he succeeded in placing "philosophic principles into intimate conjunction with propaganda . . . ."[5] Of Jefferson's propaganda technique, Saul K. Padover wrote: "With the cleverness of a subtle manipulator of public opinion, he personalized the enemy and exposed him to devastating attack." Thus rang Jefferson's famous, oversimplified charges:

196

The history of the present King of Great Britain is a history of repeated injuries and usurpations, all having in direct object the establishment of an absolute Tyranny over these States. To prove this, let Facts be submitted to a candid world.

He has refused . . . .
He has forbidden . . . .
He has refused . . . .
He has called together . . . .
He has dissolved . . . .
He has refused . . . .
He has endeavoured . . . .
He has made . . . .
He has obstructed . . . .
He has erected . . . .
He has kept among us . . . .
He has affected . . . .
He has combined . . . .
For quartering large bodies of armed troops among us:
For protecting them . . . .
For cutting off our trade . . . .
For imposing Taxes on us . . . .
For depriving us . . . .
For taking away . . . .
For suspending . . . .
He has abdicated Government here . . . .
He has plundered our seas, ravaged our Coasts, burnt our towns, and destroyed the lives of our people.
He is at this time transporting large Armies of foreign Mercenaries . . . .
He has constrained . . . .
He has excited domestic insurrections . . . .

These accusations constituted a list of grievances whose purpose was to bring King George to the bar of justice. They contained facts and truths, but not those of an impartial "history" — rather, facts and truths exaggerated, aimed at justifying the historic steps toward independence, and insuring that American "hearts and hands" would move together. The contemporary English view of this document was recorded by Ambrose Serle: "A more impudent, false and atrocious proclamation," said Serle of the Declaration, "was never fabricated by the hands of man. Hitherto, they have thrown all the blame and insult upon the Parliament and Ministry; now, they have the audacity to calumniate the King and the people of Great Britain. 'Tis impossible to read this paper without horror at the daring hypocrisy of these men, who call *God* to witness the uprightness of their proceedings." To most Britons in 1776, truth was hard to find in the famous American paper. To the Americans, of course, it was the act of declaring independence, not the Declaration of Independence, that gave meaning to the Revolution.

By July 5 copies of the document had been printed, and great effort was made to quickly distribute them throughout the colonies. The entire apparatus of the Revolution sped on its way. To the state conventions, to the Committees of Safety, to the military commanders, to ministers of the pulpit, and to private individuals, Congress directed copies of the paper. Newspaper editors also played an important role in its dissemination. On July 6, the *Pennsylvania Evening Post* was the first newspaper to print the proclamation. On the ninth it appeared in Dunlap's *Maryland Gazette* at Baltimore; on the tenth in the *New York Constitutional Gazette*; on the thirteenth in the *Providence Gazette*; on the seventeenth in the *Massachusetts Spy*; on the nineteenth in the *New England Chronicle*. Among the Southern newspapers that carried the document were the *Virginia Gazette*, on July 20, and the *South Carolina and American Gazette* on August 2.

Many Americans, who did not read the Declaration themselves, heard it read from statehouse balconies, from pulpits, or at army formations. Washington reported to Congress on July 10 that he had "caused the Declaration to be proclaimed before all the Army under my immediate command," and that

198

"the measure seemed to have their most hearty assent; the expressions and behavior both of officers and men testifying their warmest approbation of it . . . ."

By summer's end in 1776, the Declaration of Independence was known to most of the American people, to the enemy, and shortly thereafter, to the world.

"From the inception of the controversy," Professor Schlesinger wrote, "the patriots exhibited extraordinary skill in manipulating public opinion, playing upon the emotions of the ignorant as well as the minds of the educated." As propagandists, the Americans demonstrated great ability. Understanding the uses to which the printing press could be put, they embarked on devastating attacks on the "sceptered savage of Great-Britain," who was charged, by one writer, with a thirst "for the blood of America. Hessians, Hanoverians, Brunswickers, Canadians, Indians, Negroes, Regulars and Tories are invited to the carnage."[6]

That non-English and non-white persons actually became involved in the war was no exaggeration, but in the end their activities were of little service to England. Stirred to greater resistance because of such "foreign" elements, the Americans not only opposed the King's men with arms, but conducted intensive propaganda and subversive operations against them.

The leaders of the Revolution, however, even in the midst of their most angry flood of words, never lost sight of the fact that words were no substitute for "an arm of flesh." Writing of the military effort and the search for peace, John Adams noted in 1781 that only Washington, Greene, "and their colleagues in the army" could truly negotiate for America.

The British, who sent armies and fleets to these shores to persuade the Americans to forego rebellion and independence, were themselves "persuaded" to relinquish their colonies — persuaded by the stubborn resistance of Washington, Greene, "their colleagues in the army," and the potent French alliance.

Notes

CHAPTER 1

Propaganda and Military Operations

1. Reginald Hargreaves, *The Bloodybacks: The British Serviceman in North America, 1655-1783,* p. 248; Frank Moore, *Diary of the American Revolution, From Newspapers and Original Documents,* Vol. I, p. 124.

2. George Washington, *The Writings of George Washington,* ed. John C. Fitzpatrick, Vol. II, p. 490. Hereafter cited as *GW.*

3. John W. Wright, "The Rifle in the American Revolution," *American Historical Review,* Vol. XXIX, No. 2, pp. 293-95.

4. Broadside Collection, Portfolio 108, No. 16, Library of Congress.

5. Worthington C. Ford, ed., *Broadsides, Ballads, &c. Printed in Massachusetts, 1635-1800,* Massachusetts Historical Society, *Collections,* p. 266.

6. Danske Dandridge, "Sgt. Bedinger's Journal," *Historic Shepherdstown,* p. 107.

7. Peter Force, comp., *American Archives,* Fourth Series, Vol. VI, p. 242.

8. The refugee governors were: William Tryon of New York, John Murray (Earl of Dunmore) of Virginia, Josiah Martin of North Carolina, and Lord William Campbell of South Carolina.

9. Christopher Ward, *The War of the Revolution,* Vol. I, p. 209.

10. Edmund C. Burnett, ed., *Letters of Members of the Continental Congress,* Vol. II, pp. 66-67.

11. Force, *Archives,* Fifth Series, Vol. II, p. 398.

12. Bellamy Partridge, *Sir Billy Howe,* p. 111.

13. Carl Leopold Baurmeister, *Revolution in America: Confidential Letters and Journals 1776-1784 of Adjutant General Major Carl Baurmeister of the Hessian Forces,* trans. B. A. Uhlendorf, p. 75.

14. Thomas Jefferson, *The Papers of Thomas Jefferson,* ed. J.P. Boyd, Vol. I, p. 659.

15. Moore, *American Revolution,* Vol. II, p. 197.

16. George Creel, "Propaganda and Morale," *American Journal of Sociology,* Vol. XLVII, pp. 340-41.

17. John Almon, ed., *The Remembrances, or Impartial Repository of Public Events,* Vol. VI, pp. 99, 137-38.

18. B.F. Stevens, comp., *Facsimiles of Manuscripts in European Archives Relating to America, 1773-1783,* Vol. IV, p. 2094.

19. *GW*, Vol. XIII, pp. 132-33.

20. W.C. Ford and G. Hunt, eds., *Journals of the Continental Congress*, Vol. VII, pp. 1168-69. Hereafter cited as *JCC*.

21. Baurmeister, *Revolution*, p. 146.

22. Ward, *Revolution*, Vol. II, p. 703.

23. Jefferson, *Papers*, Vol. III, pp. 525, 550.

24. Carl Van Doren, *Secret History of the American Revolution*, p. 377.

25. James Thacher, *Military Journal During the American Revolution*, p. 231.

26. Henry Steele Commager and Richard B. Morris, eds., *The Spirit of 'Seventy-Six: The Story of the American Revolution as Told by Participants*, Vol. II, pp. 767-70.

27. B.F. Stevens, ed., *The Campaign in Virginia, 1781, An Exact Reprint of Six Rare Pamphlets on the Clinton-Cornwallis Controversy*, Vol. I, p. 371.

28. Great Britain, Historical Manuscripts Commission, *Report on American Manuscripts in the Royal Institution of Great Britain*, Vol. II, p. 401. Hereafter cited as American Manuscripts.

CHAPTER 2

American Propaganda and the Struggle For Canada

1. Arthur G. Bradley, *Lord Dorchester*, p. 9.

2. Force, *Archives*, Fourth Series, Vol. I, p. 853.

3. *Ibid.*, p. 1164.

4. *Ibid.*, Vol. II, p. 23.

5. Bradley, *Dorchester*, p. 90.

6. Force, *Archives*, Fourth Series, Vol. II, p. 919.

7. *Ibid.*, Vol. III, p. 1342.

8. *Ibid.*, p. 962.

9. *GW*, Vol. IV, pp. 65-66n.

10. Kenneth Roberts, ed., *March to Quebec: Journals of the Members of Arnold's Expedition*, pp. 89-90.

11. *Journal of the Most Remarkable Occurrences in Quebec, 1775-1776 by an Officer of the Garrison*, New York Historical Society, Collections, Vol. III, Pt. 2, pp. 175-76.

12. *Ibid.*, p. 177.

13. Force, *Archives*, Fifth Series, Vol. V, p. 411.

14. R.W. McLachlan, "Fleury Mesplet, The First Printer at Montreal," *Proceedings and Transactions of the Royal Society of Canada*, Second Series, Vol. XII, pp. 224-25.

15. John and Abigail Adams, *Familiar Letters of John Adams and His Wife*, ed. C.F. Adams, p. 139.

16. William R. Riddell, "Benjamin Franklin's Mission to Canada and the Causes of Its Failure," *Pennsylvania Magazine of History and Biography*, Vol. XLVIII, No. 190, pp. 111-18.

17. Force, *Archives*, Fourth Series, Vol. VI, p. 418, and Fifth Series, Vol. I, p. 1241.

18. *Ibid.*, Fifth Series, Vol. II, p. 1144.

19. *Ibid.*

20. Moore, *American Revolution*, Vol. I, p. 525.

21. *Ibid.*, Vol. II, pp. 102-04.

22. *American Manuscripts*, Vol. II, pp. 1-2.

23. *GW*, Vol. XVIII, pp. 386-88.

24. Jean N. McIlwraith, *Sir Frederick Haldimand*, pp. 352-53.

25. Benjamin Franklin, *The Writings of Benjamin Franklin*, ed., A.H. Smyth, Vol. VIII, p. 472.

CHAPTER 3

The Campaign to Win the Indians' Allegiance

1. Force, *Archives*, Fourth Series, Vol. V, pp. 525-26.

2. *Ibid.*, Fifth Series, Vol. I, p. 867.

3. *JCC*, Vol. IV, p. 412.

4. Force, *Archives*, Fifth Series, Vol. I, p. 1105.

5. John D. Barnhart, ed., *Henry Hamilton and George Rogers Clark*, pp. 27-28.

6. Samuel Cole Williams, *Tennessee During the American Revolution*, p. 272.

7. Francis J. Hudleston, *Gentleman Johnny Burgoyne: Misadventures of an English General in the Revolution*, p. 163.

8. *GW*, Vol. IX, pp. 75-76.

9. Isaac N. Arnold, *The Life of Benedict Arnold*, p. 162n.

10. Barnhart, *Hamilton*, p. 30.

11. *JCC*, Vol. IX, pp. 942-45.

12. R.G. Thwaites, and L.P. Kellogg, eds., *Frontier Defense on the Upper Ohio*, 1777-1778, p. 86.

13. *JCC*, Vol. X, pp. 110-111.

14. Burnett, *Letters*, Vol. III, pp. 129-130.

15. *JCC*, Vol. XI, pp. 587-89.

16. James A. James, *The Life of George Rogers Clark*, pp. 120-21.

17. Barnhart, *Hamilton*, pp. 180-81.

18. James A. James, *George Rogers Clark Papers, 1771-1781*,

Collections of the Illinois State Historical Library, Vol. VIII, Virginia Series, Vol. III, pp. 95-96.

19. Catherine Crary, *The Price of Loyalty: Tory Writings from the Revolutionary Era*, pp. 254-55.

20. George Otto Trevelyan, *The American Revolution*, ed.', Richard B. Morris, p. 425.

21. *American Manuscripts*, Vol. II, pp. 1-2.

22. *JCC*, Vol. XVI, p. 334.

23. *GW*, Vol. VI, pp. 192-93.

CHAPTER 4

The Incitement of Negro Insurrection

1. Joseph Galloway made the 600,000 estimate in June 1778; Stevens, *Facsimiles*, Vol. XXIV, p. 2098.

2. Moore, *American Revolution*, Vol. I, p. 24; Ivor Noel Hume, *1775: Another Part of the Field, A month-by-month account of what everyday life was in Virginia during . . . 1775*, pp. 109-10; John Adams, *The Works of John Adams, with a Life of the Author*, ed., C.F. Adams, Vol. II, p. 428.

3. Moore, *American Revolution*, Vol. I, p. 104.

4. William L. Saunders, ed., *The Colonial Records of North Carolina*, Vol. X, pp. 25, 63, 87.

5. David J. Mays, *Edmund Pendleton, A Biography*, Vol. II, p. 14.

6. Saunders, *North Carolina*, Vol. X, p. 138a.

7. Mays, *Pendleton*, Vol. II, p. 56.

8. Richard Henry Lee, *The Letters of Richard Henry Lee*, ed., J.C. Ballagh, Vol. I, p. 162.

9. Jefferson, *Papers*, Vol. I, p. 266.

10. Mays, *Pendleton*, Vol. II, p. 160.

11. *Ibid.*

12. Force, *Archives*, Fourth Series, Vol. VI, p. 811.

13. Ward, *Revolution*, Vol. II, p. 592.

14. W.B. Hartgrove, "The Negro Soldiers in the American Revolution," *Journal of Negro History*, Vol. I, No. 2, p. 126.

15. *Ibid.*, p. 128.

16. Walter Clark, ed., *The State Records of North Carolina*, Vol. XIX, pp. 911-14.

17. Moore, *American Revolution*, Vol. II, pp. 176-77.

18. After the peace treaty a group of slaves in New York City refused to return to their former status, as the Americans demanded,

insisting on their rights "under the Clinton proclamations." The British supported them in this, and hundreds of Negroes sailed away when the British fleet withdrew.

19. Hartgrove, "Negro Soldiers," p. 117.

20. Benson J. Lossing, *The Pictorial Field-Book of the Revolution,* Vol. II, p. 573n.

21. Benjamin Quarles, *The Negro in the American Revolution,* pp. 167, 171-72.

CHAPTER 5
The Campaign to Subvert the Hessians

1. Ambrose Serle, *The American Journal of Ambrose Serle, Secretary to Lord Howe, 1776-1778,* ed., Edward H. Tatum, Jr., p. 77.

2. Force, *Archives,* Fourth Series, Vol. V, pp. 525-26.

3. Franklin, *Writings,* Vol. VI, p. 448.

4. Lyman H. Butterfield, Psychological Warfare in 1776: The Jefferson-Franklin Plan to Cause Hessian Desertions," *Proceedings of the American Philosophical Society,* Vol. CXCIV, p. 234.

5. Burnett, *Letters,* Vol. II, p. 62.

6. Force, *Archives,* Fifth Series, Vol. II, pp. 203-04.

7. Edward J. Lowell, *The Hessians and Other German Auxiliaries of Great Britain in the Revolutionary War,* pp. 38-39.

8. *GW,* Vol. VI, p. 284.

9. *JCC,* Vol. IV, pp. 984-85.

10. Burnett, *Letters,* Vol. II, p. 209.

11. *GW,* Vol. VII, p. 314.

12. *Ibid.,* pp. 1-3.

13. Baurmeister, *Letters and Journals,* p. 128.

14. Burnett, *Letters,* Vol. III, p. 216.

15. *GW,* Vol. XII, pp. 149-50.

16. *Journal of Lt. John Charles Philip Von Krafft, 1776-84.* New York Historical Society, *Collections,* Vol. XV, pt. 1, p. 59.

17. Baurmeister, *Letters and Journals,* p. 228.

18. *JCC,* Vol. XII, p. 868.

19. *Ibid.,* p. 1192-93.

20. Max von Eelking, *Memoirs and Letters and Journals of Major General Riedesel,* trans., William L. Stone, pp. 266-68.

21. Under the terms of the surrender, in deference to Burgoyne called a "convention," Gates agreed that Burgoyne's army would be marched to Boston and returned to their homeland, on the guarantee that

they would never be employed again on American duty. This agreement was never fulfilled by Congress, which feared they would replace other British troops who, in turn, would be sent to fight in America.

22. Lowell, *Hessians*, p. 287.

23. *GW*, Vol. XXIV, pp. 175-76.

24. *American Manuscripts*, Vol. III, pp. 314-15.

25. *Ibid.*

26. *Ibid.*

27. *Ibid.*, Vol. II, p. 401.

28. Baurmeister, *Letters and Journals*, p. 541.

29. *Ibid.*, pp. 569, 579.

30. Lowell, *Hessians*, pp. 291, 299-301.

CHAPTER 6

Kidnappings, Rumors, and Bribery

1. Frederick Mackenzie, *Diary of Frederick Mackenzie, Giving a Narrative of His Military Service . . . during the years 1775-1781 . . .*, Vol. I, p. 150.

2. *Ibid.*, pp. 153-54.

3. *Ibid.*

4. George F. Scheer and Hugh F. Rankin, eds., *Rebels and Redcoats: The Living Story of the American Revolution*, p. 226.

5. *GW*, Vol. XI, p. 51.

6. William B. Wilcox, *Portrait of a General, Sir Henry Clinton in the War of Independence*, pp. 266-67, 331-32.

7. Baurmeister, *Letters and Journals*, pp. 406-07.

8. Thacher, *Military Journal*, p. 86.

9. Hudleston, *Burgoyne*, p. 78.

10. Force, *Archives*, Fourth Series, Vol. II, p. 1504.

11. John Sullivan, *Letters and Papers of Major-General Sullivan*, ed., Otis G. Hammond, Vol. I, p. 360.

12. Van Doren, *Secret History*, pp. 46, 48; New York Historical Society, *Collections*, Vol. XII, p. 21.

13. Burnett, *Letters*, Vol. II, p. 527.

14. Edward Duffield Neill, "Rev. Jacob Duché, the First Chaplain of Congress," *Pennsylvania Magazine of History and Biography*, Vol. II, No. 1, p. 83.

15. William R. Reed, *Life and Correspondence of Joseph Reed*, p. 377.

16. *Ibid.*, p. 384.

17. *Ibid.*, p. 388; John F. Roche, *Joseph Reed, A Moderate in the American Revolution*, p. 138.

18. The state of Pennsylvania later condemned her loyalist husband as a traitor and seized his property. Although Mrs. Ferguson separated from him, the notoriety for her "thoughtless act," carrying Duché's letter to Washington, continued to darken her later years.

19. Stevens, *Facsimiles*, Vol. VIII, p. 835.

20. Adams, *Works*, Vol. III, p. 179.

21. Jared Sparks, *The Diplomatic Correspondence of the American Revolution*, Vol. II, pp. 34-39.

22. Van Doren, *Secret History*, p. 82.

CHAPTER 7

Overseas Propaganda

1. Bernard Fay, *Franklin, The Apostle of Modern Times*, p. 412.

2. Gilbert Chinard, "Adventures in a Library," *The Newberry Library Bulletin*, Second Series, No. 8, p. 227; Paul Leicester Ford, "Affaires de l'Angleterre et de l'Amérique," *Pennsylvania Magazine of History and Biography*, Vol. XIII, No. 50, pp. 222-26.

3. Carl Van Doren, *Benjamin Franklin*, p. 572.

4. Franklin, *Writings*, Vol. VIII, p. 457.

5. Hays I. Minis, ed., *Calendar of the Papers of Benjamin Franklin in the Library of the American Philosophical Society*, Vol. I, pp. 231, 248.

6. Black propaganda emanates from a source other than the true one.

7. Durand Echeverra, " 'The Sale of the Hessians.' Was Benjamin Franklin the Author?", *American Philosophical Society Library Bulletin*, pp. 427-31.

8. Franklin, *Writings*, Vol. VII, pp. 57-58.

9. William Bell Clark, *Ben Franklin's Privateers: A Naval Epic of the American Revolution*, p. 168.

10. Franklin, *Writings*, Vol. VII, p. 398.

11. Francis Wharton, ed., *The Revolutionary Diplomatic Correspondence of the United States*, Vol. V, pp. 689-91.

12. Francis Adrian Van der Kamp, *An Autobiography, Together with Extracts from His Correspondence*, ed., Helen Fairchild, pp. 55-56.

13. Van Doren, *Franklin*, p. 673.

14. Nicholas Hans, "Franklin, Jefferson and the English Radicals at the End of the Eighteenth Century." *American Philosophical Society Library Bulletin*, pp. 406-26.

15. *Ibid.*

CHAPTER 8

Epilogue: Washington, Congress and the
Declaration of Independence

1. Gilbert Chinard, ed., *George Washington as the French Knew Him: A Collection of Texts*, p. 28.

2. Moore, *American Revolution*, Vol. I, p. 96.

3. *GW*, Vol. XXIV, p. 325.

4. Arthur M. Schlesinger, *Prelude to Independence: The Newspaper War on Britain*, pp. 256-80; Philip Davidson, *Propaganda and the American Revolution*, pp. 131-38.

5. Nathan Schachner, *Jefferson, A Biography*, Vol. I, p. 129.

6. Adams, *Familiar Letters*, pp. 397-98.

Bibliography

PRIMARY SOURCES
Letters, Journals - - -

Adams, John. *The Works of John Adams, with a Life of the Author, Notes and Illustrations.* Edited by C.F. Adams. 10 vols. Boston: Little, Brown and Company, 1850-1856.

Adams, John, and Adams, Abigail. *Familiar Letters of John Adams and His Wife.* Edited by C.F. Adams. New York: Hurd and Houghton, 1876.

Adams, Samuel. *The Writings of Samuel Adams.* Edited by Harry A. Cushing. 4 vols. New York: G.P. Putnam's Sons, 1904-1908.

Almon, John, ed. *The Remembrancer; Or Impartial Repository of Public Events.* 17 vols. London: J. Almon, 1775-1784.

Anburey, Thomas. *Travel Through the Interior Parts of America by Thomas Anburey, lieutenant in the army of General Burgoyne.* 2 vols. Boston: Houghton Mifflin Co., 1923.

Barnhart, John D., ed. *Henry Hamilton and George Rogers Clark.* Crawfordsville, Ind.: R.E. Banta, 1951.

Baurmeister, Carl Leopold. *Revolution in America; Confidential Letters and Journals 1776-1784 of Adjutant General Major Baurmeister of the Hessian Forces.* Translated by B.A. Uhlendorf. New Brunswick, N.J.: Rutgers University Press, 1957.

Brown, Marvin L., Jr., Assisted by Huth, Marta, trans. *Baroness von Riedesel and the American Revolution: Journal and Correspondence of a Tour of Duty, 1776-1783, A Revised Translation with Introduction and Notes.* Chapel Hill: University of North Carolina Press, 1965.

Burgoyne, John. *A State of the Expedition from Canada As Laid Before the House of Commons, by Lieutenant General Burgoyne.* London: J. Almon, 1780.

Burke, Edmund. *Selected Writings and Speeches . . . on Reform, Revolution and War.* Edited by Ross J.S. Hoffman and Paul Levach. New York: Alfred A. Knopf, 1970.

Burnett, Edmund C., ed. *Letters of Members of the Continental Congress.* 8 vols. Washington, D.C.: Carnegie Institution of Washington, 1921-1936.

Chinard, Gilbert, ed. *George Washington as the French Knew Him, A Collection of Texts.* Princeton, N.J.: Princeton University Press, 1940.

Clark, George Rogers. "George Rogers Clark Papers, 1771-1781." *Collections of the Illinois State Historical Library.* Edited by James A. James. Vol. 8 (1912), Virginia Series 3.

Clark, Walter, ed. *The State Records of North Carolina.* Vol. 19. Goldsboro, N.C.: Nash, 1901.

Clinton, Sir Henry. *The American Rebellion: Sir Henry Clinton's Narrative of his campaigns, 1775-1782, with an appendix of original documents.* Edited by William B. Wilcox. New Haven: Yale University Press, 1954.

Commager, Henry Steele, and Morris, Richard B., eds. *The Spirit of 'Seventy-Six: The Story of the American Revolution as told by Participants.* 2 vols. Indianapolis, Ind.: The Bobbs-Merrill Co., Inc., 1958.

Cory, Catherine S. *The Price of Loyalty: Tory Writings From the Revolutionary Era.* New York: McGraw-Hill, 1963.

Cresswell, Nicholas. *The Journal of Nicholas Cresswell, 1774-1777.* New York: Dial Press. 1924.

Curwen, Samuel. *Journals and Letters of . . . Samuel Curwen . . . An American Refugee in England, 1775-1784.* Edited by George A. Ward. New York: Levitt, Trow & Co., 1842.

Dandridge, Danske. *Historic Shepherdstown.* Charlottesville, Va.: The Michie Co., 1910.

Deane, Silas. The Deane Papers, 1774-1790. New York Historical Society, *Collections.* 5 vols. 1887-1890.

Dearborn, Henry. *Revolutionary War Journals of Henry Dearborn, 1775-1783.* Edited by L.A. Brown and H. Peckham. Chicago: The Caxton Club, 1939.

Du Roi. *Journal of Du Roi the Elder, Lieutenant and Adjutant in the Service of the Duke of Brunswick, 1776-1778.* Translated by Charlotte S.J. Epping. New York: D. Appleton and Co., 1911.

Eelking, Max von. *Memoirs and Letters and Journals of Major Riedesel.* Translated by William L. Stone. Albany: J. Munsell, 1968.

Force, Peter. comp. *American-Archives.* Fourth Series, 6 vols. Washington: St. Clair Clark and Peter Force, 1837-1846; Fifth Series, 3 vols. 1848-1853.

Ford, Paul Leicester, ed. *An Address to the Good People of Ireland on behalf of America, October 4th, 1778, by Benjamin Franklin.* Brooklyn, N.Y.: Brooklyn Printing Club, 1891.

Ford, Worthington C. *Broadsides, Ballads, &c. Printed in Massachusetts, 1639-1800.* Massachusetts Historical Society Collections. Vol. LXXV. Boston: 1922.

——————. The Washington-Duché Letters. Brooklyn, N.Y.: Private Print, 1890.

Ford, W.C., and Hunt, G., eds. *Journals of the Continental Congress.* 34 vols. Washington: Government Printing Office, 1904-1937.

Franklin, Benjamin. *The Writings of Benjamin Franklin.* Edited by A.H.

Smyth. 10 vols. New York: The Macmillan Co., 1905-1907.

Gage, Thomas. *Correspondence of Gen. Thomas Gage, 1763-1775.* Edited by Clarence E. Carter. 2 vols. New Haven, Conn.: Yale University Press, 1931-33.

Great Britain, Historical Manuscripts Commission. *Report on American Manuscripts in the Royal Institution of Great Britain.* 4 vols. London: H. M. Stationary Office, 1904-1909.

Heitman, Francis B. *Historical Register of Officers of the Continental Army.* Washington, D.C.: Rare Books Shop Publishing Co., 1914.

Howe, William. *The Narrative of Lieut. Gen. Sir William Howe, in a Committee of the House of Commons, on the 29th of April 1779.* London: H. Baldwin, 1780.

Hughes, Thomas. *A Journal by Thos. Hughes.* Edited by E.A. Benians. Cambridge, England: The University Press, 1947.

Huth, Hans. "Letters From a Hessian Mercenary," *Pennsylvania Magazine of History and Biography.* Vol. 12. No. 4 (October, 1938).

James, James Alton, ed. *George Rogers Clark Papers, 1771-1781. Collections* of the Illinois State Historical Library. Vol. 8, Virginia Series 3. Springfield, 1912.

Jefferson, Thomas. *The Papers of Thomas Jefferson.* Edited by J.P. Boyd. 14 vols. Princeton, N.J.: Princeton University Press, 1950-1958.

Journal of Lt. John Charles Philip Von Krafft, 1776-1784. New York Historical Society, *Collections,* Vol. 15, Pt. 1 (1882).

Journal of the Most Remarkable Occurrences in Quebec, 1775-1776 By An Officer of the Garrison. New York Historical Society, *Collections.* Vol. 3, Pt. 2 (1880).

Lamb, Roger. *Memoir of His Own Life.* Dublin: J. Jones, 1811.

Lee, Richard Henry. *The Letters of Richard Henry Lee.* Edited by J.C. Ballagh, 2 vols. New York: The Macmillan Co., 1914.

Mackenzie, Frederick. *Diary of Frederick Mackenzie, Giving a Narrative of His Military Service . . . during the years 1775-1781 . . . .* 2 vols. Cambridge, Mass.: Harvard University Press, 1930.

Madison, James. *The Papers of James Madison.* Edited by William M.E. Rachal and others. 9 vols. Chicago: University of Chicago Press, 1962-1975.

Minis, Hays I., ed. *Calendar of the Papers of Benjamin Franklin in the Library of the American Philosophical Society.* 5 vols. Philadelphia: The American Philosophical Society, 1906.

Moore, Frank. *Diary of the American Revolution.* 2 vols. New York: Scribner, 1859.

Morris, Richard B., ed. *Alexander Hamilton and the Founding of the Nation.* New York: Dial Press, 1957.

New Jersey. *Archives of the State of New Jersey.* Second Series, "Extracts from American Newspapers." Vols. 2 (1778) and 3 (1779).

Niles, Hezekiah, ed. *Centennial Offering, Republication of the Principles and Acts of the Revolution in America.* New York: A.S. Barnes & Co., 1786.

O'Callaghan, E.B., comp. *Documents Relative to the Colonial History of the State of New York.* Vol. 8. Albany, N.Y.: Weed, Parsons, and Co., 1857.

Paine, Thomas. *Selected Writings of Thomas Paine.* Edited by R.E. Roberts. New York: Everybody's Vacation Publishing Co., 1945.

Pomeroy, Seth. *The Journals and Papers of Seth Pomeroy, Sometimes General in the Colonial Service.* Edited by L.B. de Forest. New York: Society of Colonial Wars in the State of New York, 1926.

Popp, Stephen. *A Hessian Soldier in the American Revolution: Diary of Stephen Popp.* Translated by Reinhard J. Pope. Racine, Wis.: Private Print, 1953.

Reed, William B. *Life and Correspondence of Joseph Reed.* 2 vols. Philadelphia: Lindsay and Blakiston, 1847.

Roberts, Kenneth, ed. *March to Quebec: Journals of the Members of Arnold's Expedition.* New York: Doubleday, Doran & Co., 1938.

Rush, Benjamin. *Letters of Benjamin Rush.* Edited by L.H. Butterfield. 2 vols. Princeton, N.J.: Princeton University Press, 1951.

Ryden, George H. ed. *Letters to and from Caesar Rodney, 1756-1784.* Philadelphia: University of Pennsylvania Press, 1933.

Saffell, William T.R. *Records of the Revolutionary War.* Baltimore, Md.: Charles C. Saffell, 1894.

Saunders, William L., ed. *The Colonial Records of North Carolina.* Vol. 10. Raleigh, N.C., 1870.

Scheer, George F., and Rankin, Hugh F., eds. *Rebels and Redcoats: The Living Story of the American Revolution.* Cleveland, Ohio and New York: The World Publishing Co., 1956.

Serle, Ambrose. *The American Journal of Ambrose Serle, Secretary to Lord Howe, 1776-1778.* Edited by E.H. Tatum, Jr. San Marino, California: The Huntington Library, 1940.

Sparks, Jared, ed. *The Diplomatic Correspondence of the American Revolution.* 6 vols. Washington: J.C. Reeves, 1857.

Stevens, Benjamin F., ed. *B.F. Stevens Facsimiles of Manuscripts in European Archives Relating to America, 1773-1785.* 25 vols. London: Malby & Sons, 1889-1898.

————————. *The Campaign in Virginia, 1781. An Exact Reprint of Six Rare Pamphlets on the Clinton-Cornwallis Controversy.* London: 1888.

Stille, Charles J. *Major General Anthony Wayne.* Philadelphia: J.B. Lippincott Co., 1893.

Stone, William L. ed. *Letters of Brunswick and Hessian Officers During the American Revolution.* Albany, N.Y.: Joel Munsell's Sons, 1891.

————————. *Orderly Book of Sir John Johnson During the Oris-*

212

kany Campaign, 1776-1777. Albany, N.Y.: Joel Munsell's Sons, 1884.

Sullivan, John. *Letters and Papers of Major General John Sullivan.* Edited by O.G. Hammond. 2 vols. Concord: New Hampshire Historical Society, 1930.

"The Treason of Benedict Arnold, as Presented in Letters of Sir Henry Clinton to Lord George Germain," *Pennsylvania Magazine of History and Biography.* Vol. 22 (1898).

Thacher, James. *Military Journal During the American Revolutionary War.* Hartford, Conn.: S. Andrews & Son, 1854.

Thwaites, R.G., ed. State Historical Society of Wisconsin, *Collections.* Vol. 11. Madison, 1888.

_____ and Kellogg, L.P., eds. *Frontier Defense on the Upper Ohio, 1777-1778.* State Historical Society of Wisconsin. Madison, 1912.

Tyler, Moses Coit. *The Literary History of the American Revolution.* 2 vols. New York: G.P. Putnam's Sons, 1951.

Van der Kemp, Francis Adrian. *An Autobiography, together with Extracts from his Correspondence.* Edited by Helen L. Fairchild. New York: G.P. Putnam's Sons, 1903.

Warren-Adams Letters, Being Chiefly a Correspondence among John Adams, Samuel Adams, and James Warren. Massachusetts Historical Society, *Collections.* 2 vols. Boston, 1917-1925.

Washington, George. *The Writings of George Washington.* Edited by John C. Fitzpatrick. 30 vols. Washington: U.S. Government Printing Office, 1931-1944.

Wharton, Francis, ed. *The Revolutionary Diplomatic Correspondence of the United States.* 6 vols. Washington: U.S. Government Printing Office, 1889.

Manuscripts - - -

Washington, D.C. Library of Congress. *Broadside Collection, 1775-1783.*

Washington, D.C. Library of Congress. *Washington Papers.*

Washington, D.C. National Archives. *Papers of the Continental Congress, 1774-1783.*

SECONDARY SOURCES

Alden, John R. *General Gage in America, Being Principally a History of His Role in the American Revolution.* Baton Rouge, La.: Louisiana State University Press, 1948.

Aldridge, Alfred O. *Franklin and His French Contemporaries.* New York: New York University Press, 1957.

Anderson, Troyer S. *The Command of the Howe Brothers During the American Revolution.* London: Oxford University Press, 1936.

Aptheker, Herbert. "American Negro Slave Revolts." Ph.D. Dissertation, Columbia University, 1943.

Arnold, Isaac N. *The Life of Benedict Arnold: His Patriotism and His Treason.* Chicago: A.C. McClurg & Co. 1897.

Barnhart, John D. *Henry Hamilton and George Rogers Clark.* Crawfordsville, Ind.: R.E. Banta, 1951.

Bliven, Bruce, Jr. *Under the Guns: New York, 1775-1776.* New York: Harper & Row, 1972.

Bolton, Charles K. *The Private Soldier Under Washington.* New York: Scribner, 1902.

Bonsal, Stephen. *When the French Were Here.* New York: 1945.

Bowman, Allen. *The Morale of the American Revolutionary Army.* Washington: American Council on Public Affairs, 1943.

Bradley, Arthur G. *Lord Dorchester.* New York: Oxford University Press, 1926.

Brooks, Noah. *Henry Knox: A Soldier of the Revolution.* New York: G.P. Putnam's Sons, 1900.

Burnett, Edmund C. *The Continental Congress.* New York: W.W. Norton Co., 1964.

Butterfield, Herbert. *George III, Lord North and the People, 1779-1780.* London: Bell, 1949.

Butterfield, Lyman H. "Psychological Warfare in 1776: The Jefferson-Franklin Plan to Cause Hessian Desertions." *Proceedings of the American Philosophical Society,* 194 (June 1950), 233-241.

Chinard, Gilbert. *Honest John Adams.* Boston: Little, Brown & Co., 1933.

————————. "Adventures in a Library." *The Newberry Library Bulletin.* Second Series., No. 8 (March 1952), 223-238.

Clark, Dora M. *British Opinion and the American Revolution.* New Haven, Conn.: Yale University Press, 1930.

Clark, William B. *Ben Franklin's Privateers: A Naval Epic of the American Revolution.* Baton Rouge, La.: Louisiana State University Press, 1956.

Clarke, T. Wood. *The Bloody Mohawk.* New York: The Macmillan Co., 1940.

Dabney, W.M. *After Saratoga: The Story of the Convention Army.* Albuquerque: University of New Mexico Press, 1954.

Dandridge, Danske. *Historic Shepherdstown.* Charlottesville, Va.: The Michie Co., 1910.

Davidson, Philip. *Propaganda and the American Revolution.* Chapel Hill: University of North Carolina Press, 1941.

Dumbauld, Edward. *The Declaration of Independence and What it Means Today.* Norman: University of Oklahoma Press, 1950.

Echeverra, Durand. " 'The Sale of the Hessians,' Was Benjamin Franklin the Author?" American Philosophical Society Library Bulletin (1954), 427-431.

Elder, Friedrich. *The Dutch Republic and the American Revolution.* Baltimore: The Johns Hopkins Press, 1911.

Eelking, Max von. *The German Allied Troops in the North American War of Independence.* Translated by J.G. Rosengarten. Albany, N.Y.: Joel Munsell's Sons, 1893.

Fay, Bernard. *Franklin, The Apostle of Modern Times.* Boston: Little, Brown & Co., 1929.

Fitzpatrick, John C. *The Spirit of the Revolution.* Boston and New York: Houghton Mifflin Co., 1924.

Flexner, Thomas J. *The Traitor and the Spy: Benedict Arnold and John André.* New York: Harcourt, Brace & Co., 1953.

Ford, Paul Leicester. "Affaires de l'Angleterre et de l'Amérique," *Pennsylvania Magazine of History and Biography.* Vol. 13 (1889), 222-226.

Freeman, Douglas S. *George Washington, A Biography.* 7 vols. New York: Charles Scribner's Sons, 1948-1957.

French, Allen. *The First Year of the American Revolution.* Boston: Doubleday, Doran & Co., 1934.

Frothingham, Richard. *History of the Siege of Boston.* Little, Brown & Co., 1873.

Gottschalk, Louis. *Lafayette Comes to America.* Chicago: University of Chicago Press, 1935.

———————. *Lafayette Joins the American Army.* Chicago: University of Chicago Press, 1937.

———————. *Lafayette and the Close of the American Revolution.* Chicago: University of Chicago Press, 1942.

Hans, Nicholas. "Franklin, Jefferson, and the English Radicals at the End of the Eighteenth Century," *American Philosophical Bulletin* (1954), 406-426.

Hargreaves, Reginald. *The Bloodybacks: The British Serviceman in North America, 1655-1783.* London: Rupert Hart-Davis, 1968.

Hartgrove, W.B. "The Negro Soldier in the American Revolution," *Journal of Negro History,* Vol. I (Jan. 1916).

Hazelton, John B. *The Declaration of Independence: Its History.* New York: DeCapo Press, 1970.

Hudleston, Francis J. *Gentleman Johnny Burgoyne: Misadventures of an English General in the Revolution.* New York: The Sun Dial Press, 1939.

Hume, Ivor Noel. *1775: Another Part of the Field, A Month-by-month account of what every day life was in Virginia during the stirring year 1775.* New York: Alfred Knopf, 1966.

James, James Alton. *The Life of George Rogers Clark.* Chicago: The University of Chicago Press, 1928.

Jameson, J. Franklin. *The American Revolution Considered as a Social Movement.* Princeton, N.J.: Princeton University Press, 1940.

Kuntzleman, Oliver G. *Joseph Galloway, Loyalist.* Ph.D. dissertation, Temple University, 1941.

Lossing, Benson J. *The Pictorial Field-Book of the Revolution.* 2 vols. New York: Harper Brothers, 1852.

Lowell, Edward J. *The Hessians and the Other German Auxiliaries of*

Great Britain in the Revolutionary War. New York: Harper & Brothers, 1884.

Mays, David J. *Edmund Pendleton, A Biography.* 2 vols. Cambridge, Mass.: Harvard University Press, 1952.

McDowell, R.B. *Irish Public Opinion, 1750-1800.* London: Faber & Faber, Ltd., 1944.

McIlwraith, Jean N. *Sir Frederick Haldimand.* London: Oxford University Press, 1926.

McLachlan, R.W. "Fleury Mesplet, The First Printer at Montreal," *Proceedings and Transactions of the Royal Society of Canada.* Second Series, Vol. XII (May 1906), 197-309.

Miller, John C. *Sam Adams: Pioneer in Propaganda.* Boston: Little, Brown & Co., 1936.

——————————. *Origins of the American Revolution.* Boston: Little, Brown & Co., 1943.

——————————. *Triumph of Freedom, 1775-1783.* Boston: Little, Brown & Co., 1948.

Montross, Lynn. *The Reluctant Rebels: The Story of the Continental Congress, 1774-1789.* New York: Harper & Brothers, 1950.

Morrison, Samuel Eliot. *John Paul Jones.* Boston: Little, Brown & Co., 1959.

Neil, Rev. Edward Duffield. "Rev. Jacob Duché, The First Chaplain of Congress," *Pennsylvania Magazine of History and Biography,* Vol. II No. 1 (1878), 58-73.

Nevins, Allan. *The American States During and After the Revolution, 1775-1789.* New York: The Macmillan Co., 1924.

Padover, Saul K. *Jefferson.* New York: Harcourt, Brace & Co., 1942.

Palmer, John M. *General Von Steupen.* New Haven, Conn.: Yale University Press, 1937.

Partridge, Bellamy. *Sir Billy Howe.* London: Longmans, Green & Co., 1932.

Peckham, Howard H. *The War for Independence: A Military History.* Chicago: University of Chicago Press, 1958.

Pennypacker, Morton. *General Washington's Spies on Long Island and in New York.* Brooklyn, N.Y.: Long Island Historical Society, 1939.

Quarles, Benjamin. *The Negro in the American Revolution.* Chapel Hill: University of North Carolina Press, 1961.

Renaut, Francis P. *La Politique de Propagande des Américains durant la Guerre d'Indépendance, 1776-1783.* 2 vols. Paris: Graoli, 1922-1925.

Ruddell, William R. "Benjamin Franklin's Mission to Canada and the Causes of Its Failure," *Pennsylvania Magazine of History and Biography.* Vol. XLVIII, No. 190 (April 1924), 111-18.

Roche, John F. *Joseph Reed, A Moderate in the American Revolution.* New York: Columbia University Press, 1951.

Schachner, Nathan. *Jefferson, A Biography.* 2 vols. New York: Appleton-Century-Crofts, 1951.

216

Schlesinger, Arthur M. *Prelude to Independence: The Newspaper War on Britain.* New York: Alfred A. Knopf, 1958.

Smith, Justin H. *Our Struggle for the Fourteenth Colony.* 2 vols. New York: Putnam, 1907.

Stillé, Charles J. *Major-General Anthony Wayne.* Philadelphia: J.B. Lippincott Co., 1893.

Stryker, William S. *The Battle of Monmouth.* Princeton, N.J.: Princeton University Press, 1927.

Trevelyan, George Otto. *The American Revolution.* Edited by Richard B. Morris. New York: McKay Co., 1964.

Tyler, Moses Coit. *The Literary History of the American Revolution.* 2 vols. New York: G.P. Putnam's Sons, 1897.

Van Doren, Carl. *Benjamin Franklin.* New York: The Viking Press, 1938.

_____. *Secret History of the American Revolution.* New York: The Viking Press, 1941.

Van Tyne, Claude H. *The War of Independence.* Boston: Houghton Mifflin Co., 1929.

_____. *The Loyalist in the American Revolution.* New York: The Macmillan Co., 1929.

Wade, Mason. *The French Canadians, 1760-1945.* New York: The Macmillan Co., 1955.

Wallace, Willard M. *Traitorous Hero: The Life and Fortunes of Benedict Arnold.* New York: Books for Libraries Press, 1954.

Ward, Christopher. *The War of the Revolution.* 2 vols. New York: The Macmillan Co., 1952.

_____. *The Delaware Continentals, 1776-1783.* Wilmington, Del., The Historical Society of Delaware, 1941.

Wertenbaker, Thomas J. *Father Knickerbocher Rebels, New York City During the Revolution.* New York: Charles Scribner's Sons, 1948.

Wickshire, Franklin and Mary. *Cornwallis: The American Adventure.* Boston: Houghton Mifflin Co., 1970.

Wilcox, William B. *Portrait of a General, Sir Henry Clinton in the War for Independence.* New York: Alfred A. Knopf, 1968.

Wright, John W. "The Rifle in the American Revolution," *American Historical Review*, Vol. XXIX. No. 2 (January 1924) 293-99.

Wrong, George M. *Canada and the American Revolution.* New York: The Macmillan Co., 1935.

Index

219